THE EPISTLE OF SAINT PAUL
TO THE PHILIPPIANS

THE EPISTLE OF
SAINT PAUL
TO THE PHILIPPIANS

JEAN-FRANÇOIS COLLANGE
Docteur ès sciences religieuses

Translated from the First French Edition by
A. W. Heathcote

LONDON
EPWORTH PRESS

FIRST PUBLISHED BY

DELACHAUX and NIESTLÉ, NEUCHATEL and PARIS

TRANSLATION © EPWORTH PRESS 1979

FIRST ENGLISH EDITION PUBLISHED BY

EPWORTH PRESS 1979

Enquiries should be addressed to
The Methodist Publishing House
Wellington Road
Wimbledon
London SW19 8EU

7162 0270 0

PRINTED AND BOUND IN ENGLAND BY
HAZELL WATSON AND VINEY LTD
AYLESBURY, BUCKS

TO MY WIFE

This commentary, originally published in French in 1973, is a successor to the one by P. Bonnard which appeared as no. 10 in the same series, *Commentaire du Nouveau Testament* in 1950.

Dr E. Trocmé, Dean of the Faculty of Protestant Theology in the University of Human Sciences at Strasbourg, Pierre Bonnard, Professor in the Faculty of Theology at the University of Lausanne, and the Revd Donald S. Deer have been kind enough to give critical scrutiny to certain parts of the manuscript. We offer them sincere thanks for their valuable suggestions and comments.

J.-F. COLLANGE

TRANSLATOR'S NOTE

I am deeply indebted to my friend Mr P. J. Allcock, with his sensitive knowledge of the French language, for carefully scrutinising the manuscript and thereby removing many blemishes and gross errors. Needless to say, I am entirely responsible for those errors which remain.

The text of the epistle which is given here is not a strict translation of the French but is rather a translation of the Greek made in the light of the exegesis contained in the body of the commentary.

A. W. HEATHCOTE

CONTENTS

INTRODUCTION

CERFAUX, L., 'L'épître aux Philippiens', in *Introduction à la Bible* (A. Robert and A. Feuillet, eds.), II, 1959, pp. 477–86.
FEINE, P., BEHM, J., *Einleitung in das NT*, 12th. ed. W. G. Kümmel, 1963.
GOGUEL, M., *Introduction au NT*, IV/1, 1925.
GRANT, R. M., *Historical Introduction to the NT*, 1963.
GUTHRIE, D., *NT Introduction, The Pauline Epistles*, 1961.
JAY, B., *Introduction au NT*, 1969.
KÜMMEL, W. G., cf. Feine-Behm.
MCNEILE, A. H., *An Introduction to the Study of the NT*[2], 1953.
MARXSEN, W., *Einleitung in das NT. Eine Einführung in ihre Probleme*,[3] 1964 (ET, *Introduction to the NT. An Approach to its Problems*, 1968).
MICHAELIS, W., *Einleitung in das NT*, 1946.
PRICE, J. L., *Interpreting the NT*, 1961.
— *Epître aux Philippiens. Introduction* (pp. 583–85, TOB).
WIKENHAUSER, A., *Einleitung in das NT*[5], 1965.

1. PHILIPPI AND THE PHILIPPIAN CHRISTIAN COMMUNITY

COLLART, P., *Philippes, ville de Macédoine, depuis ses origines jusqu'à la fin de l'époque romaine*, 1937.
LEMERLE, P., *Philippes et la Macédoine orientale à l'époque chrétienne et byzantine*, 1945.
PICARD, C., 'Les dieux de la colonie de Philippes vers le premier siècle de notre ère d'après les ex-voto rupestres', *RHR*, 86, 1922, pp. 117–201.

The first European city reached by the Gospel (Acts 16[9ff]), Philippi was not at that time of great importance but was the administrative centre for a rural area. It was founded about 360 B.C. by the exiled Athenian Callistratus, and a few years later was annexed by Philip II of Macedon who gave it his own name, fortified it, and drew from it a substantial revenue by exploiting the gold mines discovered nearby. These, however, were rapidly exhausted so that when the Roman consul Aemilius Paulus divided Macedonia into administrative districts in 167 B.C. it was Amphipolis (Acts 17[1]) which was chosen as the capital of the first district of the province ('Macedonia I') and not Philippi, which was further handicapped because its port, Neapolis, was so far away.

The year 42 B.C., however, marked an important turning-point in the life of this Macedonian city, not far from which occurred a memorable battle between the troops of Cassius and Brutus on the one hand and Antony and Octavian on the other. Immediately after the victory of the latter pair Antony discharged on the spot a considerable number of his veterans and settled them at Philippi which he made a Roman colony. Later, in the year 31 B.C., when Octavian in his turn had defeated the united forces of Antony and Cleopatra at Actium, the colony increased again, taking the name of *Colonia Julia (Augusta) Philippensis*, and apparently it was endowed with the *jus italicum* which gave it the privileges of a Roman city. Lying as it did on the *via Egnatia*, which was an important military and commercial route linking southern Italy with Asia Minor, Philippi was to experience two centuries of peaceful existence.

Apart from a basic indigenous Thracian strain, its population comprised various Greek elements, to which were added veterans of the Roman army and their descendants. The organisation of these last was modelled on that of Rome (quaestors, aediles, legates, etc.; cf. Acts $16^{36,38}$) and their language was Latin. Their religion was marked in particular by a distinctive syncretism (P. Collart, *op. cit.*, pp. 389–486; C. Picard., *art. cit.*). Alongside the indigenous Thracian cults which never lost their attraction (Dionysus, Artemis-Bendis, etc.) there flourished classical Graeco-Latin cults and a collection of foreign cults—Egyptian, Syrian and Anatolian—but in the first century a certain dominance of official Imperial religion is to be observed.

Between A.D. 49 and 52 Paul arrived in Philippi for the first time and in that way the Gospel came to Europe (Acts 16^{11-40}; 1^5; 4^{15}). A certain Lydia, a pagan attracted by Judaism, who 'feared God', was soon converted and offered hospitality to the Apostle and his colleagues. [Subsequently women seem to have continued to play an important part in the Christian community once it was established (4^{2f}). But so far as Paul was concerned the situation rapidly deteriorated. Even if the narrative of Acts 16^{16ff} is in large part legendary, it nonetheless corresponds to the testimony of 1 Thess. 2^2 (cf. 1^{30}) where the writer speaks of 'the injury and outrage which we had suffered at Philippi'. Having shortly to leave the city, Paul made his way to Thessalonica. The brevity of the time spent at Philippi only makes the more remarkable the special loyalty and affection binding the small church of that city to its apostle, to which this epistle bears lively testimony.

On two further occasions Paul was to have the opportunity of passing through Philippi. The second visit, mentioned in 1 Cor. 16^{5f}, does not seem to have been particularly peaceful to judge by the note in 2 Cor. 7^5 (cf. 2 Cor. 2^{13}; Acts 20^{1ff}), although 2 Cor. 8^2 still shows the good relationship existing between the apostle and the Macedonian congregations. It was the mere chance of a Jewish plot that brought Paul on a final visit to Philippi (Acts 20^6), and then it was the Passover period and he very soon set sail for Jerusalem via Troas.

We have to wait some decades until the Epistle of Polycarp to the Philippians in the first quarter of the second century before we hear again of the Christian community at Philippi, upon which the memory of the great apostle remained deeply impressed (9^{1f}; 3^2; 11^{2f}). Nothing, on the other hand, can be deduced from the apocryphal Acts of Paul (cf. W. Schneemelcher in E. Hennecke and W. Schneemelcher, *New Testament Apocrypha*, II, 1965, pp. 322ff).

2. AUTHENTICITY AND UNITY

A. *Authenticity*

BAUR, F. C., *Paulus, der Apostel Jesu Christi*, II², 1867, pp. 50–88.
MORTON, A. Q.-MCLEMAN, J., *Paul, the Man and the Myth: a Study in the Authorship of Greek Prose*, 1966.

The authenticity of the letter is no longer in dispute and the attacks of F. C. Baur and his followers seem things of the past. It is difficult to appreciate the motive a forger could have had in writing so disjointed a letter, which continually refers to a definite situation (but with so little precision) and the message of which does not stand out clearly. The further fact that Paul here shows himself hesitant and humble (1^{21ff}) and makes no appeal to his apostolic authority (cf. *ad* 1^1) excludes the suggestion that anyone could be using his name as a 'cover'. The epistle is therefore authentic. It is true that recently A. Q. Morton and J. McLeman, having recourse to the good offices of a computer, have believed it impossible to rank *Philippians* alongside *Romans*, *Galatians* and *1* and *2 Corinthians*. But in fact the brevity of the epistle, composed of several different fragments, makes futile any use of a computer the conclusions of which are based upon the statistics of large numbers. A bulldozer is of no use for digging a garden! The fact remains that Polycarp of Smyrna, as we have already pointed out, alludes in his own Epistle to the Philippians to letters (note the plural) which Paul had written to them (3^2), as well as to certain specific passages in our epistle (9^{1f}; 3^2; 11^2).

B. *Unity*

BORNKAMM, G., 'Der Philipperbrief als paulinische Briefsammlung', in *Neotestamentica et patristica. Freundesgabe O. Cullmann*, 1962, pp. 192–202.
— *Paul*, ET 1971, p. 246f.
BUCHANAN, C. O., 'Epaphroditus' sickness and the letter to the Philippians', *EVQ*, 36, 1964, pp. 157–66.
DELLING, G., art. 'Philipperbrief', *RGG*³, V, cols. 333–6.
FURNISH, V., 'The place and purpose of Phil. III', *NTS*, 10, 1962–3, pp. 80–8.
JEWETT, R., 'The epistolary thanksgiving and the integrity of Philippians', *NT*, 12, 1970, pp. 40–53.

KÖSTER, H., 'The purpose of the polemic of a Pauline fragment (Philippians III)', *NTS*, 8, 1961–2, pp. 317–32.

MACKAY, B. S., 'Further thoughts on Philippians', *NTS*, 7, 1960–61, pp, 161–70.

MÜLLER-BARDORFF, J., 'Zur Frage der literarischen Einheit des Philipperbriefes', *WZJ*, 7, 1957–58, pp. 591–604.

POLLARD, T. E., 'The integrity of Philippians,' *NTS*, 14, 1966–67, pp. 57–66.

RAHTJEN, B. D., 'The three letters of Paul to the Philippians', *NTS*, 6, 1959–60, pp. 167–73.

SCHMITHALS, W., *Paulus und die Gnostiker. Untersuchungen zu den kleinen Paulusbriefen*, 1965, pp. 48–58 (reprint of an article which had already appeared in *ZTK*, 54, 1957, pp. 297ff).

The integrity of the epistle, having been put in doubt in the 17th century,[1] was hardly discussed until about the middle of the 20th century. But the climate of opinion seems to have changed today so that there is a wealth of studies which regard the epistle as a composite collection of texts which were originally independent.[2] However, it is unnecessary to list the different patterns of dissection, for in fact they turn upon two fundamental problems: the marked break at 3^1 and the question of 4^{10-20}.

That a break occurs at 3^1 is obvious. The exhortation to rejoice in 3^{1a} is directly followed by a most stern warning (3^{1bff}), and the peculiarly virulent tone of **3** stands in contrast to the cordiality of **1** and **2**. It is true that the target for the virulence is not the Philippians themselves but particular opponents. No matter! The first two chapters give no hint of any pressing danger to the community and, on the other hand, none of the apostle's preoccupations about his own fate, which form a good part of **1** and **2**, reappear in **3**. Remembering then that Polycarp mentions several letters from the apostle to the Philippians, one can but ask whether **1–2** and **3** did not originally belong to different letters.[3]

Clearly, all these arguments are not irrefutable, and supporters of the unity of the epistle[4] point out that some time must have elapsed between the writing of **1–2** and **3–4**; that when at last Paul touches on the question of opponents, he becomes very heated; and are we not familiar elsewhere with these sudden changes of temper which are totally devoid of transition? It is, moreover, wrong to suppose

[1] By Le Moyne, according to M. GOGUEL (*op. cit.* p. 404f) who gives, moreover, a brief but very good historical survey of the question to the beginning of the 20th century.

[2] Among the works cited above by Bornkamm, Köster, Müller-Bardorff, Rahtjen, Schmithals; among the introductions, Marxsen; among the commentaries: Beare, Benoit, Friedrich, Gnilka, Michael.

[3] The *catalogus Sinaiticus* (c. A.D. 400) also has mention of two letters to the Philippians. But this testimony has little certainty.

[4] In studies cited by Delling, Furnish, Jewett, Mackay, Pollard; in introductions by Goguel, Grant, Guthrie, Kümmel, Michaelis, Price. Most commentators hold the same view.

that the opening of the letter is unmarked by any polemic when we remember the 'adversaries' ('*antikeimenoi*') of 1^{28}. The letter as a whole is certainly marked by a lack of organised plan; Paul talks to his dear Philippian friends and says just what he thinks as the ideas come into his mind—unless we join C. J. Bahr in thinking that the apostle who was used to dictating his letters took the pen himself at 3^1.[1] In no case are there any grounds for doubting the unanimity of the manuscript tradition of the letter.

What can we think of all this? It would be right to hesitate if the first two chapters in actual fact looked like a kind of aimless chit-chat, but reading them with a little attentiveness shows that this is not the case. Although Paul makes no academic composition of the chapters, he does certainly follow, in a coherent manner, a definite aim. After the fine opening lines of his introduction (1^{3-11}) he first gives news of his own circumstances (1^{12-26}), then his opinion of the situation developing at Philippi ($1^{27}-2^{18}$), and he ends with plans for the future (2^{19-30}). On the other hand, the argument of 3 in itself is particularly compact and does not lack a measure of theological profundity. We are faced, then, with two homogeneous and coherent blocks, but the coherence is disrupted if we put the two sections together. All that we then get is a rather clumsy juxtaposing the purpose of which we try in vain to discover. In face of the evident break at 3^1 and the obvious artificiality of all attempts so far to bridge the gap, the conclusion is clear; our epistle is a composite work. The only substantial argument in favour of its unity is the continuity of themes between 3 and $1^{27}-2^{18}$. But this difficulty must be resolved otherwise than by the unity of the letter, as we shall show further on.

The second problem is posed by 4^{10-20} which is a self-sufficient pericope only loosely connected with its context. The apostle is here thanking the Philippians for material assistance which they have sent to him in prison. But is a place at the end of a letter at all likely for an expression of thanks? This is the more questionable if account is taken of the fact that 1^{3-11} and 2^{19-30} allude to a gift for which the apostle seems to have rendered thanks already. Moreover, 2^{19-30} shows that quite a long time must have elapsed between the arrival of Epaphroditus, who brought the offering, and the writing of the same passage.[2] Would Paul have waited so long before expressing his thanks? and, moreover, does not 2^{19-30} allow us to suppose frequent exchanges between Paul and Philippi? Thus, most writers we have mentioned who think that our epistle arose from originally distinct letters add to the two fragments already defined a third one, viz. 4^{10-20}. It was a mere note, doubtless prior to the rest of our epistle, in which Paul acknowledged the receipt of the gift which had

[1] 'The Subscriptions in the Pauline Letters', *JBL*, 1968, pp. 27–41.
[2] The period still remains very important even if one attempts to reduce it by supposing that Epaphroditus fell ill before he reached Paul (C. O. BUCHANAN, *art. cit.*, p. 160f; B. S. MACKAY, *art. cit.*, p. 169).

just reached him. Alone among scholars Gnilka and Friedrich reject this deduction yet without producing specific arguments. Yet such arguments could have a bearing on the way in which Paul understood the initiative of the Philippians. So it is that C. O. Buchanan (*art. cit.*, pp. 161ff) thinks that Paul having forbidden the sending of material gifts welcomed Epaphroditus' mission with a certain coolness, hence the not very enthusiastic reference to it at the end of the letter. Yet however attractive, this interpretation does not give a sound account of the whole passage 4^{10-20}. We therefore believe that our epistle is composed of three different letters, namely, 4^{10-20}; a letter comprising essentially 1 and 2; and a letter consisting principally of 3.

Is it possible to be more definite? Putting vv. 10–20 aside, 4 consists of exhortations and recommendations which could equally well be taken as the ending of any of the above mentioned letters. And it is essentially on this point that one notices divergences among advocates of the composite structure of the epistle; any conclusion about it is tentative (Köster). But among the mass of exhortations and recommendations in 4 four different sections can be distinguished: (a) vv. (1) 2–3; (b) vv. 4–7; (c) vv. 8–9; (d) vv. 21–23. Vv. 4–7, or (b), are to be attached to the first two chapters because they continue the dominant theme of joy, absent from 3 and interrupted at 3^{1a}, and moreover in both instances we have injunctions to prayer and thankfulness ($4^6 = 1^{3ff} = 2^{12ff}$) and reference to the nearness of the Lord ($4^4 = 1^{7,11} = 2^{16}$). The first section, vv. 2–3, cannot be separated from vv. 4–7 without unnecessarily complicating the intervention of the final redactor of the epistle and failing to recognise the striking coincidence between the references to the theme of striving on behalf of the Gospel, frequent in 1 and 2, present in 4^3 ($=1^{5,7,12,16}$; 2^{22}), but absent from 3. Thus $4^{(1)2-7}$ belongs to the same letter as the first two chapters.[1]

On the other hand, 4^{8-9} (section *c*) re-echoes and refers back to the beginning of 4 and has more in common with the tone of 3^{1b-21}, especially in what touches on the example offered by the apostle ($4^9 = 3^{17ff}$; cf. however 1^{29ff}). The greetings of 4^{21-23} by their reference to 'those of Caesar's household' link either with the 'praetorium' of 1^{13} or to the note 4^{10-20} which, so far as the imprisonment of the apostle goes, presupposes an analogous situation to 1 and 2. We therefore arrive at the following allocation of the various sections of the epistle:[2]

A = 4^{10-20} (or 4^{10-23});
B = $1^1–3^{1a}+4^{2-7}+(4^{21-23})$;
C = $3^{1b}–4^1+4^{8-9}$.

---

[1] Beare, Bornkamm, Marxsen, Müller-Bardorff, Rahtjen, attach 4^{21-23} to the first two chapters; Schmithals and—with more reservations Benoit—to 4^{10-20}.

[2] The dissection may seem baffling to the uninitiated, so in the detailed commentary we have nevertheless preferred to follow the canonical order of the chapters and verses.

The chronological order of these three letters presents little difficulty. By its nature as a brief note of thanks letter A is earlier than
letter B. In letter C there is no reference to imprisonment. It could
then have been written before the apostle's imprisonment, but in such a
case it is hard to conceive that the later letters A and B should have
retained no single echo of the violent polemic underlying 3 (=C),
unless with Beare we assume that the letters were not all addressed
to Philippi. It seems much more likely to us that when Paul wrote
letter C he had left prison and was attacking an alarming state of
affairs in the Philippian community, a state already discernible in
germ from the contents of letter B.

C. Compilation

FEINE, P. —BEHM, J., *Einleitung*, 12th ed. by W. G. Kümmel, 1963,
    pp. 352ff.
GNILKA, J., *Der Philipperbrief*, 1968, pp. 10f, 14–18.
MICHAELIS, W., 'Teilungshypothesen bei Paulusbriefen', *ThZ*, 14,
    1958, pp. 321–26.
MITTON, C. L., *The Formation of the Pauline Corpus of Letters*, 1955.
MOULE, C. F. D., *The Birth of the New Testament*, 1962, pp. 199–206.
SCHMITHALS, W., 'Zur Abfassung und ältester Sammlung der paulinis-
    chen Hauptbriefe', *ZNW*, 51, 1960, pp. 225–45.

Every hypothesis about the composite structure of the epistle,
finally implies the possibility of some redactional activity, a possibility against which W. Michaelis cautions us (*art. cit.*). Yet the
evidence is strong. Very early on the Pauline epistles were put into
circulation, doubtless being read during worship and so forming
gradually a collection which would give birth to our existing canon.
Certainly, the attempt to develop the hypothesis further and to name
the people concerned in this event is to move into pure speculation
and it would be better to affirm with C. F. D. Moule that what
occurred was a 'slow, anonymous process' (*op. cit.*, p. 203). We must
put redaction of our epistle within this process. It is quite understandable that when writings of the apostle passed into circulation
the Philippian community, which was in possession of three quite
modest notes, may have thought it useful to assemble them into a
more imposing whole. Behind this was the wholly practical reason
of circulation but also certainly the motive of prestige—the apostle's
letters were acquiring an eminently respectable status.

In no way must the honesty of the act of composition be put in
question; it took place with texts which were regarded as almost
sacred and, whatever may have been said at various times, the epistle
bears no trace of interpolations. The simple fact is that in wanting
to make one letter out of three, all the passages of exhortation with
which Paul usually ends his letters were put at the end. The plan of
the edited work is therefore clear: Introduction (1^{1-12})—Body of the
letter (1^{12}–4^{1})—Exhortations and recommendations (4^{2-23}). Each of

these chapters re-grouped the corresponding sections of the original letters. From this viewpoint letter A (4^{10-20}) is merely regarded as a component of the collection of 'recommendations' which close the epistle.

3. THE LETTERS AND THE CIRCUMSTANCES
THEY PRESUPPOSE

A. *Letter A* (4^{10-20})

The apostle is in prison and the Philippians have sent a gift to supply his needs through the mediation of Epaphroditus, one of their company (4^{18}; cf. 2^{25ff}). Paul, no doubt beset by more urgent preoccupations, sent brief thanks for the assistance. But one detects that the apostle is not without certain reservations about the matter.

B. *Letter B* ($1^1-3^{1a}+4^{2-7}+4^{21-23}$)

This letter comprises the greater part of our present epistle. Paul is still in prison ($1^{7,13ff}$); but what are his circumstances? An answer to this question seems of prime importance for a correct understanding of the text, likewise also that of the circumstances of the apostle's correspondents. We shall therefore first of all devote some care to the closer examination of these two issues.

(a) *The apostle's circumstances*

MANSON, T. W., 'St Paul in Ephesus. The date of the Epistle to the Philippians', *BJRL*, 23, 1939, pp. 182–200.

It is generally believed that the imprisoned apostle stood in danger of death but did not know precisely the fate which awaited him. For this reason the letter would be rather like a last will and testament sent by Paul to the congregation he had founded. In it he would once again affirm that his over-riding concern is the advancement of the Gospel ($1^{5,7,12,16,27}$; 2^{22}) and emphasise the humility which is a mark of the Christian community (2^{1ff}). From such a perspective his own imprisonment (or even, with Lohmeyer, his martyrdom) could seem profitable (1^{12}) and *joy* at the progress of the work of God could largely override his personal sufferings.[1]

Such an analysis rests upon 1^{21-24} and 2^{17} where it seems possible to detect allusions to an imminent death. This is so generally accepted that nowadays the study by T. W. Manson listed in the Bibliography in which he tries to show that Paul had already left prison when he wrote the letter is passed over without comment. Manson is certainly far from carrying us with him completely since we think that Paul indeed writes as a prisoner and that the allusions to legal proceedings (1^{13}) cannot refer to his appearance before Gallio at Corinth (Acts 18^{12-17}).[2] But Manson (joined at this point by Michaelis)

[1] 1^4, ^{25}; 2^2, ^{29}; 4^1; 1^{18}; 2^{17}, ^{28}; 3^1.
[2] Manson's views seem to have been taken up again recently in the Dutch commentary by Matter.

carries conviction when he shows that there is nothing in the themes taken up or in the tone employed which fits in with a letter of final farewell. On the contrary, what we find are rather anticipations of a renewed meeting ($1^{25f,27}$; $2^{12,24}$), and the dominant theme of joy is at least as intelligible in a context of expected liberation as in that of the imminence of death.

It is true that the situation underlying 1^{12-26} is not easy to assess and that vv. 21–24 seem to imply that the apostle awaited sentence without knowing whether he would be acquitted or condemned to death. But the style of these verses has hardly any other parallels in Paul except in rhetorical passages where he is influenced by the technique of the diatribe, so that we can quite properly ask whether, far from expressing an actual state of mind, the author is not giving vent to a rhetorical and theological defence of a certain stance. The suggestion is given further weight when it is observed that the preceding verses (vv. 15–18) put the reader in a polemical situation. This is a fact generally ill-understood. Some, as Barth, Dibelius and Gnilka, are happy to regard vv. 15–18 as a rather superfluous parenthesis. Such a judgement has no support from the text, and the link between vv. 15–18 and vv. 21–24 is confirmed by the '*gar*' ('in fact') in v. 19. Moreover, the identity of the persons envisaged in 1^{15ff} is not without embarrassment for commentators. It is agreed nowadays that genuine Christian preachers were in mind, because Paul raises no objection to them on doctrinal grounds.

In our view we must go further and we will venture a suggestion which is obviously tentative but which does not lack evidence as will soon be seen.

After being in prison for some time Paul has just decided to bring about his liberation by revealing his qualification of Roman citizenship.[1] But this initiative has not been uniformly well received by the Christian community of the city where he is. Some may have accused him of cowardice and made it clear that the true vocation for a disciple of Christ and an apostle of the Cross was martyrdom. Hence the apostle's defence in 1^{12-26} which shows that his sole concern has been the Gospel. Furthermore, the results of his action have been in accordance with his hopes. As his trial dragged along all the praetorium were stirred by what he revealed (v. 12f); the Christian community in the city, hitherto paralysed by his imprisonment, found the courage to speak out once more (v. 14); even those who reproached him for taking this initiative proclaimed the authentic Gospel, that is the Cross, though their motives might be suspect (vv. 15–18); and because of his earnestness, his appearing before the judges will be a unique opportunity for glorifying Christ (vv. 19f). Martyrdom, indeed, would have been an easy option (vv. 21–24); henceforward a new mission field and new horizons of work are opened up.

To this rapid glance at the purpose of 1^{12-26}, supporting our

[1] We presuppose by this that Paul was not writing from Rome; *v. infra* pp. 15ff.

hypothesis of Paul's initiative, can be added further points of detailed exegesis, the most notable of which to be mentioned here are that three times over (vv. 15, 17, 18) it is said of the malicious preachers that they preached 'Christ'. Now for Paul, to proclaim Christ could only be to proclaim the Cross. In v. 17 the drift of these preachers is quite clearly stated: 'They think to raise up affliction (*'thlipsis'*) for me in my bonds'. Also in v. 22 Paul says he does not know which to *choose* (*'airēsomai'*), whether death or life; he does not say which to *wish for*, in the way one too readily assumes. How is the choice to be explained on the traditional lines of interpretation?

When these exegetical points are brought to light does the hypothesis we are propounding seem historically viable? It is, indeed, the only defensible one unless one accepts the suggestion of a Roman imprisonment, for outside the capital the apostle's Roman citizenship would protect him from any death sentence (cf. Acts 25¹¹) unless Paul himself decided to conceal his true identity. Now the exchanges between Paul and the Philippians of which our epistle is the echo show that imprisonment had already lasted for some time, just as 1²¹⁻²⁴ shows that the apostle's intention had been to 'magnify Christ' (v. 20) by his death and sufferings. But indeed the situation was to become gloomier; the trial ran the risk of proceeding unnoticed; the intimidated local church was fearful (v. 14); and alarming news arrived of other congregations like the one at Philippi (vv. 25ff). Hence the turn-about by the apostle who, in his constant concern for the Gospel, decided to achieve his liberation by revealing his true citizenship. The circumstance is in no way incredible and Acts gives us three comparable occasions (16³⁷ᶠᶠ; 22²⁵; 25¹¹). Nevertheless, there and then among some of the Christians this change of mind aroused the hostile reaction which we have seen. 'No matter! Christ is proclaimed . . .' (v. 18).

There is, of course, 2¹⁷ which is also usually understood in the context of martyrdom, but perhaps we may be allowed to refer the reader to the detailed exegesis where it will be shown that the sense is quite different.

(b) *The Philippian community*

In spite of the tone of cordiality towards the Christian community at Philippi, it is clear that it was not without difficulties and problems. Appeals to humility and mutual regard (2¹ᶠᶠ) point to internal rivalries, dissensions and jealousy. And one can go further. The fact that the section 1²⁷–2¹⁸ presents analogies with 3¹ᵇ–4¹ has often been stressed by those who uphold the unity of the epistle. We agree with W. Schmithals (*op. cit.*, p. 54) that the opponents, who have come from outside and who are attacked so violently in letter C, had already started their work of propaganda when Paul wrote letter B. This view finds definite confirmation in 1²⁸ which poses a difficult exegetical problem only to be disposed of from this viewpoint. Where we differ from Schmithals is in determining the identity of the opponents, a matter we shall try to clarify in the study of letter C (3^{1b}–4^{1}); but we can say here that the letter puts before us Judaeo-Christian itinerant preachers who give themselves out as splendid patterns to be copied and in marked contrast to the wretched appearance of the apostle of the Cross. So it is understandable that their action would lead to troubles and rivalries, and in particular it can be appreciated how welcome the Christological hymn (2^{5-11}) would be in this context. For the Christian one 'pattern' alone is possible, a pattern which anchors the Christian life to *history*. It is a way which leads from humiliation to exaltation, from misery to glory; the glory is promised with certainty, but the way to it passes necessarily through the abasement and humiliation of the Cross.

(c) *The apostle's response; outline and contents of letter B.*

The apostle's attitude of mind which this second Philippian letter reveals can be characterised, against the backcloth which we have just sketched, by joy, affection and vigilance. By joy, because yet again Paul is on the way to experiencing the dynamism of the Gospel ('*prokopē euanggeliou*', 1^{12}) and affection because the Philippian gesture of generosity has revived an old friendship. And so he does not take advantage of his apostolic authority (*ad* 1^{1}) and in a very long prologue (1^{3-11}) he gives every assurance as to his feelings. These apply to *all* his readers ('*pantes*' occurs a number of times, cf. *ad* 1^{1}) without exception, and this stress introduces from the start another side to the apostle's attitude, namely vigilance. Aware of the grave problems presenting themselves at Philippi, he nevertheless thinks that persuasion would serve rather better than unyielding authoritarianism. But in this case the transition from letter B to letter C shows that the gentle method has not wholly succeeded.

The following features may be discerned in the plan of the letter:

Address (1^{1-2}). Paul addresses himself humbly and warmly to all the Philippians.

Prologue (1^{3-11}). A new and solemn assertion of affection. Everything must be viewed in the searching light of God's action in Jesus Christ and in the light of prayer and of the action of grace.

The apostle's own situation (1^{12-26}). Whatever envious people may think of it (1^{15ff}), action by the apostle to gain his freedom had for its sole motive the advancement of the Gospel. In this respect his hopes are on the way to being realised (cf. v. 12b).

The situation at Philippi (1^{27}–2^{18}). The unity of the church itself is being threatened by the intrusion of adversaries ('*antikeimenoi*', 1^{28}) by whom the Cross, the very sign of salvation, is robbed of meaning and faith of its striving and suffering (1^{27-30}). Thus uprooted from what gives it specific character, the Christian community is no more than any other community of people in which each makes use of the other for the sake of self-aggrandisement (2^{1-4}). This is why it is of the first importance to anchor it once again in the events

which alone gave it birth and which can sustain it, namely, in the
unparalleled voluntary humiliation of one who wanted nothing for
himself and yet received everything from God (2⁵⁻¹¹). These events
are both dynamic and constraining, so that the Philippians are called
upon to abandon their present fanciful ideas and to 'work for their
salvation with fear and trembling'. Then, on both sides, joy will be
made perfect (2¹²⁻¹⁸).

Immediate problems and personal questions (2¹⁹–3¹ᵃ+4²⁻⁷+4²¹⁻²³).
Since he himself is unable to visit Philippi in the immediate future
the apostle proposes to send Timothy there (2¹⁹⁻²⁴); and he preferred
to have Epaphroditus, the Philippian representative, return home
because of his state of health (2²⁵⁻³⁰). The letter ends with various
personal recommendations (4²⁻³), a fresh exhortation to joyfulness
(4⁴⁻⁷) and greetings (4²¹⁻²³).

C. *Letter C* (3¹ᵇ–4¹+4⁸⁻⁹)

BETZ, H. D., *Nachfolge und Nachahmung Jesus Christi im NT*, 1967,
    pp. 145–53.
COLLANGE, J. F., *Enigmes de la deuxième épître de Paul aux Corin-
    thiens*, 1972, pp. 320–24.
GEORGI, D., *Die Gegner des Paulus im 2. Korintherbrief. Studien zur
    religiösen Propaganda in der Spätantike*, 1964.
GNILKA, J., 'Die antipaulinische Mission in Philippi', *BZ*, 1965, pp.
    258–76.
— Excursus no. 4 to the *Commentary*, 1968, pp. 211–18.
JEWETT, R., 'Conflicting movements in the early church as reflected
    in Philippians', *NT*, 12, 1970, pp. 362–90.
KLIJN, A. F. J., 'Paul's opponents in Phil. III', *NT*, VII, 1964–65,
    pp. 278–84.
KÖSTER, H., 'The purpose of the polemic of a Pauline fragment
    (Philippians III)', *NTS*, 8, 1961–62, pp. 317–32.
LÜETGERT, W., '*Die Vollkommenen im Philipperbrief und die Enthu-
    siasten in Thessalonich*, 1909.
SCHMITHALS, W., 'Die Irrlehrer des Philipperbriefes' in *Paulus und
    die Gnostiker*, 1965, pp. 47–87 (the article appeared in its first
    form in 1957 in *ZTK*, 54, pp. 297–341.

The apostle's final letter to the Philippians bears the stamp of
violent polemic, Paul even going so far as to brand his opponents
as 'dogs' (3²). So it is impossible to understand the true intention
of the text before first attempting to particularise these opponents.

(a) *The adversaries of the Gospel at Philippi*

The initial problem which the attempt at clarification poses is
whether we are dealing with a single group of opponents or two
different groups (perhaps even three, according to Michael). 3¹⁸ᶠ
could indeed be interpreted as an attack on an immoral laxity which
stood in singular contrast to the niggling legalism implied by 3²ᶠᶠ. In
that case Paul would be fighting on two distinct fronts in our letter,

against Jews or Judaisers on the one hand and libertines,[1] materialistically minded Christians (Scott; H. D. Betz, *op. cit.*, p. 151) or even *lapsi* who had given way under persecution (Lohmeyer) on the other. Yet such a division corresponds to no clear distinction in the text itself. On the contrary, the arguments are linked to one another; thus, eschatology, death and resurrection are mentioned in vv. 10ff as in vv. 20ff; and the figure of the race-track which occurs first at v. 12 is continued in the *'peripatein'* ('walk') of v. 17f. Furthermore, the interpretation of v. 18f is not very assurred and A. F. J. Klijn (*art. cit.*) even goes so far as to apply these verses to a purely Jewish attitude; it is therefore both arbitrary and risky to separate them from the beginning of the chapter. Paul is in fact attacking on a single front.

Incontestably, the foremost characteristic of the Philippian heresy concerns its Judaistic nature which is evident in the whole argument of the first part of the chapter and in the allusion to circumcision (3[2f]). Is this Judaism or Judaistic Christianity? The question is debatable, and we can only return to it later.

The second certainty one can have is that these people are outsiders. Nowhere in fact does the apostle try to win them over or to get them to abandon their views. They are 'outside the circle of the recipients of the epistle', as Goguel says. They are presenting themselves as nothing less than patterns to be copied since the insistence with which Paul puts himself forward as such is striking to the degree that the whole chapter could be viewed from this perspective alone—'become imitators of me' (*'summimētai mou ginesthe'*, v. 17; cf. 1[30])! The pattern thus offered to the Philippians was to be a perfectionistic one and the word 'perfect' (*'teleios'*, v. 15) certainly figured in the language of the propaganda.

Could these people have been gnostics? This is the suggestion of Schmithals and Köster. But Schmithals' argument rests entirely upon an exegesis which sees a libertine group behind vv. 18ff, and gnosticism as the one melting-pot able to fuse together Judaism (3[2ff]) and libertinism. We have already said that such exegesis lacks evidence. Köster however even goes so far as to speak of a rigoristic gnosticism. Everything turns on the question of what gnosticism is but nothing in this chapter shows features characteristic of it.

The Judaistic thesis[2] lacks probability also, if only because it would be hard to envisage Gentile Christians nurtured on Pauline teaching readily abandoning the freedom of the Gospel. In fact what is most striking, as Gnilka has rightly seen and in part Jewett also (*art. cit.*, pp. 364ff), is the resemblance between the polemic in this chapter and that of *2 Corinthians*. There too we are in the presence of opponents who were itinerant preachers, boasting of their Jewish ancestry (11[22f]) and particularly interested in the Old Covenant

---

[1] Beare, Dibelius, Haupt, Jewett, Lightfoot, W. LÜTGERT (*op. cit.*, pp. 10–14), Michael, Michaelis, Staab.
[2] Goguel, A. F. J. Klijn (*art. cit.*), Müller.

(3^{1-18}). The analogy runs even to the vocabulary: *'ergatēs'* ('work-man'; 3^2 and 2 Cor. 11^{13}), and *'hebraios'* ('Hebrew', 3^5 and 2 Cor. 11^{22}) both of which D. Georgi has definitely shown belong to Jewish and indeed Jewish-Christian missionary propaganda (*op. cit.*, pp. 49–60). Now the Jewish-Christian missionaries at Corinth presented themselves, just like the numerous propagators of various religions and philosophies at that period, as representatives of the deity (*'theioi andres'*) and put on many a display of ecstasy and extraordinary acts as the guarantee of their 'apostleship'.

Such a theology could be built upon an apparently seductive Christology, that of the miracles and the resurrection. It in fact meant the decline of Christology. With the scandal of the Cross and the perspective of a long pilgrimage of faith towards a world yet to come, it was Christ himself who was being pushed aside to the ad-vantage of the 'glory' belonging to his 'apostles' (cf. our study of *2 Corinthians*). It is remarkable to notice how often Paul seems in *Philippians* to confront the same dangers. He talks of 'enemies of the Cross' (3^{18}); he stresses the sufferings and the death of Christ as well as the Christian's conformity therewith ($3^{10ff,21}$; cf. 1^{28ff}; 2^{12ff}). For the apostle the Christian is still 'en route' (3^{12ff}) and the glory is yet to come (3^{11}; 3^{20f}); and above all there is for him but one pattern—Christ himself (2^{5-11}) or that of men who humbly follow in the steps of their master (3^{17}).

However, it is not certain that we should totally identify Paul's opponents in *2 Corinthians* with those in *Philippians*. In the latter, apostleship does not seem to be directly in dispute; everything occurs on the community level itself. Even reflections upon the Covenant are absent (2 Cor. 3), so that our epistle gives the impression of opponents who were certainly akin to those of *2 Corinthians*, but less prestigious, mere followers (here) in comparison with masters (there).

The missionary movement which launched the early Christians upon the roads of the Empire was no isolated phenomenon. It was part of a vast religious movement in the history of the first century of our era which created a host of itinerant preachers, miracle-workers and bearers of hitherto unknown revelations who brought to a Graeco-Roman civilisation, where ancient beliefs no longer sufficed, the marvel and mystery for which it hungered. The very originality of Christianity, nay more its essence and its very survival are at stake; hence the importance of defining it as the message of the Crucified and Risen One and that alone. Hence, also, the virulence and the violence of the apostle in this chapter.

(b) *The apostle's reply; plan and contents of letter C*

No longer is Paul in prison, and on the other hand the situation at Philippi is much aggravated ('I repeat it', $3^{1b,18}$). So the tone is pas-sionate, violent ('dogs', 3^2) and uneasy ('with tears', 3^{18}). There is nothing academic about the argument. The apostle gives solemn

warning of the machinations of the intruders (vv. 1b–4a) whose
title to glory has not enough substance to impress him (vv. 4b–6). On
the contrary, the Gospel of the Cross represents an overturning of
values, as the 'catechesis' of salvation by faith and divine righteousness shows (vv. 7–11). Moreover, the Christian life, rooted in time
and in history, runs out towards a goal which though assured is not
yet attained (vv. 12–16).

3^{17}–4^1 only repeat these various points (imitation of the apostle,
cautions, appeal to the glory which lies ahead) while 4^{8-9} ends the
letter with an urgent appeal for an attitude which is 'reasonable' and
confident.

4. PLACES AND DATES OF COMPOSITION

ANTOINE, P., art., 'Ephèse', *DBS*, 11, 1934, cols. 1076–1104.

COLSON, J., *Paul. Apôtre et martyr*, 1971, pp. 145–55.

DEISSMANN, A., 'Zur ephesenischen Gefangenschaft des Apostels
Paulus', *Anatolian Studies. Mélanges W. M. Ramsey*, 1923, pp.
121–27.

DODD, C. H., *New Testament Studies*, II, 1953, p. 83–128.

DUNCAN, G. S., *St Paul's Ephesian Ministry*, 1929.

— 'Were St Paul's imprisonment epistles written from Ephesus?',
ExpT, 1955–56, pp. 163–66.

— 'Paul's ministry in Asia; the last phase', *NTS*, 3, 1956–57, pp.
211–18.

— 'Chronological table to illustrate Paul's ministry in Asia', *NTS*,
5, 1958–59, pp. 43–5.

HARRISON, P. N., 'The Pastoral Epistles and Duncan's Ephesian
theory', *NTS*, 2, 1955–56, pp. 250–61.

JOHNSON, L., 'The Pauline Letters from Caesarea', *ExpT*, 68, 1956–57,
pp. 24–6.

LISCO, H., *Vincula sanctorum. Ein Beitrag zur Erklärung der Gefangenschaftsbriefe des Apostels Paulus*, 1900.

MALHERBE, A. J., 'The beasts at Ephesus', *JBL*, 87, 1968, pp. 71–80.

MICHAELIS, W., *Die Datierung des Philipperbriefes*, u.d.

SCHMID, J., *Zeit und Ort der paulinischen Gefangenschaftsbriefe*,
1931.

To regard our epistle as an edited collection may complicate a
little the controversial question of where and when the letters were
written. Dispute really centres on letter B, written in prison. Letter
A came slightly earlier and letter C which no longer suggests imprisonment may have been written some months or even a year after
the main letter, the problems referred to in this latter having had
time to come to a head.

Until the beginning of this century and encouraged by the super-
scriptions which introduce it in the manuscripts, expositors have
thought that our epistle originated in the apostle's Roman captivity

(Acts 28[16ff]) and that it therefore belonged to the end of his life. Along with the imprisonment at Caesarea (Acts 24ff), this is the only one taken account of in the *Acts*, and the allusions to the 'praetorium' (1[13]) and to 'those of Caesar's household' (4[22]) seem unmistakable. Still today a Roman origin has many supporters,[1] and has been particularly well defended by J. Schmid and C. H. Dodd (*op. cit.*). Placing the writing of the epistle thus, so much later than the bulk of the Pauline letters, it is all the more possible to detect a development in the apostle's thought, especially in his eschatology (cf. 1[20ff]).

But this view runs up against various objections of which the strongest concerns the distance between Rome and Philippi. We must reckon four or five weeks at that period for travelling from the one city to the other (discussed by Lightfoot, p. 38). Now our epistle implies a whole series of exchanges between the apostle and the church at Philippi. The latter had been informed of Paul's imprisonment; they had sent Epaphroditus; they had learned of his illness (2[25ff]) and he in his turn had heard that his compatriots were anxious about him (2[26]). Even if we suppose with Mackay (*NTS*, 7, pp. 161ff) and C. O. Buchanan (*EvQ*, 36, 1964, pp. 157–66) that Epaphroditus had fallen ill on the journey the problem is not resolved.

The plans voiced by the apostle reflect the same ease of communication: he is ready to send Epaphroditus back (2[25ff]), to dispatch Timothy a little later (2[19ff]) who will return to reassure him about the state of the congregation at Philippi, after which he contemplates coming himself to his readers. This last point, moreover, stands in contradiction to Rom. 15[24–28] where Paul says he wants to set out for Spain after travelling to Rome. So if our epistle had been written in that city we should have to suppose that his plans concerning Spain had been completely abandoned and that far from continuing to look towards the West he turns back to the East. It is true that the argument does not have compelling force any more than does the difficulty of identifying the very free detention described in Acts 28[16ff] with the threat of death which seems to press (or rather, had pressed) upon the apostle according to *Philippians*. But when it is further realised that the 'praetorium' ('*praitorion*' 1[13]) can signify the residence of any provincial governor (the sole use of the term in the New Testament; Mt. 27[27] par.; Acts 23[35]) and that slaves or freedmen in 'the imperial service' (4[23]) were to be found throughout the Empire it can be appreciated that the hypothesis of a Roman origin is not really compelling. Then the fact that our epistle may be the reflection of a sustained correspondence

---

[1] In the commentaries by Barth, Beare, Haupt, Jones, Müller, Scott, Staab, Vincent; in the introductions by L. CERFAUX, *op. cit.*, p. 485f; R. M. GRANT, *op. cit.* p. 192f; D. GUTHRIE, *op. cit.*, pp. 144ff; B. JAY, *op. cit.*, p. 208f; and among the special studies by P. N. HARRISON (*NTS*, 2, 55–56, pp. 250–61); B. S. MACKAY (*NTS*, 7, 60–61, p. 168); RAHTJEN (*NTS*, 6, 59–60, p. 169f).

speaks against it further because of the distance between Rome and Philippi. This explains why almost all who hold to the redactional composition of the letter are opposed to a Roman origin.[1]

If it was not Rome, was it then Caesarea? This view, first aired by H. E. G. Paulus (1799; cf. J. Schmid, *op. cit.*, p. 2, n1), notably upheld by E. Lohmeyer in his commentary and, more recently, by L. Johnson (*ExpT*, 68, 1956–57, pp. 24–6), has not in fact gained much support to the present time.[2] The reason is easily explained. Philippi is as far from Caesarea as Rome, so that a Caesarean theory has all the defects of a Roman one without any advantages.

At this point a third possibility emerges, namely that of an Ephesian imprisonment. The interest of this view is obvious at once —Ephesus was only a week's sail from Philippi. To say with Scott that communications between Rome and Philippi were easier than between Ephesus and Philippi verges on the dishonest. Paul had stayed in Ephesus for almost two years on his third missionary journey (Acts 19) and obviously the single chapter in the Acts devoted to this period is far from giving an exhaustive account of all the things that happened there, and even if the narrative makes no mention of an imprisonment it nevertheless does not fail to indicate that it was not all easy going (Acts 19[21ff]) and later when Paul wanted to bid farewell to the 'elders' of the church of Ephesus it was Miletus and not Ephesus which had to be the place for the final meeting (Acts 20[17ff]). Again, passages such as 2 Cor. 6[5]; 11[23] and Rom. 16[7] (cf. 1 Clem. 5[6]) allude to several Pauline imprisonments *prior* to those of Caesarea and Rome. We may add that Ephesus was the provincial capital and that the residence of the Roman governor (*DBS*, II, 1934, col. 1086) as well as of men 'in the Imperial service' was to be found there, as an inscription discovered in 1877 testifies: '*curam agunt collegia lib(ertorum) et servorum domini n(ostri) Aug(usti) i(nfra) s(cripta)*' (G. S. Duncan, *op. cit.*, p. 110). Ephesus may therefore be said to meet in every way the requirements for being the place of origin of our epistle.

First suggested by H. Lisco in 1900 and taken up by A. Deissmann, this theory has been particularly defended on the German side by W. Michaelis and on the British by G. S. Duncan. It has gained support today not only from those who uphold the redactional origin of our letter (*v. supra*) but also from a not inconsiderable group of scholars who champion the unity of *Philippians*.[3] It does however

---

[1] B. D. RAHTJEN (*art. cit.*) is about the only exception to this rule. The commentaries by Beare, Benoit (to some extent; *BJ*, p. 19), Friedrich, Gnilka (pp. 18–25), Michael; the studies by G. BORNKAMM (*op. cit.*, p. 199), J. MÜLLER-BARDORFF (*art. cit.*, p. 598f), W. MARXSEN (*Introduction*, ET 1968, pp. 64ff), W. SCHMITHALS (*Paulus* . . ., 1965, p. 84) are opposed to a Roman origin. Michaelis and Gnilka also detect in our epistle some indications of the recent origin of the Philippian church (cf. 1[30]; 2[12–16]; 4[15f]).

[2] W. G. KÜMMEL (P. Feine—J. Behm—W. G. Kümmel, *Einleitung*, pp. 236, 239) is not unfavourably disposed towards it.

[3] Bonnard; G. DELLING (*RGG*[3], V, col. 335); Goguel; P. LEMERLE (*Philippes*

confront us with two serious difficulties. There is no direct evidence for this imprisonment; and, if Paul had been imprisoned, would he have risked death since he had the privilege of an appeal to Caesar on the basis of his Roman citizenship?

The second objection is removed at once by our suggestion concerning the actual predicament of the apostle at the time when letters A and B were written. Paul did not at first reveal his Roman citizenship because he thought that the time had come to die as a martyr and thereby to glorify Christ. It was only in the face of a different course of events that he changed his mind and took steps to procure his freedom by revealing his true identity. The difficult verse 1 Cor. 15[32] further supports this theory and at the same time appears as a clear allusion to an Ephesian captivity.

The Jerusalem Bible translates the verse: 'If my motives were only human ones, what good would it do me to fight the wild animals at Ephesus?' (*'ei kata anthrōpon ethēriomachēsa en Ephesō, ti moi to ophelos;*') But the difficulty of this interpretation is apparent. If Paul had actually fought with beasts how had he lived to tell the tale, and, furthermore, did not his citizenship protect him from such a combat? It has therefore been suggested to take the verb *'thēriomacheō'* ('to fight with wild beasts') figuratively, e.g. 'to fight with adversaries as ferocious as wild beasts'. A. J. Malherbe (*art. cit.*) has recently accorded his support to this interpretation, but it comes to grief because of the regular use of the verb which has nothing metaphorical about it and because of the context of Cor. 15[26ff]. In fact Paul gives as 'proofs' of his faith in the resurrection a list of mortal dangers to which he has been exposed. How would he come to include with these a reference to a theological combat? So we agree with J. Weiss and J. Héring[1] that we must take the phrase as hypothetical, which is grammatically correct: 'If I had fought, "as a man",with wild beasts . . .' The apostle means: 'If there is no resurrection of the dead, how do you explain that I contemplated fighting with beasts at Ephesus and dying a martyr?' But the idea was only a human notion (*'kata anthrōpon'*) and accorded rather with his personal aspirations to 'be with Christ' than with the progress of the Gospel, as 1[21-24] so well explains. We therefore regard an Ephesian imprisonment, in the terms in which we have defined it above, as beyond dispute; and it was in these circumstances that our letters A and B were written.

One further point supports the argument for Ephesus, namely the similarity of which we have already spoken in the previous section between the polemic of **3** in our epistle and that of *2 Corinthians*. This observation, indeed, leads Gnilka (p. 22f) to put the composi-

---

et la Macédoine orientale . . ., 1945, pp. 45–58). On the other hand the commentaries by Dibelius, Michael and Martin, and the introductions by McNeile, J. L. PRICE (*op. cit.* pp. 419–22), A. WIKENHAUSER (*op. cit.*, p. 311f) claim to be unable to pronounce an opinion on these various theories.
[1] J. WEISS, *Der Erste Korintherbrief*,[10] 1925; J. HÉRING, *The First Epistle of Saint Paul to the Corinthians*, ET, 1962: *ad* 1 Cor. 15[32].

tion of *Philippians* a little before *2 Corinthians*, seeing also in the 'affliction' (*'thlipsis'*) of 2 Cor. 1⁸ᶠᶠ an allusion to the Ephesian imprisonment (cf. also G. Bornkamm, *art. cit.*, p. 199f; Michael, pp. xviff). We ourselves have concluded that in spite of any affinity there may be, the two polemics nonetheless present notable divergences, so that we prefer to put the writing of our epistle before *1 Corinthians*, at least in so far as letters A and B are concerned. The opponents whom Paul will attack with full knowledge in *2 Corinthians* started by putting in an appearance at Philippi, at first cautiously (letter B), then with more violence (letter C), and then at length reached Corinth (*2 Corinthians*). The clear allusion in 1 Cor. 15³² expressly invites this inference, which is further strengthened by the fact that at the time of writing *1 Corinthians* the apostle was already on the point of leaving Ephesus (1 Cor. 16⁹ and 5⁶⁻⁸). The affliction of 2 Cor. 1⁸ is therefore a different trial, later than the one afforded by the imprisonment in question.

Therefore, with W. Michaelis (*op. cit.* pp. 60ff) we conclude that letters A and B of our epistle were written before *1 Corinthians* while the apostle was staying in Ephesus, either between the autumn of A.D. 52 and the spring of A.D. 55 or between the autumn of A.D. 54 and the spring of A.D. 57, according to which chronology of Paul's life we adopt.

5. THE THEOLOGY OF THE EPISTLE

The Christological hymn 2⁵⁻¹¹ has always been regarded as the gem of this epistle. This reputation remains unchallenged and it is no mere chance that such a hymn occurs at the heart of this document. For the striking feature of *Philippians* is the tenacity with which the apostle rejects any flight away from human history, a flight suggested either by the idea of a death 'with Christ' (1²¹⁻²⁴) or by the temptation to some 'glorious' Christian life (3). For Paul an unending submersion in time and history is necessary; that is where work is done and progress made.

For it is precisely there where Christ himself worked and made progress (2⁶⁻¹¹), disrupting but not destroying human history, transforming it utterly only to establish his own rule over it (2¹⁰ᶠ). But this rule is no abstraction; it is living, incarnate in the lives of men who have been struck overwhelmingly by the shattering challenge of the Cross and the Resurrection (3⁴ᶠᶠ), set moving by it (3¹²ᶠᶠ), and who strive towards a goal still in the future (3²⁰ᶠ). It is just because there is salvation only within history that the apostle concerns himself with the ceaseless proclamation of the Gospel (1¹²⁻²⁶) and the Christian community is exhorted to flee from any artificial paradise in order to construct a solidly based ethic (1²⁷⁻2⁵,¹²⁻¹⁶; 4²⁻⁹). But this radically new history also carries the mark of the event which gave it birth, the event that is which is actually experienced in the apostolic preaching and in the life of the Christian community.

This is why the Gospel experienced in history is characterised in the first place by its dynamic, the dynamic of Christ's resurrection (3^{10}). Indeed, the entire letter vibrates with the joy arising from the vision of a new departure in missionary activity (1^{12-26})—except where it vibrates with indignation in face of the danger of falsification which the Gospel encounters (3). But in both cases it is the same dynamic which makes it possible to look death in the face, to accept imprisonment, suspicions, betrayals and, in the long run, the possible collapse of years of work and prayer; the same dynamic which makes it possible to persevere, even to advance, facing difficulties and tensions and obstinately refusing to compromise or retreat.

For just as the Resurrection is rooted in the dark night of the Cross, so the dynamic of the Christian can only arise from 'fellowship with the sufferings of Christ and conformity with his death' (3^{10}). This is why the apostolate bears no other mark than humility and weakness, and why the ethic of the Christian community rests only upon death to self and a love which regards another's welfare as superior to one's own (2^3).

So the Christian is led to live out day by day the true meaning of the revolution brought into human affairs by the intervention of Christ: everything is the free gift of God, the miraculous work of a Father who makes strength spring forth from weakness, love from discord, life from death ($2^{9ff,13}$; 3^{8ff}).

On three particular issues the epistle raises specific problems which have not been without important influence in the history of theology, namely, the reference to ' "bishops" and deacons' in 1^1, to life 'with Christ' after death in 1^{23}, and the Christological hymn of 2^{6-11}. These problems are too complex for treatment in the limits of an introduction, and in each case an appropriate *excursus* is devoted to them in the body of the commentary.

6. THE TEXT

ALAND, K., *Kurzgefasste Liste der griechischen Handschriften des NT*, 1, 1963.
— *Studien zur Überlieferung des NT und seines Textes*, 1967 (especially pp. 58–80; 91–136).
ALAND, K., BLACK, M., METZGER, B. M., WIKGREN, A., *The Greek New Testament*, 1966.
GNILKA, J., *Commentary*, pp. 25–7.
Novum Testamentum Graece cum apparatu critico curavit E. Nestle novis curis elaboraverunt E. Nestle et K. Aland, 25th edn., 1963.

So far as the text is concerned the epistle raises no particular difficulties. *The Greek New Testament* retains only 16 variants of which eight alone are regarded as problematic; 73 of the 104 verses undergo no variation throughout the manuscript tradition. Before studying each paragraph we have, however, mentioned any relevant text-critical problems.

Almost the whole of the epistle is attested from the beginning of the 3rd. century by the Chester Beatty papyrus kept at Dublin (P 46). Two other papyri (P 16 and P 61), which date respectively from the 3rd/4th and 7th/8th centuries, preserve only fragments of 3 and the beginning of 4. As to the uncial witnesses to the epistle, of which there are 18, the three earliest (א, B, A) present a complete text dating respectively from the 4th and 5th centuries. According to Gnilka, on the 20th September 1967 more than 620 minuscules were listed, ranging from the 9th to the 18th century.

BIBLIOGRAPHY

I *Commentaries on the Epistle to the Philippians*

BARTH, K., *Erklärung des Philipperbriefes*, 1928,[6] 1947.
BEARE, F. W., *A Commentary on the Epistle to the Philippians, BNTC*, 1959.
BENGEL, J. A., *Gnomon Novi Testamenti*,[3] 1773, 1860, pp. 765–82.
BENOIT, P., Epître aux Philippiens, *BJ*, 1949,[2] 1956.
BONNARD, P., *L'épître de saint Paul aux Philippiens, CNT*, X, 1950.
CALVIN, J., *Commentaires sur le NT*, edn. Meyrueis et Cie. 1855.
DE BOOR, W., *Die Briefe des Paulus an die Philipper und an die Kolosser*, Wuppertaler-Studienbibel, 1957.
DIBELIUS, M., *An die Philipper, HNT* 11,[3] 1937.
EWALD, P., *Der Brief des Paulus an die Philipper*, ZKNT, 3rd. edn. by G. Wohlenberg, 1917.
FRIEDRICH, G., *Der Brief an die Philipper, NTD*,[8] 1965.
GNILKA, J., *Der Philipperbrief, HTK*, X/3 1968.
HAUPT, E., *Die Gefangenschaftsbriefe, MKNT*,[7] 1902.
HEINZELMANN, G., *Der Brief an die Philipper, NTD* 8, 1935.
HENDRIKSEN, W., *A Commentary on the Epistle to the Philippians*, Geneva Series Commentary, 1963.
HUBY, J., *Saint Paul, les épîtres de la captivité, VS*, 8,[14] 1947.
JONES, M., *The Epistle to the Philippians*, Westminster Commentary, 1918.
LIGHTFOOT, J. B., St Paul's Epistle to the Philippians,[6] 1881.
LOHMEYER, E., *Die Briefe an die Philipper, Kolosser und an Philemon, MKNT*, [9]1953.
MARTIN, R. P., *The Epistle of Paul to the Philippians, TNTC*, 1959.
MATTER, H. M., *Die Brief aan de Philippenzen en de Brief aan Philemon*, commentaar op het NT, 1965.
MEDEBIELLE, *Epître aux Philippiens, PC*, XII, pp. 77–126, 1938.
MICHAEL, J. H., *The Epistle of Paul to the Philippians, MNTC*, 1928.
MICHAELIS, W., *Der Brief des Paulus an die Philipper, THK*, 11, 1935.
MÜLLER, J. J., *The Epistles of Paul to the Philippians and to Philemon*, The New International Commentary of the NT, 1955.
PÉRY, A., *L'épître aux Philippiens*, 1958.
SCHMAUCH, W., *Beiheft* to Lohmeyer's Commentary,[13] 1964.
SCOTT, E. F., *The Epistle to the Philippians, IB*, XI, 1955.
STAAB, K., *Die Thessalonikerbriefe; die Gefangenschaftsbriefe, RNT*, 1959.
STRACK, H. —BILLERBECK, P., *Kommentar zum NT aus Talmud und Midrasch*, III, pp. 618–25, 1926.
SYNGE, F. C., *Philippians and Colossians, TBC*, 1951.

TILLMANN, F., 'Der Philipperbrief', in *Die Gefangenschaftsbriefe des hl. Paulus, die Heilige Schrift des NT*, VII (H. Meiner and F. Tillmann), 1931.

VINCENT, M. R., *Critical and Exegetical Commentary on the Epistles to the Philippians and to Philemon*, ICC, [1]1897; [3]1922.

II. *Other works mentioned*

ALAND, K., *Kurzgefasste Liste der griechischen Handschriften des NT*, I, 1963.

— *Studien zur Überlieferung des NT und seines Textes*, 1967.

— BLACK, M., METZGER, B. M., WIKGREN, A., *The Greek New Testament*, 1966.

ANTOINE, P., art. 'Ephèse', *DBS*, II, 1934, cols. 1076–1104.

ARNDT, W. F., and GINGRICH, F. W., *A Greek-English Lexicon of the NT and Other Early Christian Literature*, ET 1957, being a trans. and adaptation of W. Bauer's *Wörterbuch* ([4]1952).

ASTING, R., *Die Heiligkeit im Urchristentum*, 1930.

BAHR, C. J., 'The subscriptions in the Pauline letters', *JBL*, 87, 1968, pp. 27–41.

BAIRD, W., 'Pauline eschatology in hermeneutical perspective', *NTS*, 17, 1971, pp. 314–27.

BAKKEN, N. K., 'The new humanity: Christ and the modern age', *Interpretation*, 22, 1968, pp. 71–82.

BARCLAY, W., 'Great themes of the NT: Phil. 2.1–11', *ExpT*, 70, 1958–59, pp. 4–7, and 40–4.

BARDY, G., *Oeuvres de saint Augustin*, 33; *La Cité de Dieu*, Bks. 1–5, General Introduction and notes by G. Bardy, 1939.

BARTH, K., *Church Dogmatics*, IV, Pt. 1, ET 1956.

BAUER, W., see ARNDT, W. F.

BAUERNFEIND, art. '*strateuomai*, etc.', *TWNT*, VII, 1964, pp. 701–13 (ET *ibid.*).

— art. '*trecho*, etc.' *TWNT*, VIII 1969, pp. 225–35 (ET VIII, pp. 226–35).

BAUMERT, N., 'Ist Ph.4.10 richtig übersetzt?', *BZ*, 13, 1969, pp. 256–62.

BAUR, F. C., *Paulus der Apostel Jesus Christi*, II, 1867.

BEHM, J., art. '*koilia*', *TWNT*, III, 1938, pp. 786–89 (ET *ibid.*).

— art. '*morphē*', *TWNT*, IV, 1942, pp. 750–60 (ET IV, pp. 750–59).

BENOIT, A., *Le baptême chrétien au second siècle*, 1953.

BENOIT, P., *Exégèse et théologie*, II, 1961.

— 'Préexistence et incarnation', *RB*, 77, 1970, pp. 5–29.

BERTRAM, art. '*sunergos*, etc.' *TWNT*, VII, 1964, pp. 869–75 (ET VII, pp. 871–76).

— art. '*hupsos*, etc.', *TWNT*, VIII, 1969, pp. 600–19 (ET VIII, pp. 602–20).

— art. '*phrēn*, etc.', *TWNT*, IX, 1970, pp. 216–31 (ET IX, pp. 220–35).

BEST, E., 'Bishops and deacons: Ph. 1.1', in *Studia Evangelica i.e. Texte und Untersuchungen*, 102 (ed. F. L. Cross), 1968, pp. 971–76.

BETZ, H. D., *Nachfolge und Nachahmung Jesu Christi im Neuen Testament*, 1967.

BEYER, H. W., art. *'diakoneō*, etc.', *TWNT*, II, 1935, pp. 81–93 (ET *ibid.*).

— art. *'episkopos'*, *TWNT*, II, 1935, pp. 604–17 (ET II, pp. 608–20).

BIETENHARD, art. *'onoma*, etc', *TWNT*, V, 1954, pp. 242–83 (ET *ibid.*).

BONHOEFFER, A., *Epiktet und das Neue Testament*, 1911.

BONHOEFFER, D., *Ethics*, ET 1955.

BONNARD, P., 'Vivre et mourir avec J. C. selon saint Paul', *RHPR*, 1956, pp. 101–12.

— 'La justice de Dieu et l'histoire. Remarques exégétiques sur une controverse récente', *ETR*, 1968, pp. 61–8.

— 'L'intelligence chez saint Paul', in *L'Evangile hier et aujoud'hui* (*Mélanges F. J. Leenhardt*), 1968, pp. 13–24.

BORNHAUSER, K., *Jesus Imperator Mundi*, 1938.

BORNKAMM, G., *Paul* ET 1971.

—'Zum Verständnis des Christus-Hymnus, Phil. 2.6–11', in *Studien zu Antike und Urchristentum. Gesammelte Aufsätze*, II, 1959, pp. 177–87.

— 'Der Philipperbrief als paulinische Briefsammelung', in *Neotestamentica et Patristica* (*Freundesgabe O. Cullmann*), 1962, pp. 192–202.

BOUTTIER, M., *En Christ. Etude d'exégèse et de théologie pauliniennes*, 1962.

— *La condition chrétienne selon saint Paul*, 1964.

BOUYER, L., *'Harpagmos'*, *RSR*, 39, 1951, pp. 281–88.

BREWER, R. R., 'The meaning of *"Politeuesthe"* in Phil. 1.27', *JBL*, 76, 1954, pp. 76–83.

BUCHANAN, C. O., 'Epaphroditus' sickness and the Letter to the Philippians', *EvQ*, 36, 1964, pp. 157–66.

BULTMANN, R., *Theology of the New Testament*, ET 1952–55.

— art. *'gignōskō*, etc.', *TWNT*, I, 1933, pp. 688–719 (ET I, pp. 689–719).

— art. *'elpis*, etc.', *TWNT*, II, 1935, pp. 513–31 (ET II, pp. 515–33).

— art. *'kauchaomai*, etc.', *TWNT*, III, 1942, pp. 646–54 (ET III, pp. 645–54).

CAMPENHAUSEN, H. v., *Ecclesiastical Authority and Spiritual Power in the Church of the First Three Centuries*, ET 1969.

CERFAUX, L., *Recueil L. Cerfaux*, I and II, 1954.

— 'L'épître aux Philippiens', *Introduction à la Bible* (pub. under the direction of A. Robert and A. Feuillet), II, 1959, pp. 477–86.

CHEVALLIER, M. A., *Esprit de Dieu, paroles d'hommes. Le rôle de l'esprit dans les ministères de la parole selon l'apôtre Paul*, 1966.

CHRISTOU, P., ' "*Isopsuchos*"; Ph. 2.20', *JBL*, 70, 1951, pp. 293–96.

COLLART, P., *Philippes, ville de Macédoine, depuis les origines jusqu'à la fin de l'époque romaine*, 1937.

COLSON, J., *Paul, apôtre et martyr*, 1971.

COLLANGE, J. F., *Énigmes de la deuxième épître de Paul aux Corinthiens. Etude exégétique de 2 Cor. 2.14–7.4*, 1972.

CONZELMANN, H., *An Outline of the Theology of the New Testament*, ET 1969.

COPPENS, J., 'Phil. 2.7 et Is. 53.12', *ETL*, 41, 1965, pp. 147–50.

— 'Une nouvelle structuration de l'hymne christologique de l'épître aux Philippiens', *ETL*, 43, 1967, pp. 197–202.

CRESPY, G., *La guérison par la foi*, 1952.

CULLMANN, O., *Peter. Disciple—Apostle—Martyr*, ET 1953.

— *The Christology of the New Testament*, ET 1959.

— *The Earliest Christian Confessions*, ET 1949.

— *Immortality of the Soul or Resurrection of the Dead?* ET 1958.

DANIÉLOU, J., *The Theology of Jewish Christianity*, ET 1964.

DAWE, D. G., 'A fresh look at the Kenotic Christologies', *SJT*, 15, 1962, pp. 337–49.

DEICHGRAEBER, R., *Gotteshymnus und Christushymnus in der frühen Christenheit*, 1967.

DEISSMANN, A., 'Zur ephesenischen Gefangenschft des Apostels Paulus', in *Anatolian Studies (Festschrift W. M. Ramsey)*, 1923, pp. 121–27.

DELLING, G., *Worship in the New Testament*, 1962.

— 'Monos theos', *TLZ*, 77, 1952, pp. 469–76.

— art. 'Philipperbrief', *RGG³*, V, cols. 333–36.

— art. '*plērēs*, etc.', *TWNT*, VI, 1959, pp. 283–309 (ET VI, pp. 283–311).

— art. '*suzugos*', *TWNT*, VII, 1964, pp. 749–50 (ET VII, pp. 748–50).

— art. '*telos*, etc.', *TWNT*, VIII, 1969, pp. 50–88 (ET VIII, pp. 49–87).

— 'Zum steigernden Gebrauch von Komposita mit "*huper*" bei Paulus', *NT*, 11, 1969, pp. 127–53.

DENIS, A. M., 'La fonction apostolique et la liturgie nouvelle en Esprit. Etude thématique des métaphores pauliniennes du culte nouveau', *RSPT*, 42, 1958, pp. 401–36 and 617–56.

DIDIER, G., *Désintéressement du chrétien. La rétribution dans la morale de saint Paul*, 1955.

DIX, G., *The Shape of the Liturgy*, 1946.

DODD, C. H., *New Testament Studies*, II, 1953.

DUNCAN, G. S., *Saint Paul's Ephesian Ministry*, 1929.

— 'Were Saint Paul's imprisonment epistles written from Ephesus?', *ExpT*, 67, 1955–56, pp. 163–66.

— 'Paul's ministry in Asia; the last phase', *NTS*, 3, 1956–57, pp. 211–18.

— 'Chronological table to illustrate Paul's ministry in Asia', *NTS*, 5, 1958–59, pp. 43–5.

DUPONT, J., *Gnosis. La connaissance religieuse dans les épîtres de saint Paul*, 1949.
— '*Sun christōi*'. *L'union avec le Christ suivant saint Paul*. Pt. 1: '*Avec le Christ*' *dans la vie future*, 1952.
— 'Jésus-Christ dans son abaissement et son exaltation d'après Phil. 2.6–11', *RSR*, 37, 1950, pp. 500–14.
EHRHARDT, A. A. T., 'Jesus and Alexander the Great', *JTS*, 46,1945, pp. 45–51.
EICHHOLZ, G., 'Bewahren und Bewähren des Evangeliums: der Leitfaden von Phil. 1–2', in *Hören und Handeln. Festschrift für E. Wolf* (ed. H. Goldwitzer and H. Traub), 1962, pp. 85–105.
ESCANDE, A., '*Kurios Iēsous Christos*', 1970.
FAIRWEATHER, E. G., 'The "kenotic Christology" ', appendix to Beare's Commentary, 1959, pp. 159–74.
FEINE-BEHM, *Einleitung in das Neue Testament*, 12th end. by W. G. Kümmel, 1963.
FEUILLET, A., *Le Christ Sagesse de Dieu d'après les épîtres pauliniennes*, 1966.
— 'Mort du Christ et mort du chrétien d'après les épîtres pauliniennes', *RB*, 66, 1959, pp. 481–513.
— 'L'hymne christologique de l'épître aux Philippiens (2.6–11)', *RB*, 72, 1965, pp. 352–80 and 481–507.
FITZMYER, J. A., 'To know him and the power of his resurrection; Ph. 3.10' in *Mélanges B. Rigaux* (ed. A. Descamps and A. de Halleux), 1970, pp. 411–25.
FOERSTER, W., '*harpagmos*', *TWNT*, I, 1933, pp. 472–74 (ET *ibid.*).
— Rad, G. von., art. '*eirēnē*, etc', *TWNT*, II, 1935, pp. 398–418 (ET II, pp. 400–20).
— Fohrer, art. '*sōzō*, etc.', *TWNT*, VII, 1964, pp. 966–1024 (ET *ibid.*).
FRIEDRICH, G., 'Lohmeyer's These über das paulinische Briefpräskript kritisch beleuchtet', *TLZ*, 81, 1956, pp. 343–46.
FURNESS, J. M., '*Harpagmos k.t.l. heauton ekenōsen*', *ExpT*, 69, 1957–58, pp. 93–4.
— 'The authorship of Phil. 2.6–11', *ExpT*, 70, 1958–59, pp. 240–43.
— 'Behind the Philippians Hymn', *ExpT*, 79, 1967–68, pp. 178–82.
FURNISH, V., 'The place and purpose of Phil. III', *NTS*, 10, 1962–63, pp. 80–8.
GAMBER, K., 'Der Christushymnus im Philipperbrief in Liturgiegeschichtlicher Sicht', *Bibl*, 51, 1970, pp. 369–76.
GEORGI, D., *Die Gegner des Paulus im 2. Korintherbrief. Studien zur religiösen Propaganda in der Spätantike*, 1964.
— 'Der Vorpaulinische Hymnus Phil. 2.6–11', in *Zeit und Geschichte (Dankesgabe an R. Bultmann zum 80. Geburtstag)*, 1964, pp. 263–93.
GEWIESS, J., 'Zum altkirchlichen Verständnis der Kenosisstelle (Phil. 2.5–11)', *ThQ*, 120, 1948, pp. 463–87.

— 'Die Philipperbriefstelle 2.6b', in *Neutestamentliche Aufsätze* (*Festscrift für J. Schmid*), 1963, pp. 69–85.

GIBBS, J. G., *Creation and Redemption*, 1971.

GIGLIOLI, A., 'Mihi enim vivere Christus est. Congettura al testo di Phil. 1.21', *RB*, 16, 1968, pp. 305–15.

GLOMBITZA, O., 'Mit Furcht und Zittern. Zum Verständnis von Phil. 2.12', *NT*, 3, 1959, pp. 100–6.

— 'Der Dank des Apostels. Zum Verständnis von Phil. 4.10–20', *NT*, 7, 1964, pp. 135–41.

GLOTZE, G., art. 'Hellenodikai', in *Dictionnaire des antiquités grecques et romaines* (ed. C. Daremberg and E. Saglio), III/1, 1900–63, pp. 60–4.

GNILKA, J., 'Die antipaulinische Mission in Philippi', *BZ*, 1965, pp. 258–76.

GOGUEL, M., *Introduction au NT*, IV/1, 1925.

GRANT, R. M., *Historical Introduction to the New Testament*, 1963.

GREEVEN, art. '*deomai*, etc.', *TWNT*, II, 1935, pp. 39–42 (ET II, pp. 40–42).

GRIFFITHS, D. R., ' "*Harpagmos*" and "*heauton ekenōsen*" in Phil. 2.6–7', *ExpT*, 69, 1957–58, pp. 337–39.

GRUNDMANN, W., 'Überlieferung und Eigenaussage im eschatologischen Denken des Apostels Paulus', *NTS*, 8, 1961–62, pp. 12–26.

— art. '*stephanos*, etc.', *TWNT*, VII, 1964, pp. 615–35 (ET VII, pp. 615–36).

— art. '*sun, meta* mit Genitiv', *TWNT*, VII, 1964, pp. 766–98 (ET VII, pp. 766–97).

GUTHRIE, D., *New Testament Introduction. The Pauline Epistles*, 1961.

GUETTGEMANNS, E., *Der leidende Apostel und sein Herr. Studien zur paulinischen Christologie*, 1966.

HAHN, F., *The Titles of Jesus in Christology. Their History in Early Christianity*, ET 1969.

HARDER, G., *Paulus und das Gebet*, 1936.

HARNACK, A. v., ' "*Kopos* (*kopian, hoi kopiōntes*)" im frühchristlichen Sprachgebrauch', *ZNW*, 27, 1928, pp. 1–10.

HARRISON, P. N., 'The Pastoral Epistles and Duncan's Ephesian theory', *NTS*, 2, 1955–56, pp. 250–61.

HAUCK, art. '*koinos*, etc.', *TWNT*, III, 1938, pp. 798–810 (ET III, pp. 798–809).

HAWTHORN, T., 'Philippians 1.12–15', *ExpT*, 62, 1950–51, p. 316f.

HENNECKE, E., (ed. W. Schneemelcher), *New Testament Apocrypha*, II, ET 1965.

HENRY, P., art. 'Kénose', *DBS*, V, 1950, cols. 7–161.

HÉRING, J., *The First Epistle of Saint Paul to the Corinthians*, ET 1962.

— *Le Royaume de Dieu et sa venue*², 1959.

— 'Kyrios Anthropos', *RHPR*, 16, 1936, pp. 196–209.

HOFFMANN, P., *Die Toten in Christus. Eine religionsgeschichtliche und exegetische Untersuchung zur paulinischen Eschatologie*, 1966.

HOOVER, R. W., 'The Harpagmos enigma: a philological solution', *HTR*, 64, 1971, pp. 95–119.

JAY, B., *Introduction au Nouveau Testament*, 1969.

JEREMIAS, J., *Jerusalem in the Time of Jesus*, ET 1967.

— *New Testament Theology*, I, ET 1971.

— 'Zur Gedankenführung in den paulinischen Briefen', in *Studia Paulina in honorem J. de Zwaan*, 1953, pp. 152ff.

— 'Zu Phil. 2.7: "*heauton ekenōsen*" ', NT, 6, 1963, pp. 182–88.

— art. '*pais Theou*', *TWNT*, V, 1954, pp. 653–713 (ET V, pp. 654–717).

JERVELL, J., *Imago Dei. Gen. 1.26s, im Spätjudentum, in der Gnosis und in den paulinischen Briefen*, 1960.

JEWETT, R., 'The epistolary thanksgiving and the integrity of Philippians', *NT*, 12, 1970, pp. 40–53.

— 'Conflicting movements in the early Church as reflected in Philippians', *NT*, 12, 1970, pp. 362–90.

JOHNSON, L., 'The Pauline Letters from Caesarea', *ExpT*, 68, 1957–58, pp. 24–6.

KÄSEMANN, E., 'Kritische Analyse von Phil. 2.5–11', in *Exegetische Versuche und Besinnungen*, I, 1960, pp. 51–95.

KATTENBUSCH, F., ' "*Harpagmon? Árpagmon*"! Phil. 2.6. Ein Beitrag zur paulinischen Christologie', *Theologische Studien und Kritiken*, 104, 1939, pp. 372–420.

KERTELEGE, K., '*Rechtfertigung' bei Paulus. Studien zur Struktur und zum Bedeutungsgehalt des paulinischen Rechtfertigungsbegriff*, 1966.

KILPATRICK, G. D., ' "*Blepete*", Philippians 3.2', in *In memoriam P. Kahle* (ed. M. Black and G. Fohrer), *Beiheft ZAW*, 103, 1968, pp. 146–48.

KITTEL, G., art. '*lego*', *TWNT*, IV, pp. 100–40 (ET IV, pp. 100–41).

KLIJN, A. F. J., 'Paul's opponents in Phil. III' *NT*, VII, 1964–65, pp. 278–84.

KNOX, W. L., 'The "divine-hero" Christology in the NT', *HTR*, 41, 1948, pp. 229–49.

KÖSTER, H., 'The purpose of the polemic of a Pauline fragment (Philippians III)', *NTS*, 8, 1961–62, pp. 317–32.

— art. '*splangchnon*, etc.', *TWNT*, VII, 1964, pp. 548–59 (ET. *ibid.*).

KRAMER, W., *Christos, Kyrios, Gottessohn*, 1963.

KRINETZKI, L., 'Der Einfluss von Jes. 52.13–53.13 par. auf Phil. 2.6–11', *ThQ*, 139, 1959, pp. 157–93 and 291–336.

KÜMMEL, W. G., see FEINE-BEHM.

LAMARCHE, P., *Christ vivant*, 1966.

LARSSON, E., *Christus als Vorbild. Eine Untersuchung zu den paulinischen Tauf- und Eikontexten*, 1962.

LEMAIRE, A., *Les ministères aux origines de l'Eglise. Naissance de la triple hiérarchie: évêques, presbytres, diacres*, 1971.

LEMERLE, P., *Philippe et la Macédoine orientale à l'époque chrétienne et byzantine*, 1945.

LIGIER, L., L'hymne christologique de Phil. 2.6–11, la liturgie eucharistique et la bénédiction synagogale nishmat kol hat', in *Analecta Biblica*, 17–18, II, 1963, pp. 65–74.

LISCO, H., *Vincula sanctorum. Ein Beitrag zur Erklärung der Gefangenschaftsbriefe des Apostels Paulus*, 1900.

LOHMEYER, E., '*Sun Christō*', in *Festgabe für A. Deissmann*, 1927, pp. 218–57.

— 'Briefliche Grussüberschriften', *ZNW*, 26, 1927, pp. 158ff.

— *Kyrios Jesus. Eine Untersuchung zu Phil. 2.5–11*, 1928.

LONGENECKER, R. N., 'Early Christological motifs', *NTS*, 14, 1967–68, 526–45.

LOOF, A., 'Une ancienne exégèse de Phil. 2.6–11 dans la ketàbà demasqàtà (livre des Degrés)', in *Analecta Biblica*, 17–18, II, pp. 523–33.

LOOFS, F., 'Das altkirchliche Zeugnis gegen die herrschende Auffassung der Kenosisstelle; Phil. 2.5 bis 11', *Theologische Studien und Kritiken*, 100, 1927–28, pp. 1–102.

LUETGERT, W., *Die Vollkommenen im Philipperbrief und die Enthusiasten in Thessalonich*, 1909.

LUTHER, M., *Letters of Spiritual Counsel* (T. G. Tappert, ed. and trans., in *Library of Christian Classics*, vol. 18, 1955).

MACKAY, B. S., 'Further thoughts on Philippians,' *NTS*, 7, 1960–61, pp. 161–70.

MALHERBE, A. J., 'The beasts at Ephesus', *JBL*, 37, 1968, pp. 71–80.

MANSON, T. W., 'St Paul in Ephesus. The date of the Epistle to the Philippians', *BJRL*, 23, 1939, pp. 182–200'

MARTIN, R. P., *Carmen Christi. Philippians 2.5–11 in Recent Interpretation and in the Setting of Early Christian Worship*, 1967.

MARXSEN, W., *Introduction to the New Testament. An Approach to its Problems*, ET 1968.

MATTERN, L., *Das Verständnis des Gerichtes bei Paulus*, 1966.

MCNEILE, A. H., *An Introduction to the Study of the NT*, 2nd, edn. rev. by C. J. C. Williams, 1953.

MENOUD, P. H., *L'Eglise et les ministères selon le NT*, 1949.

— *Le sort des trépassés d'après le NT²*, 1966.

MICHAELIS, W., art. '*mimeomai*, etc.' *TWNT*, IV, 1942, pp. 661–78 (ET IV, pp. 659–74).

— *Einleitung in das NT*, 1946.

— *Die Datierung des Philipperbriefes*, u.d.

— 'Teilungshypothesen bei Paulusbriefen', *ThZ*, 14, 1958, pp. 321–26.

MICHEL, O., 'Zur Exegese von Phil. 2.5–11', in *Theologie als Glaubenswagnis. Festschrift für K. Heim zum 80. Geburtstag*, 1954 pp. 79–95.

— art. '*homologeō*', *TWNT*, V, 1954, pp. 199–220 (ET *ibid.*).

MITTON, C. L., *The Formation of the Pauline Corpus of Letters*, 1955.

MOEHRING, H. R., 'Some remarks on "*sarx*" in Phil. 3.3ff', in

Studia Evangelica, IV, *Texte und Untersuchungen*, 102 (ed. F. L. Cross), 1968, pp. 432–36.

MORRIS, L., *'Kai hapax kai dis'*, *NT*, 1, 1956, pp. 205–8.

MORTON, A. Q., MCLEMAN, J., *Paul. The Man and the Myth. A Study in the Authorship of Greek Prose*, 1966.

MOULE, C. F. D., *The Birth of the New Testament*, 1962.

MÜLLER-BARDORFF, J., 'Zur Frage der literarischen Einheit des Philipperbriefes', *WZJ*, 7, 1957–58, pp. 591–604.

MUNCK, J., *Paul and the Salvation of Mankind*, 1959.

NEUFELD, V. H., *The Earliest Christian Confessions*, 1963.

NEUGEBAUER, F., *In Christus. 'En Christōi'. Eine Untersuchung zum paulinischen Glaubensverständnis*, 1961.

PARROT, A., *Abraham et son temps*, 1962.

PÉTAVEL-OLLIF, E., 'La kénose après la transfiguration. Etude exégétique sur Phil. 2.5–11', *RTP*, 29, 1896, pp. 138–64.

PETERSON, E., 'Zur Bedeutungsgeschichte von *"parrhēsia"* ', in *R. Seeberg Festschrift*, I, 1929, pp. 283–97.

PFITZNER, V. C., *Paul and the Agon Motif*, 1967.

PICARD, C., 'Les dieux de la colonie de Philippes vers le premier siècle de notre ère d'après les ex-voto rupestres', *RHR*, 86, 1922, pp. 117–201.

POLLARD, T. E., 'The integrity of Philippians', *NTS*, 13, 1966–67, pp. 57–66.

PREISKER, H., art. *'epeikeia'*, *TWNT*, II, 1935, pp. 585–87 (ET II, 588–90).

PRICE, J. L., *Interpreting the New Testament*, 1961.

QUELL, FOERSTER, art. *'kurios, etc'*, *TWNT*, III, 1938, pp. 1038–98 (ET III, pp. 1039–98).

RAD, G. V., KUHN, K. G., GUTBROD, art. *'Israēl, etc.'*, *TWNT*, III, 1938, pp. 356–94 (ET III, pp. 356–91).

RAHTJEN, B. D., 'The three letters of Paul to the Philippians,', *NTS*, 6, 1959–60, pp. 167–73.

REICKE, B., 'Unité chrétienne et diaconie: Ph. 2.1–11', in *Neotestamentica et patristica. Freudesgabe O. Cullmann*, 1962, pp. 203–12.

RENGSTORF, K. H., art. *'gongguzō, etc.'*, *TWNT*, I, 1933, pp. 727–37 (ET I, pp. 728–37).

REY, B., *Créés dans le Christ Jésus. La nouvelle création selon saint Paul*, 1966.

ROBINSON, D. W. D., ' *"Harpagmos"*: the deliverance Jesus refused?' *ExpT*, 80, 1968–69, pp. 253–54.

ROLLER, O., *Das Formular der paulinischen Briefe. Ein Beitrag zur Lehre von antiken Briefen*, 1933.

ROMANIUK, K., 'De themate Ebed Yahve in soteriologia Sancti Pauli', *CBQ*, 22, 1961, pp. 14–25.

SAGLIO, E., art. 'Agonothètes', in *Dictionnaire des antiquités grecques et romaines* (ed. E. Saglio and C. Daremberg), I, 1, 1877–1962, pp. 148–150.

SAND, A., *Der Begriff 'Fleisch' in den paulinischen Hauptbriefen*, 1967.

SANDERS, J. T., *The New Testament Christological Hymns*, 1971.

SASS, G., 'Zur Bedeutung von "*doulos*" bei Paulus', *ZNW*, 1941, pp. 24–32.

SCHLIER, H., *Der Brief an die Epheser*, 1963.

— art. '*thlibō*, etc.', *TWNT*, III, 1938, pp. 139–148 (ET *ibid.*).

— art. '*parrhēsia*, etc.', *TWNT*, V, 1954, pp. 869–84 (ET V, pp. 871–86).

— 'Das Menschenherz nach dem Apostel Paulus', *Lebendiges Zeugnis*, 1965, pp. 110–24.

SCHMID, J., *Zeit und Ort der paulinischen Gefangenschaftsbriefe*, 1931.

SCHMITHALS, W., *Paulus und die Gnostiker. Untersuchungen zu den kleinen Paulusbriefen*, 1965.

— 'Zur Abfassung und ältester Sammlung der paulinischen Hauptbriefe', *ZNW*, 51, 1960, pp. 225–45.

SCHNACKENBURG, R., *Baptism in the Thought of Paul*, 1964.

— *Das Johannesevangelium*, I, 1965, pp. 290–302.

SCHNEEMELCHER, W., see HENNECKE, E.

SCHNEIDER, J., art. '*homoios*, etc.', *TWNT*, V, 1954, pp. 186–98 (ET V, pp. 186–99).

— art. '*schēma*, etc.', *TWNT*, VII, 1964, pp. 954–59 (ET VII, pp. 954–58).

SCHRENK, art. '*patēr*', *TWNT*, V, 1954, pp. 946–1024 (ET V, pp. 945–1022).

SCHUBERT, P., *Form and Functions of the Pauline Thanksgivings*, 1939.

SCHULZ, A., *Nachfolgen und Nachahmen. Studien über das Verhältnis der neutestamentlichen Jüngerschaft zu urchristlichen Vorbildethik*, 1962.

SCHWEIZER, E., *Church Order in the New Testament*, 1961.

— *Erniedrigung und Erhöhung bei Jesus und seiner Nachfolgern*, 1962.

— 'Zur Herkunft der Präexistenzvorstellung bei Paulus', in *Neotestamentica*, 1963, pp. 105–109.

— 'Die "mystik" des Sterbens und Auferstehens mit Christus bei Paulus', *EvT*, 26, 1966, pp. 239–57.

— art. '*pneuma*', *TWNT*, VI, 1959, pp. 330–453 (ET VI, pp. 332–455).

— art. '*sarx*, etc.', *TWNT*, VII, 1964, pp. 98–151 (ET *ibid.*).

SEVENSTER, J. N., *Paul and Seneca*, 1961.

SIBER, P., *Mit Christus leben. Eine Studie zur paulinischen Auferstehungshoffnung*, 1971.

SPICQ, C., 'Epipothein. Désirer ou chérir?', *RB*, 1957, pp. 184–95.

— *Agapè dans le Nouveau Testament*, 3 vols., 1958–59.

STRATHMANN, art. '*leitourgeō*, etc.', *TWNT*, IV, 1942, pp. 221–38 (ET IV, pp. 215–31).

— art. '*polis*, etc.' *TWNT*, VI, 1959, pp. 516–35 (ET *ibid.*).

STRECKER, G., 'Redaktion und Tradition im Christushymnus. Phil. 2.6–11', *ZNW*, 55, 1964, pp. 63–78.

STUHLMACHER, P., *Gerechtigkeit Gottes bei Paulus*, 1965.
— *Das paulinische Evangelium*, I, *Vorgeschichte*, 1968.
SUGGS, M. J., 'Concerning the date of Paul's Macedonian ministry', *NT*, 4, 1960, pp. 60–8.
TALBERT, C. H., 'The problem of pre-existence in Phil. 2.6–11', *JBL*, 86, 1967, pp. 141–53.
TANNEHILL, R., *Dying and Rising with Christ: a Study in Pauline Theology*, 1967.
TAYLOR, V., *The Person of Christ in New Testament Teaching*, 1959.
THOMAS, T. A., 'The Kenosis question', *EvQ*, 42, 1970, pp. 142–51.
THUESING, W., *Per Christum in Deum. Studien zum Verhältnis von Christozentrik und Theozentrik in den paulinischen Hauptbriefen*, 1965.
TROCMÉ, E., 'L'épître aux Romains et la méthode missionnaire de l'apôtre Paul', *NTS*, 7, 1960–61, pp. 148–53.
TRUDINGER, P., ' "*Harpagmos*" and the Christological significance of the Ascension', *ExpT*, 79, 1967–68, p. 279.
UNNIK, W. C. van, *De semitische achtergrond van 'parrhēsia' in het NT*, 1962.
VALLOTTON, P., *Le Christ et la foi*, 1960.
VOEGTLE, 'Der Menschensohn und die paulinische Christologie', in *Analecta Biblica*, 17–18, I, 1961, pp. 199–218.
VOKES, P. E., ' "*Harpagmos*" in Phil. 2.6', in *Studia Evangelica*, II (ed. F. L. Cross), 1964, pp. 670–75.
WALLACE, D. H., 'A note on morphè' *ThZ*, 22, 1966, pp. 19–25.
WARREN, W., 'On "*heauton ekenōsen*" ', *JTS*, 12, 1911, pp. 461–63.
WEGENAST, K., *Das Verständnis der Tradition bei Paulus und in den Deuteropaulinen*, 1962.
WEISS, J., *Der erste Korintherbrief*[10], 1925.
WIBBING, S., *Die Tugend- und Lasterkataloge im NT und in ihre Traditionsgeschichte unter besonderer Berücksichtigung der Qumran-Texte*, 1959.
WIKENHAUSER, A., *Einleitung in das NT*[5], 1963.

ABBREVIATIONS

When the names only of authors are given the reference is usually to commentaries listed in the first section of the Bibliography.

Bibl   *Biblica*
Billerbeck   (H. L. Strack-) P. Billerbeck, *Kommentar zum NT aus Talmud und Midrasch*, 6 vols., 1922–63.
BJRL   The Bulletin of the John Rylands Library.
B–D   F. Blass and A. Debrunner, Trans. and rev. of the 9th–10th German edn. incorp. suppl. notes of A. Debrunner—by R. W. Funk, *Grammar of NT Greek*, 1967.
BNTC   *Black*'s *New Testament Commentary*.
BZ   *Biblische Zeitschrift*.
CBQ   *Catholic Biblical Quarterly*.
CNT   *Commentaire du Nouveau Testament*.
DBS   *Dictionnaire de la Bible, Supplément*, ed. L. Pirot, A. Robert, then H. Cazelles, 1928 onwards.
ETL   *Ephemerides Theologicae Lovanienses*.
ETR   *Etudes Théologiques et Religieuses*.
EvQ   *Evangelical Quarterly*.
EvT   *Evangelische Theologie*.
ExpT   *The Expository Times*.
HNT   *Handbuch zum Neuen Testament*.
HTK   *Herders Theologischer Kommentar zum Neuen Testament*.
HTR   *The Harvard Theological Review*.
IB   *The Interpreter's Bible*.
ICC   *International Criticial Commentary*.
JBL   *Journal of Biblical Literature*.
JTS   *Journal of Theological Studies*.
MKNT   *Meyers Kritisch-exegetischer Kommentar über das Neue Testament*.
MNTC   *Moffat New Testament Commentaries*.
NTD   *Neues Testament Deutsch*.
NT   New Testament.
NT   *Novum Testamentum*.
NTS   *New Testament Studies*.
PC   L. Pirot and A. Clamer, *La Sainte Bible*.
RB   *Revue Biblique*.
RBi   *Rivista Biblica*.
RSR   *Recherches de Science Religieuse*.
RGG[3]   *Die Religion in Geschichte und Gegenwart*, 3rd. edn., 1957 onwards.

RHPR	*Revue d'Histoire et de Philosophie Religieuses.*
RHR	*Revue de l'Histoire des Religions.*
RNT	*Regensburger Neue Testament.*
RSPT	*Revue des Sciences Philosophiques et Théologiques.*
RTP	*Revue de Théologie et de Philosophie.*
SJT	*Scottish Journal of Theology.*
TBC	*Torch Bible Commentaries.*
THK	*Theologischer Hand-Kommentar zum Neuen Testament.*
TLZ	*Theologische Literaturzeitung.*
ThQ	*Theologische Quartalschrift.*
TWNT	*Theologisches Wörterbuch zum Neuen Testament*, G. Kittel and G. Friedrich (ed.); ET by G. W. Bromily (ed.), *Theological Dictionary of the New Testament*, 1964–74.
ThZ	*Theologische Zeitung.*
TNTC	*Tyndale New Testament Commentaries.*
TOB	*Traduction Oecuménique de la Bible; Nouveau Testament*, 1972.
VC	*Verbum Caro.*
VS	*Verbum Salutis.*
WZT	*Wissenschaftliche Zeitschrift Jena.*
ZAW	*Zeitschrift für die alttestamentliche Wissenschaft.*
ZKNT	Th. Zahn, *Kommentar zum Neuen Testament.*
ZNW	*Zeitschrift für die neutestamentliche Wissenschaft.*

COMMENTARY

Address and Greetings (1$^{1-2}$)

(1) *Paul and Timothy, slaves of Christ Jesus, to all the saints in Christ Jesus who are at Philippi, as well as to the bishops and deacons:* (2) *grace to you and peace from God our Father and the Lord Jesus Christ.*

FRIEDRICH, G. 'Lohmeyer's These über das paulinische Briefprä-skript kritisch beleuchtet', *TLZ*, 81, 1956, pp. 343–46.
LOHMEYER, E., 'Briefliche Grussüberschriften', *ZNW*, 26, 1927, pp. 158ff.
ROLLER, O., *Das Formular der paulinischen Briefe. Ein Beitrag zur Lehre von antiken Briefen*, 1933.

On account of the uncertain meaning of the words at the end of v. 1 some manuscripts (B^3, K, etc.) and St. John Chrysostom read '*sunepiskopois*' ('co-bishops' with Paul and Timothy) instead of '*episkopois*'.

In the introductions to his letters Paul adopts the tripartite form of his time: introduction of the writer, recipient, greetings. But with him the form is notably enriched in comparison with classical usage. It is difficult to decide whether this was through eastern (Friedrich) or liturgical (Lohmeyer) influence, but what is certainly clear is the theological profundity and the rich humanity with which the apostle infuses the conventional formulae. The characteristics of each of his letters are perceptible as soon as we read the words of greeting. In this case he does not put himself forward as an apostle but as a slave, and he includes Timothy as well. His message is addressed to *all* the Philippians up to and including a group of people whose nature is hard to determine, namely 'the "bishops" and deacons'. But the principal note is sounded above all in the name 'Jesus Christ' which occurs three times.[1] Everything uniting the apostle to the community at Philippi, as well as the spirit in which they must listen to what he is going to say to them, is to be located 'in Christ' and in him alone.

1^1 All the apostle's letters open with a mention of his name, 'Paul'. In eight instances other names are linked with his, in five of them that of Timothy; but never is he as closely associated with the author of the letter as here.[2] Why is this? To begin with it is certain that

---

[1] For the placing and meaning of the terms 'Christ' and 'Jesus' cf. A. ESCANDE, *Kurios Iēsous Christos*, 1970.
[2] In *1 and 2 Thessalonians* Timothy is again mentioned together with Silvanus

Timothy could not have been co-author of the epistle; it is much too personal and the 'I' predominates. Further, when Timothy reappears in 2^{19ff} it is in clear distinction from the author of the letter. He could have been the apostle's secretary (Müller), however, or even jointly responsible with him for some element of the contents which might have been discussed before writing (Bonnard, Ewald, Michaelis), unless Paul merely names him here in order to suggest a wider scope or more solid basis for what is said (Friedrich), or simply because he shared in the founding of the church at Philippi (Gnilka). It is certainly true that Timothy, who originated from Lystra in Lycaonia and was enlisted by Paul when he passed through the city on his second missionary journey (Acts 16^1), was a member of the group which worked at Philippi (Acts 16^{12ff}), though the *Acts of the Apostles* does not distinguish him by name on that occasion and he seems to have played a more important role at Corinth (Acts 18^5; cf. 1 Cor. 4^7; 16^{10}; 2 Cor. 1^1; Rom. 16^{21}). It could be precisely because Timothy appeared at Philippi only as one of the apostle's assistants, no more, that right from the start he invests him with his own authority in view of the mission as his plenipotentiary to that city which he is going to entrust to him (2^{19ff}; Haupt). By so doing Paul further shows the Philippians—a lesson they may have needed to learn—that relationships in the bosom of the church between collaborators were not those of authority, superiority or inferiority but of humble equality.

This is why Paul and Timothy present themselves as no more than slaves ('*douloi*') of Jesus Christ. This is in contrast to most of the other epistles where the author appears as an apostle; it indicated without doubt the quality of the personal relationships which Paul means to maintain with the church at Philippi. But it would be a pity to be content with this observation or, still worse, only to be willing, with G. Sass,[1] to take the term '*doulos*' ('slave-servant') in the Old Testament sense of a privileged envoy of God. In fact the word has pejorative force here. Linked with Jesus Christ, it cannot but evoke echoes of the 'slavery' applied in 2^7 to the condition of the incarnate Christ. To readers in danger of 'vainglory' (2^3) the apostle presents the Christian's status as placed under the sign of one Lordship only, the Lordship of Christ Jesus (cf. 2^{11}) and therefore stamped with the seal of humility. This is also why he does not claim to lecture them but simply puts himself at their side as one humble person among others.

The Philippians are indeed addressed as 'saints in Christ Jesus'. In the Pauline letters the term used for the recipients is either 'the church' or 'saints'. To be a 'saint' is therefore certainly not the result of peculiarly moral conduct but simply the corollary of membership

---

and no qualification follows the mention of the three 'authors' of the letters; in *2 Corinthians, Colossians* and *Philemon* he appears only in a secondary position carefully distinguished from the apostle who uses this title for himself.

[1] 'Zur Bedeutung von "*doulos*" bei Paulus', *ZNW*, 40, 1941, pp. 24–32.

of the people of God; for as in the Old Testament, the source of holiness can be none other than God himself who confers it gracciously.[1] It is the same rootage which marks the 'in Christ Jesus' here (Barth). The long history of interpretation of the Pauline '*en Christō*' is familiar enough,[2] and it is sufficient for the present to say that the '*en*' ('in') has temporal and historical, not spatial, force here. The state of being '*en Christō*' is marked by an historical event—the death and resurrection of Jesus Christ. So the church is only holy because it is called by the Crucified and Risen One to witness to this event which is at the same time eschatological and humbly historical. It is further the reason why holiness is a mark of *all* ('*pasin*') Christians. The factions and the struggles for prestige to which the church of Philippi is a prey are thus a betrayal of the Gospel.

Still from this perspective, the apostle then makes special reference among the Christians at Philippi to the ' "bishops" and deacons'. This is unique within the entire Pauline corpus and for that reason has evoked much comment. Who are these people and why does Paul mention them here? Were they a characteristic peculiar to the church at Philippi or are we to suppose that other Pauline congregations were also equipped with them? And further, must we see an indication here of the origin of the monarchical episcopate of Catholicism or, on the other hand, something added later to the original text precisely to justify this episcopacy? Because of the complexity of the issues we are devoting an *excursus* to try to clarify them.

Excursus 1: Bishops and Deacons

BEYER, H. W., art. '*diakoneō*, etc.', *TWNT*, II, 1935, pp. 81–93 (**ET** II, pp. 81–93).

— art. '*episkopos*', *TWNT*, II, 1935, pp. 604–17 (ET II, pp. 608–20).

BEST, E., 'Bishops and deacons: Phil. 1.1', in *Studia Evangelica IV*, i.e. *Texte und Untersuchungen*, 102 (ed. F. L. Cross), 1968, pp. 971–76.

CAMPENHAUSEN, H. v., *Kirchliches Amt und geistliche Vollmacht in den ersten drei Jahrhunderten*, 1953 (ET *Ecclesiastical Authority and Spiritual Power in the Church of the First Three Centuries*, 1969).

CHEVALLIER, M. A., *Esprit de Dieu, paroles d'hommes*, 1966.

DIX, G., *The Shape of the Liturgy*, 1946.

GEORGI, D., *Die Gegner des Paulus im 2. Korintherbrief*, 1964, pp. 31–8.

GNILKA, J. *Commentaire*, Excursus I, pp. 32–40.

---

[1] Cf. R. ASTING, *Die Heiligkeit im Urchristentum*, 1930, pp. 133–51.
[2] BORNKAMM, G., *Paul*, ET 1971, pp. 154–56; BOUTTIER, M., *En Christ. Eiude d'exégèse et de théologie pauliniennes*, 1962; CONZELMANN, H., *An Outline of the Theology of the New Testament*, ET 1969, pp. 199–212; NEUGEBAUER, F., *In Christus. 'En Christōi'. Eine Untersuchung zum paulinischen Glaubensverständnis*, 1961.

LEMAIRE, A., *Les ministères aux origines de l'Eglise. Naissance de la triple hiérarchie évêques, presbytres, diacres*, 1971.
LIGHTFOOT, J. B., 'The Christian ministry' appendix to *St Paul's Epistle to the Philippians*,[6] 1881.
MENOUD, P. H., *L'Eglise et les ministères selon le NT*, 1949.
SCHWEIZER, E., *Gemeinde und Gemeinde Ordnung im NT*, 1959.

The reference here to bishops and deacons is particularly striking because the former term appears nowhere else in Paul and it affords the earliest attestation we have of the existence of an 'episcopate'. But the meaning of the words must not be misunderstood; they have little to do with the episcopate and diaconate known to the church subsequently. This, as Protestant scholars have not failed to stress, is shown by the use of the plural '*episkopoi*' and by the secondary position to which Paul assigns the bishops and deacons after first addressing the 'saints'. Even Catholic commentaries no longer look on the word as evidence for a monarchical episcopate, but its quite extraordinary use here also makes improbable the view that it was a later addition to the original text (against Michael).

One is further well aware of the extreme difficulty of forming anything like a clear and consistent idea of the organisation of the early church or, rather, churches. The topic is nowhere treated specifically in the documents of the time, and the arrangements must have differed strikingly at various times and from place to place. So the same term could have varied connotations—think, for example, of the title 'apostle'!—and this only shows how perilous and tentative any attempt to give clear shape to the terms 'bishops' and 'deacons' must be, though as they are under discussion the effort to clarify them must be made.

1. The terms[1]

From its etymology '*epi-skopos*' denotes 'over-seer' or 'inspector'. In secular Greek as in Hellenistic Judaism the word was used for a variety of purposes which differed according to the socio-historical context but had in common the idea of inspection or oversight. To this extent one cannot speak of a unique or well defined office.

The same is true of the diaconate, with the difference that the common element in the various uses of '*diakonos*' is service, so that a 'deacon' is chiefly defined by his relationship to a master to whom he is subordinate. But his service need have nothing degrading about it. Thus, Plato speaks of political leaders as servants of the city ('*diakonoi poleōs*, Gorg. 517b) and Epictetus of the Cynic philosopher as a servant and messenger of the gods.

2. The juxtaposition of 'bishops and deacons'

Analysis of the terms themselves does not take us very far, but A. Lemaire (*op. cit.*, pp. 97–103), taking up a proposal already made

[1] Cf. BEYER, *art. cit.*; A. LEMAIRE, *op. cit.*, pp. 27–34.

by Haupt, has recently maintained that 'bishops and deacons' looks like a ready-made expression. Actually, apart from **1**[1], the coupling occurs in three early Christian texts, viz. *Didache* xv. 1, Clement of Rome *To the Corinthians*, 42[4-5] and *Hermas*, Vis. III. 5.1.[1] The difficult conjunction is hardly explicable except by the existence of a group of people called '*episkopoi kai diakonoi*'. This is further confirmed by John Chrysostom's exegesis of our verse, which he supports precisely by certain usages still current in his own day (cf. Lemaire, p. 100f).

Now Chrysostom himself thinks that this group of people corresponded to elders or presbyters. Here again we must admit that he is correct. Indeed, the *Didache*, Clement and the *Shepherd of Hermas* are unanimous in presenting the bishops and deacons as *lieutenants* of the apostles within a congregation.[2] It must further be remarked that in Acts 20[28] Luke makes Paul say when he addresses the Ephesian elders ('*presbuteroi*'), 'Take heed . . . to all the flock, over which the Holy Spirit has made you overseers ("*episkopous*") to shepherd the church of God.' The same identification of 'bishops' and 'elders' is found in 1 Pet. 5[1f] and Tit. 1[5-7]. There does not seem to be any doubt that at a certain stage in the tradition the elders of a congregation must have been called 'bishops and deacons'.[3]

But why then the double appellation? Lemaire (p. 98f) sees its origin in the formula 'judges and officers' who according to Deut. 16[18] are to be put at the head of each Israelite city. Such a theory is far from convincing and there is no indication that Deut. 16[18] would have had any influence over the organisation of early Christian communities. Indeed, the reason for the dual reference need be sought no further than in Pauline theology and also in the particular circumstances presented by the Philippian community at the time when the letter was written. Here again Chrysostom puts us on the right road when he says that 'in those days bishops were called deacons'.

3. The organisation of the Pauline churches

One fact is at once striking. Paul never used the term 'presbyter'— which we have seen must have corresponded to that of 'bishop'— well attested as it is outside Pauline usage.[4] The case is quite

---

[1] It is true that this last is not very clear; yet even if the reconstruction Lemaire gives (p. 156) is not accepted the evidence is nevertheless significant. It will also be observed that 1 Tim. 3[1-13] gives instructions about bishops (vv. 1–7) and instructions about deacons (vv. 8–13).

[2] For Clement they are the firstfruits of the congregation, comprising therefore its earliest nucleus. For the *Didache*, which in this respect reflects a later development, they have to be elected by their peers.

[3] The identification of presbyters (elders) with bishops is carefully demonstrated by LIGHTFOOT (pp. 95–9; cf. also BEYER *TWNT*, II, p. 612 (ET II, pp. 615–17). Moreover, Polycarp in his letter to the Philippians (5[3]) also speaks of 'presbyters and deacons' whom he does not seem to distinguish from mere 'deacons' (5[2]; cf. however 6[1]).

[4] Cf. Acts 11[30]; 14[23]; 20[17] . . .; 1 Tim. 5[17, 19]; Tit. 1[5]; Jas. 5[14], etc.

different for the term 'deacon' which Paul uses very frequently.

Absence of the term, however, does not mean absence of the reality; for it seems clear that as the community expanded so the need for a measure of organisation appeared, as well as the appointment of a nucleus of elders composed of the first converts. Paul did not disguise the fact, but he preferred to give them the title 'first-fruits' ('*aparchē*', Rom. 16[5]; 1 Cor. 16[15], where the suggestion of a 'diaconate' also occurs) or, perhaps, 'leaders' ('*proïstamenoi*', 1 Thess. 5[12ff], a term used of presbyters in *Hermas*, Vis. II. 4.3). So the apostle deliberately rejected the term presbyter which was too historically loaded and too static (cf. Lemaire, pp. 21–7; Gnilka, pp. 36ff); he preferred to use words carrying more of a functional sense. He was not thinking in terms of self-sufficient structures into which men could be fitted (H. v. Campenhausen, pp. 55ff; E. Schweizer, pp. 87ff). The Spirit who worked for the edification ('*oikodomē*') of the community by distributing *charismata* (1 Cor. 12[4-11,31]) was everything. Now M. A. Chevallier (pp. 148ff) has rightly demonstrated that these 'grace gifts' were not 'super-gifts' at the disposal of particular people but *functions* ordained by the Spirit for the building up of the community and it is a matter of indifference to determine who exactly exercised them. Thus, according to circumstances, the same man could be equipped for apostolic and prophetic functions, or for prophecy and teaching. The prophet, for example, is not a specific individual but someone who on some occasion is led to fulfil the prophetic function.

It is just here that we can understand the doubling made by Paul of the terms 'deacon' and 'bishop'. We have seen that he favoured '*diakoneō*' ('to serve') and its cognates. He used this group of words for various ministrations (including his own[1]), but each time to stress that the ministrations are *in the service* of God's great work in Christ and that the *service* implies humility and modesty.

That the 'elders' of the Philippian church and perhaps of other Pauline churches bore the title 'overseers' is in no way surprising, given the secular usage of '*episkopos*'. But Paul did not want to limit it to that; he wanted to make it clear that the function of oversight was of value only as a *service* for the building up of the community and that therefore it would require much humility.

4. The 'bishops and deacons' in the Epistle to the Philippians

The interpretation just given of the conjunction 'bishops and deacons' applies particularly to our epistle. The usual explanation of their appearance here is by suggesting that bishops and deacons had played a leading part in organising the gift for the apostle (Barth, Beare, Benoit, Dibelius, Jones, Friedrich, etc.). Some even go so far as to think that 4[10-20] was originally a note of thanks sent

---

[1] We must not then limit the term as a designation for itinerant preachers as would GEORGI (*op. cit.* p. 34f) who furthermore gives the same denotation to the word 'bishops'.

only to the responsible people of the community, the reference to whom in **1¹** would be due to the final editor of the epistle (W. Marxsen, *Introduction*, ET 1968, pp. 59ff; cf. W. Schmithals, *Paulus und die Gnostiker*, p. 55). But there is nothing either in Paul or in other early writings of the church which allows us to limit bishops and deacons to the role of financial stewardship, rather the contrary.

Indeed, as we have already said, Paul found himself in a delicate situation in relation to the Philippian church. On the one hand he could only be pleased with them and their attitude towards himself; on the other, he could not ignore the dissensions breaking out there, caused precisely by lack of humility (cf. **2¹ᶠᶠ**), perhaps particularly among the leadership. So to begin with the apostle tried gentleness and persuasion—and at once he started by giving a title to the leaders of the church, something which normally he avoided. At the same time he reminds them that authority before all else means responsibility, and he addresses them only after 'all the saints' whose edification (as '*diakonoi*') they have been called *to serve* (so Haupt).

1² The greetings in Pauline epistles, which follow a very stereotyped form, are characteristic of the apostle's context within the Graeco-Roman world. The pattern is actually Greek, with the *intitulatio* and *adscriptio* followed by the *salutatio* (A. Roller, *op. cit.*, p. 61), and a hint of the simple '*chairein*' typical of this last may be seen in the '*charis*' ('grace') which occurs here. But the scope of this introduction is suggestive of the East and not of Greece (E. Lohmeyer, *art. cit.*, pp. 158ff; O. Roller, *op. cit.* p. 457). The terminology itself is typically Semitic and the 'grace and peace' echo the wording of the Jewish benediction 'mercy and peace'.¹

Yet the verse offers more than mere syncretism. 'Peace', '*shālôm*', expressive of the whole relationship between God and men, is an historical, incarnate reality inasmuch as its source is the One whom Jesus revealed as Father, and it has for guarantee the lordship of this same Jesus over his own and over all else. Hence, furthermore, this peace is 'grace' ('*charis*')— a key term in Pauline thought. The *salutatio* is therefore essentially 'Christian', and this is further confirmed by Lohmeyer's suggestion when he sees a liturgical formula being used here. The rhythmic structure of the verse (with three members), the reference to the fatherhood of God and the lordship of Christ (cf. **2⁶⁻¹¹** and the Lord's Prayer), the echo of a Jewish benediction, and the fact that the Pauline epistles were no doubt read during worship, all make it likely that the apostle was using and wished to invoke upon his readers a liturgical blessing (against Friedrich, *art. cit.*). Henceforward we are therefore put within the perspective opened up by the activity of Jesus of Nazareth and now continued by the Lord of the church.

¹ Tob. 7¹²; Apoc. Bar. 78²; and also 1 Tim. 1²; 2 Tim. 1²; 2 Jn. 3; Jude 2; Gal. 6¹⁶.

FIRST PART

Acts of Thanksgiving and Prayer (1³⁻¹¹)

EICHHOLZ, G., 'Bewahren und Bewähren des Evangeliums: der Leit-
faden von Philipper 1–2' in *Hören und Handeln. Festschrift für
E. Wolf* (ed. H. Golwitzer and H. Traub), 1962, pp. 85–105.
HARDER, G., *Paulus und das Gebet*, 1936.
SCHUBERT, P., *Form and Functions of the Pauline Thanksgivings*, 1939.

All the Pauline epistles except *Galatians* open with an act of
thanksgiving generally expressed by the verb '*eucharisteō*'. This is
developed in largely comparable forms, more or less extended
according to circumstances (P. Schubert, *op. cit.*, pp. 10–39).
Although this usage carries strong marks of the apostle it nevertheless finds parallels in the papyri and inscriptions of the time, and
therefore merely from a literary point of view places the Pauline
'letters' between ordinary personal letters and official administrative
documents (P. Schubert, *op. cit.*, pp. 142–79).
Of all the Pauline thanksgivings that of *Philippians* is the most
extensive, and this is an indication at the same time of his real joy
at the remembrance of the Philippian community, his affection for
them (vv. 4, 7, 8), the suspicion which weighs down upon his affection and his concern for them (vv. 6, 9, 11). Furthermore, in conformity with current usage, the thanksgiving introduces the main
themes of the letter. So vv. 9–11 give the first glimpse of the situation at Philippi and of the themes which will be pursued from 1²⁷.
But the apostle goes further: the joy and affection which stamps all
he will say is the fruit of his conviction concerning the work of God
in human affairs (Eichholz). This is why the disconcerting hazards
which will be mentioned must fall into their proper place and find
their meaning between the 'first day' (v. 5) and the 'last' (vv. 6, 10).
Then everything in truth will simply be directed 'by Jesus Christ to
the glory and praise of God' (v. 11).
For clarity of exposition, though not without a hint of the arbitrary, we may distinguish the following sections within this prologue:
1. Act of thanksgiving, vv. 3–6;
2. The apostle's affection, vv. 7–8;
3. Intercession, vv. 9–11.

1. *Act of thanksgiving* (1³⁻⁶)

(3) *I give thanks to my God whenever I think of you*; (4) *it is with
joy that I pray for you all, always, in all my prayers,* (5) *because of*

your participation in the Gospel from the first day until now; (6) *and*
I am confident that he who began this good work among you will
continue it to completion at the day of Christ Jesus.

The only important though ill-attested variant is: 'I myself give thanks
to our Lord . . .' (D*, G, it., Ambst.). It emphasises the contrast between
Paul's concern for the Philippians and his joy, and it is accepted by Barth,
Ewald-Wohlenberg and Haupt. But Paul never mentions the 'Lord'
(*'kurios'*) in thanksgiving formulae; these are always directed to 'God'. It
could perhaps be insisted that Paul is speaking for himself to the exclusion
of Timothy.—At the end of v. 6 manuscript tradition hesitates between
'Christ Jesus' (P46, B, *Koiné*, D . . .) and 'Jesus Christ' (*Hesych.*, G, K).

However serious the problems are which are going to be treated,
they are to be dealt with only in the light of a thanksgiving which at
one and the same time presents the problems to God and receives in
return for them consolation (*'pepoithōs'*, v. 6) and joy (*'chara'*, v. 4).
Everything turns out to be *theologically* centred around the faithfulness of the One who is at work in history (cf. 'from the first day until
now') through the proclamation of the Gospel (vv. 5-6).

1³ The first verb (*'eucharisteō'*) involves the first person 'I' which
excludes Timothy from the writing of the letter. As with most
Pauline thanksgivings, it is addressed to God. In a significant way
Paul here particularises, saying 'my God', an appellation very rare
for him which doubtless is an echo of the language of the Psalter
(Bonnard, Lohmeyer, Michaelis). This thoroughly personal note
also throws doubt on the suggestion of Lohmeyer who detects the
presence of a liturgical fragment (with Friedrich, Gnilka). In the
second part of the verse we could have either a subordinate expression of time ('every time I remember you') or of cause ('because of
your remembrance of me'). In the second case there could be an
allusion to the material assistance the Philippians have sent the
apostle and not for the first time as **1⁵** and **4¹⁵** reveal. While this interpretation agrees well with the context (Ewald-Wohlenberg, Tillmann,
P. Schubert, *op. cit.*, pp. 74-81) it is out of harmony with the fact
that almost every Pauline instance of *'mneia'* ('remembrance') occurs
at the beginning of epistles and in a sense which is not open to
ambiguity.

1⁴ Several constructions are possible. If the end of the previous verse
is taken as a clause expressing cause then here we have the temporal
clause for the verb 'to give thanks'. But we have seen that this latter
is more probably expressed from v. 3b so that this verse shows the
frequency and intensity of the apostle's prayer for the Philippians
(so most commentaries). Moreover, it is uncertain whether 'for you
all' should be linked with what precedes or what follows, though the
meaning of the phrase would be the same (cf. Michaelis); but it

would be difficult to take the words as qualifying the verb '*eucharis-teō*' (v. 3, Lightfoot).

The heaping up of 'always' ('*pantote*'), 'in *all* my prayers' ('*en pasē*'), besides the genuine discipline of prayer (Haupt; Friedrich; Herder, *op. cit.*), expresses very clearly the real preoccupation which the community at Philippi was for the apostle. The emphasis rests, however, on the fact that this concern far from being tinged by bitterness is above all marked by joy ('*chara*'): 'joy predominates whenever I pray for you'. Such prayers are essentially intercessions, as is made plain by the repetition of '*deēsis*' instead of '*proseuchē*' which is usual in the opening of Pauline letters (cf. Greeven, *TWNT*, II, 1935, pp. 39–42 (ET II, pp. 40–2)). The intercessions are also on behalf of *all* the Philippians ('*huper pantōn humōn*'), for again the apostle does not want to take sides in the dissensions which have arisen in the Philippian church.

Joy, therefore, is the dominant note. It springs up as in 2 Cor. 2³; 6¹⁰; 7⁴,¹³; 8²; etc., against a background of difficult circumstances which it transforms and thus it is a manifestation of the Spirit and a sign of the Kingdom of God (Rom. 14¹⁷; 15¹³; Gal. 5²²; 1 Thess. 1⁶). For this reason also it characterises above all the mutual relationships between Christians, so that Paul can write 'Brothers, you are my joy and my crown' (4¹; cf. 1 Thess. 2¹⁹ᶠ). It is not therefore surprising that 'joy' is one of the keynotes of this letter, where no less than 14 of the 50 Pauline instances of '*chara/chairō*' occur. It is the more striking here because it is unusual among Paul's prologues (P. Schubert, *op. cit.*, pp. 78ff). It is due not so much to the material value of the gift the Philippians have sent to Paul as to what it betokens—an actualising of God's purpose in history, of which brotherhood in the struggle on behalf of the Gospel is the sign.

1⁵ Whether this is the reason for the thanksgiving as such (Gnilka, Michaelis, Müller) or for the intercession and joy (Haupt, Lohmeyer, Michael) which is mentioned here is really theologically irrelevant (Bonnard). The two possibilities seem inseparable. The reason for thanksgiving lies in the 'participation of the Philippians in the Gospel' which G. Eichholz (*art. cit.*), Hendriksen and Martin rightly claim to be the key to what is said in these two first chapters.

The Christian life indeed is essentially stamped with the seal of fellowship ('*koinōnia*'); fellowship with Christ (1 Cor. 1⁹; 1 Thess. 4¹⁷), with the Spirit (2 Cor. 13¹³; 2¹), with the brethren (Rom. 15²⁷; Phm. 17), whence also the special use of the term for Holy Communion (1 Cor. 10¹⁶ᶠᶠ). But this 'fellowship' expresses itself also in action and in Rom. 15²⁶ and 2 Cor. 9¹³ the word signifies material assistance. In both these instances as here the construction is with '*eis*' ('fellowship in/with'). So again we are led to see an allusion to the material help sent by the Philippians (Tillmann) and especially as in 4¹⁴ᶠᶠ we have '*sunkoinōnēsantes*', '*ekoinōnēsen*' and a remark about the constancy of the Philippians 'from the first day'. But this interpretation cannot be taken in a restrictive way; it neither excludes a reference to the recipients' faith (Friedrich; Hauck, art. '*koinos*, etc.', *TWNT*, III, 1938, p. 805 (ET III p. 798)), to their own missionary activities (Gnilka), nor yet to their intercession (Lightfoot, Martin). Like any contemporary church collection it carries with it the idea of uniting together to assist the work of the Gospel.

This term 'gospel' plays a considerable part in Pauline theology.[1] In nearly half the instances Paul uses it without qualification, as though it were an entity in its own right. In essence it means the free and mighty intervention of God in history through the events of the Cross and Resurrection, an intervention made effective through apostolic proclamation, which therefore also forms a part of the final eschatological act of God. It is this proclamation which underlies the argument of the first section of the letter (1^{12-26}) wherein the word 'gospel' will again appear three times over ($1^{7,12,16}$; cf. 1^{27}), as a fixed reference point by which the apostle determines his behaviour.

As a corporate activity, the 'gospel' makes its mark in time; hence the reference to the 'first day' when the Good News reached Philippi for the first time (cf. also 1 Cor. 1^{4-6}; Gal. 1^{6-8}; 1 Thess, 1^{5-10}) and when the Philippians first took an active part in the apostle's work (cf. Acts 16^{4ff} and 4^{14ff}). The 'day' is not regarded as a subjective and personal event, contrary to what one might suppose from some pietistic and revivalistic circles, but as an objective, communal fact. Moreover, to recall the beginning has value only in so far as it involves the enlightening and revitalising of the present ('*nun*' of 1^{30}; 2^{12}).

1^6 Thanksgiving engenders a confidence and an assurance which owe nothing to reason but are an act of faith in God's trustworthiness (Calvin, Bonnard), although such faith can be supported by what God has already done (cf. Dibelius, Lohmeyer).[2] The appeal to divine faithfulness is in the purest biblical and Jewish tradition (Billerbeck), commencing with the fact that God is not named but merely alluded to as 'he who began' ('*ho enarxamenos*').[3] And the 'good work' he has commenced is precisely the Philippian church's participation in the Gospel wherein, despite the difficulties of the moment, the apostle hopes the church will continue to the very end. Furthermore, the expression 'good work' with reference to God in biblical and Jewish tradition primarily means in Creation (cf. Gen. 2^2; Gnilka; Bertram *TWNT*, II, 1935, p. 633f (ET II, p. 629f)). For Paul, therefore, the Gospel, rooted in the Cross and Resurrection,

[1] Cf. P. STUHLMACHER, *Das paulinische Evangelium*, I, *Vorgeschichte*, 1968.

[2] '*Auto touto*' can be related either to what precedes ('confident of that very thing, because . . .'; HAUPT) or to what follows ('confident in this that . . .'; so most commentators); cf. B–D §290. But we cannot, with Vincent and Michael, take the '*en humin*' as meaning 'in your hearts', but rather 'among you'.

[3] The verb is found only three times in the NT, in Paul; each time it is linked with '*epiteleō*' ('to complete'): 2 Cor. 8^6; Gal. 3^3.

made living in the apostolic proclamation and the communal life of
the church, is the new creation which God has rightly determined to
bring to its consummation. This consummation is spoken of as the
'day of Christ', the goal of history, which the Old Testament already
designated the 'Day of the Lord'. In striking contrast with some
apocalyptic tendencies, appeal to this 'day' has no inherent value and
does not warrant any grandiose description. It occurs only to give
meaning to 'today' ('*nun*', v. 5) of which more will be said in the
remainder of the letter; no longer does it arouse either terror or distress (the Cross has already brought these upon humanity) but on
the contrary the plenitude and joy which one would expect since the
One awaited is both Saviour and Friend.

2. *The apostle's affection* (1⁷⁻⁸)

(7) *Indeed, it is right for me to feel in this way about you all, because
I have you in my constant care, and in my bonds as in the defence and
confirmation of the Gospel you are all sharers in the grace given to me.
(8) For God is my witness that it is with the tenderness of Christ Jesus
(himself) that I cherish you.*

In v. 7 Eb. Nestle suggests reading '*chreias*' instead of '*charitos*', an
unconvincing conjecture. In v. 8 some manuscripts read '*moi*' for '*mou*',
omitted by P 46 and others, while the *Koiné* inserts '*estin*' between '*mou*'
and '*ho theos*'. These variants have no influence on the meaning of the
text.

It is strange to find the apostle again protesting his attachment to
the Philippians. He would emphasise that this relates to *all* his
readers ('all' is used three times in these two verses); he wants at all
costs to preserve the threatened unity of the congregation at Philippi.
Moreover, as Calvin has rightly said, 'he affirms the warm affection
he has for them so that what he goes on to say will be better received.'
In fact, the Philippians must be convinced that the recent initiative
which the apostle has just made for obtaining his liberty (1¹²⁻²⁶) was
in part out of concern for them (1²⁴). Even the exhortations to
humility and unity in the verses immediately following and developed
in 1²⁷⁻²⁸ must not be taken as a lecture on morals or as reprimands
but solely as the outcome of a father's affection for his children. This
affection, of which God is the guarantor (v. 8a), is again shown as
arising from a common striving on behalf of the Gospel and springing
from the love of Christ himself.

1⁷ The sentence opens with a '*kathōs*' ('even as'), frequent in Pauline
prologues (1 Cor. 1⁶; Col. 1⁶ᶠ; 1 Thess. 1⁵; 2 Thess. 1³; cf. Lohmeyer) and with a weakened comparative sense of which Bonnard
rightly says that it has followed the same semantic development as

the French '*ainsi*'. The connection thus made is not particularly with v. 6 (Dibelius, Haupt, Vincent), nor with v. 4 (Bonnard), but with the whole passage vv. 3–6 (Ewald-Wohlenberg, Gnilka, Michaelis). What has been said in the preceding verses is now characterised as a set of 'dispositions' of the author's with respect to his correspondents. The verb '*phroneō*', so difficult to translate, must not be limited to the realm of feeling.[1] It conveys at once, something very profound and its definite, tangible consequences; perhaps one could speak of a 'plan' or 'scheme' actualised in some definite act. The idea is especially frequent in this epistle (of the 23 Pauline instances of the verb, 10 occur in Philippians; cf. particularly **2**[2ff]) where it takes a distinctive flavour well expressed in this instance: Christian '*phronein*' is essentially an outgoingness to other people and with no exclusiveness ('*huper pantōn*'). As such it is therefore 'right' ('*dikaion*'), that is, in the original biblical meaning of the word, 'in conformity with the norm, right, sound' (cf. also Acts 4[19]; Eph. 6[1]; Col. 4[1]).

The reason for this right attitude is to be found in the apostle's 'heart' ('*kardia*'), meaning the ground of the will and of action rather than of feeling.[2] From this sensitive spot, touched by the Spirit, the Christian life is co-ordinated (e.g. 2 Cor. 3[3]). Paul stresses again that still more than his affection for the Philippians it is for their benefit that he makes his own attitudes and position very clear. How, indeed, could it be otherwise, given their direct participation in the grace ('*charis*') given to him for the service of the Gospel in his apostolate (Bonnard; cf. *ad* 1[5,12,18] etc.)? From the fact that this apostolate has just been exercised also during his imprisonment ('*en tois desmois mou*'), a 'fellowship with the sufferings of Christ' (3[10]),[3] the Philippians have been particularly involved in this through their aid and their prayers. But Paul was also called to exercise his apostleship in the 'defence and confirmation of the Gospel'. We see no reason to detect here, as Lohmeyer does, a reference to martyrdom. On the contrary, '*apologia*' often in the New Testament means the defence made by an accused person before a tribunal (Acts 19[33]; 22[1]; 25[16], etc.). So Paul is alluding to his imminent appearance in court at Ephesus (Jones) brought about by the revealing of his true citizenship (cf. Introduction, pp. 8ff) which because of the defence

[1] Cf. BERTRAM, art. '*phrēn*, etc.', *TWNT*, IX, 1970, pp. 216–31 (ET IX, pp. 220–35).

[2] Cf. H. SCHLIER, 'Das Menschenherz nach dem Apostel Paulus', *Lebendiges Zeugnis*, 1965, pp. 120–24. It could also be taken as 'because *you* have *me* in your heart', though the word order would be unusual (cf. Lightfoot, Vincent). Calvin no doubt forces the meaning of the text when he translates it 'for I feel in my heart that you are all sharers with me . . .'

[3] Dibelius rightly observes that the apostle regards his bonds not as tokens of suffering but of grace. It must be noted, however, that in distinction from Phm. 1, 9 Paul does not present himself directly as a prisoner ('*desmios*'), he only makes reference to his 'bonds' ('*desmoi*'; as in 1[13, 14, 17]). Certainly this is not fortuitous, and T. W. MANSON ('St Paul in Ephesus. The date of the Epistle to the Philippians', *BJRL*, 23, 1939, p. 184) has even been able to deny any reference to imprisonment and to retain only a general allusion to suffering.

he will put up before his judges and because of his probable acquittal will be a 'confirmation' of the Gospel. No doubt the Philippians who have been closely associated with his work hitherto will continue to be so in the events which next befall him.

1⁸ God and Christ themselves are the final guarantee of the depth of the apostle's affection for the Philippians. Resort to an oath is unusual in the epistles and shows all the more the seriousness of what is being said (Rom. 1⁹; 2 Cor. 1²³; 1 Thess. 2⁵,¹⁰); the formula used here is not Rabbinic (the divine name would not be mentioned) but derived directly from the Old Testament (cf. LXX Gen. 31⁴⁴; 1 Kgs. 12⁵ᶠ; 20²³,⁴²; Billerbeck, Gnilka, Lohmeyer). The verb used ('*epipotheō*') reinforces the depth of feeling; borrowed from the *koiné* and clearly carrying the stamp of the apostle, it always indicates in his usage the quality of affection which binds him to his brethren in Christ (C. Spicq, 'Epipothein. Désirer ou chérir?', *RB*, 64, 1957, pp. 184–95). Indeed, in the light of most of the Pauline instances (notably 2²⁶) it is not impossible that it should be understood here as 'I long above all to see you all again' (cf. 1²⁵ᶠᶠ; 2¹²,²³). This strong desire is always said to arise from the 'bowels of Christ himself', so that a more 'visceral' love could not be conceived (cf. *ad* 2¹) and, as Bengel well puts it, 'It is not Paul who lives within Paul, but Jesus Christ, which is why Paul is not moved by the bowels of Paul but by the bowels of Jesus Christ' (*op. cit.*, p. 767).

3. *Intercession* (1⁹⁻¹¹)

(9) *And this is my prayer: that your love may increase more and more in understanding and in all perception* (10) *so that you can discern true values, in order that you may be pure and without reproach for the day of Christ,* (11) *bearers of that fruit which is the righteousness obtained through Jesus Christ, to the glory and praise of God.*

In v. 9 some manuscripts (B, D, *al.*) have an aorist ('*perisseusē*') instead of the present '*perisseuē*'. In v. 11 the *Koiné* has the plural 'the fruits of righteousness' ('*karpōn*' for '*karpon*', the genitive being more frequent after '*plēroō*'). The closing doxology ends in D with 'Christ' instead of 'God' (no doubt because of the preceding 'through Jesus Christ'), with 'my praise' in G, and with 'to the glory of God and my praise' in P 46. In spite of weak attestation, the last seems so strange that we can only ask whether it was not the original reading (cf. 1 Cor. 4⁵).

Since the apostle has so vigorously expressed his affection in the preceding verses then it is appropriate, in the epistolary style of the time, for him to announce at this point the recommendations which he will elaborate from 1²⁷ onwards. Make no mistake, the prayer of v. 9 is actually not far removed from exhortation (Scott); recognising the readers' love ('*agapē*'), the apostle asks that they increase in knowledge and discernment in view of the false doctrines which are infiltrating their community. Here again are encountered the fundamental themes which emerged in the earlier verses: the theological and Christological basis of the Christian life (v. 11) producing a community ethic (v. 10), the only response conceivable within the framework of a theology of history (cf. 'the Day of Christ').

1⁹,¹⁰ Disguised or not, the exhortation of these verses avows itself first of all as a prayer (*'proseuchomai'*) wherein the apostle's affection for the Philippians is again expressed and also his confidence in divine action (Michael). Formally considered, the prayer develops in three subordinate clauses (two final and one participial) each ending with a phrase introduced by *'eis'* (Lohmeyer).

First of all the prayer is about 'love' (*'agapē'*), not so much as of absolute value (Barth, Beare, Gnilka, Lohmeyer) but as the love which the Philippians have just shown to Paul (Bonnard) and which yet does not suffice; 'discrimination' must be added. We might think also of the brotherly and communal spirit which we know he found somewhat lacking at Philippi (Michael, Vincent). This essentially Christian virtue is here shown to be dynamic since it can be expected to 'abound yet more and more' (cf. 1 Thess. 3⁹). As C. Spicq has well put it: 'One never loves enough, or rather, is never sufficiently receptive of the gift of love' (*Agapè*, II, 1959, p. 235). Hence agapé is an object of prayer (*'proseuchomai'*), the Spirit is the source of it (Rom. 5⁵; Gal. 5²²) supplying this eschatological bounty (*'perisseuē'*; Rom. 5¹⁵; 1 Cor. 14¹²; 2 Cor. 3⁹; etc.) which is typical of the ultimate acts of God. As the norm of the new life agapé thus plays the same part as the Law in Judaism or 'Reason' in Stoicism (Spicq); it far exceeds the domain of mere feeling, and here comes to embrace 'knowledge and discernment' (Friedrich).

These two last terms (*'epignōsis kai aisthēsis'*) have a very wide meaning. The first of them, 'knowledge' or 'comprehension', bears no suggestion of the technical sense of *gnosis* nor is it found with this force in the Corinthian correspondence. The second, a New Testament *hapax*, basically means 'sensation', 'perception', whence the meaning of moral or spiritual discernment which it conveys in the Bible, particularly in the Book of Proverbs (22 occurrences out of 27). Mobilised by love these two abilities of man must 'test things which differ' (*'eis to dokimazein ta diapheronta'*) or, as Bonnard and Jones well translate it, 'discern what is vital'. Frequent in Stoicism (cf. A. Bonhöffer, *Epiktet und das NT*, 1911, p. 298f), the verb *'dokimazō'* here means 'to examine, hold an enquiry or make a test, in order to evaluate and to judge and finally to retain what is of value' (C. Spicq, *Agapè*, II, p. 238). The present participle *'diapheronta'* was also current in Greek and Hellenistic philosophy to denote what was important or essential. So the Philippians are asked, from material presented by alien preachers, to separate what has its source in the Gospel or in *'agapē'* from what is of merely human origin.[1]

---

[1] For the importance of 'discernment' in Christian ethics today, see D. BONHOEFFER on 'Proving' in his *Ethics*, ET 1955, pp. 161–66.

The majority of Greek Fathers therefore understood the text correctly when they found a reference here to distinguishing carefully between 'heresy' and the apostolic teaching (cf. Barth, Bonnard, Calvin), although as we shall see the debate was essentially on an ethical level.

All this must take place in the light of (dynamic *'eis'*, Müller) the Day of Christ (cf. *ad* **1⁶**) which thus lends direction and seriousness to ethics. Hence also the demand to be 'flawless', (*'eilikrinēs'*, Pauline *hapax*, but cf. 1 Cor. 5⁸; 2 Cor. 1¹²; 2¹⁷) and 'without reproach' (*'aproskopos'*)—the latter no doubt implying that the Philippians are called to avoid becoming stumbling-blocks (*'proskomma'*; 1 Cor. 8⁹ᶠ) for one another (1 Cor. 10³²; so Beare, Michael, Vincent; against Calvin). In this respect the situation is akin to that of ɪ Cor. 8.

1¹¹ The apostle's final request concerns the 'fulness' (*'peplēromenoi'*) of the Philippians. In view of the context in **3** (cf. also *ad* **2⁷**) it is not impossible that the word is borrowed from his opponents' propaganda. Hence the insistence that the only 'fulness' is that which comes from the righteousness attained through Jesus Christ. Righteous here then has the properly Pauline force of 'divine righteousness' and not the more ethical sense of righteousness in the Old Testament (contrary to most commentaries). The qualification—'obtained through the work of Christ' (*'dia christou'*)—and the background afforded by **3** prevent any other interpretation. Itself a 'fruit' (*'karpos'*; most commentaries) or 'producing fruit' (C. Spicq, *op. cit.*, p. 242), righteousness is also to the glory and praise of God. It is usual for a simple stylised phrase of doxology to conclude a prayer (cf. Billerbeck; 2 Sam. 22⁵⁰; Ps. 21¹⁴; 35²⁸; etc.); the words here are nonetheless pregnant with meaning. Readers who are prone to glory in other things than God alone are reminded by the apostle of the basis and the limits of all Christian living—'through Jesus Christ to the glory of God'.

As we have said, the reading in P 46 is surprising enough in character to be original, while those of D* and G are surely emendations. Moreover there is in its support the fact that in classical Greek as in Paul the word 'praise' (*'epainos'*) is chiefly associated with felicitations addressed to human beings. This final phrase might then be apologetic and polemical: let the Philippians act in the way Paul has just requested, at least in friendliness towards himself so that he may not have run or laboured in vain (2¹⁶). Taken in this way a transition is provided to the passage which follows.

SECOND PART

The Apostle's Circumstances (1^{12-26})

Paul then devotes the first part of his letter to giving news of his own circumstances. Yet he offers no abundance of details, and his 'miserliness' in this respect has often caused surprise. But it has also often been quite rightly stressed that this was due to the fact that the Philippians must have been aware of the dangers of his position through the frequent exchanges between themselves and him and from the bearer of the letter himself. It is also true that Paul's chief concern is to bring into relief the basic significance of the events which he has experienced, that they serve for the advancement of the Gospel. Hence the centrality of v. 18 (Bonnard, Gnilka). But what has not previously been sufficiently understood is that the course of events, and that alone, produced a real problem. The dangers of the situation did not of themselves warrant a written catalogue, but the purpose which had activated them and the significance which they were taking certainly did.

Indeed, that purpose and significance provoked opposition. We have already said (cf. Introduction, p. 9f) that the only way of fitting the references in vv. 15 and 17 to those who were preaching out of ill-will and to account for what is said about them is to regard them as genuine preachers of the Cross who alleged against the apostle an attitude of infidelity to the Cross. We have also shown that in order to agree with the general tone of the letter, with historical probabilities and with detailed exegesis, this attitude could only be an initiative which the imprisoned apostle has taken in order to be set free, doubtless by revealing his Roman citizenship. Having himself perhaps entertained the idea of 'glorifying Christ' (v. 19) by martyrdom, Paul realised as time went by that the occasion had not yet arrived and that for the present the Gospel demanded his life rather than his death. It is easy to see that this sudden turn about could have opened him to the charge of cowardice, especially in the light of the Cross itself.

Paul therefore explains here that he has but one concern—to proclaim Christ. This is his whole life, and the preaching is not by words alone; it involves a total commitment which could even lead to death (vv. 21ff). Other of the apostle's writings, and here too 1^{27ff} and 3, clearly show that he did not hesitate to fight for this view of the Gospel, and this alone, as the life-pattern for the congregations he was founding. But here he recognises that various ways open up even within the range of a genuine preaching of the Gospel. On the one side is the radicalism or purism of his detractors, a stance he himself had taken up at one time and perhaps even encouraged; on the other, a certain 'realism' which rather lets itself be guided by the movement of events, to which in the end he has surrendered himself.

It must be added that Paul offers no theological justification for his choice—it is merely '*anangkaioteron*' (v. 24), more profitable or more necessary; and this is no more than to state a subjective principle of opportunism. The apostle does not challenge the validity and weight of the arguments of his detractors; at most he shows a presentiment that they do not always correspond to motives which are as pure as they might first appear (but might not the same doubt arise in his own case?). The important thing is that Christ should be really proclaimed in one way or another. From this springs the joy which sweeps aside shocks and doubts and friction (v. 18).

Radical, doctrinaire commitment or 'realistic', opportunistic commitment—the choice is still just as burning a one today, and the way Paul handles it is perhaps not uninstructive.[1]

We distinguish the following scheme:

1. The progress of the Gospel: 1^{12-20}.
2. The alternatives: death or continuance of apostolic work: 1^{21-24}.
3. Prospect of reunion: 1^{25-26}.

1. *The Progress of the Gospel* (1^{12-20})

(12) *I would have you know, brothers, that my affairs have contributed rather to the progress of the Gospel;* (13) *that is to say, it has become clearly apparent, through the praetorium and elsewhere, that my bonds are bonds in Christ,* (14) *and the majority of the brethren, encouraged in the Lord by my bonds and freed from all fear, have redoubled their bold proclamation of the word of God.* (15) *Some, it is true, preach Christ from malevolence and contention, and others with a good disposition;* (16) *the latter proclaim Christ out of love, knowing that I am here for the defence of the Gospel,* (17) *the former from a spirit of rivalry with ulterior motives imagining to add even greater affliction to my imprisonment.* (18) *What are we to think? Only that whether in pretence or in truth Christ is proclaimed in every way, and in that I rejoice and will rejoice.* (19) *I know, indeed, that thanks to your prayer and the help of the spirit of Jesus Christ, this will lead on to my salvation;* (20) *what I long and hope for is that I may be confounded by nothing but that today as always I may openly glorify Christ in my own person whether by life or by death.*

---

[1] An analogous problem can be found in Luther's reply to the pastors of Breslau who asked him whether he ought not to flee from the plague: an open letter on 'whether it is proper for a Christian to flee when in danger of death', *Library of Christian Classics*, vol. 18, 1955, pp. 230–44.

In v. 14 P 46 and the *Koiné* use 'word' without qualification; G has 'word of the Lord'. The Textus Receptus reverses the order of vv. 16 and 17 and introduces an '*epipherein*' ('to bring upon', 'to increase') which is clearly a correction of the difficult '*egeiren*' ('to raise up'). Similarly the '*plēn hoti*' ('except that') of v. 18 is altered in B to a simple '*hoti*' ('because') and in the *Koiné* and Claromontanus to '*plēn*' ('yet'). The end of the same verse is also punctuated differently in different editions of the text and P46 links it particularly to what precedes by adding an '*alla*' ('but'). It seems that the Nestle-Aland punctuation, which does not make v. 18b a fresh departure should be accepted. The link between v. 19 and v. 18 ('*gar*') is weakened in some manuscripts ('*de*': P 46, B, 69). Other variants are without weight.

The apostle's recent initiative concerning the revealing of his Roman citizenship ('*ta kat'eme*'; v. 12), far from betraying the Gospel has contributed rather ('*mallon*'; v. 12) to its advance ('*prokopē*'). The results have been positive both outside the Christian community (v. 13) and within it (vv. 14–18), although it must be observed that the position Paul has taken up has set in motion conflicting currents of opinion which are not all in his favour (vv. 14–18). At least, the criticisms are based upon a theology of the Cross and thereby in one way or another Christ is proclaimed (vv. 15ff), and the apostle can only rejoice (v. 18). Furthermore, it is quite clear that the public trial which is about to open will give him fresh opportunity for witnessing to Christ (vv. 19–20). His life is therefore as profitable for the Gospel as his death might have been (v. 20b).

1[12] Presenting the proposition which will be argued in the following passage, the verse opens with a rather trite formula frequent in other letters of the time as well as Paul's ('I would have you know . . .').[1] The proposition consists in this, that the apostle's 'affairs' ('*ta kat'eme*')—which there is no reason to identify merely with his imprisonment—have contributed to the 'advancement' ('*prokopē*', a rare and late Greek word) of that which gives life meaning, namely the Gospel (cf. *ad* 1[5]). Weight must be given to the '*mallon*' ('has contributed *rather* to . . .'). The adverb is not opposing personal difficulties, such as the rigours of an imprisonment, to interests regarded as superior (those of the Gospel; against Barth, Bonnard, Lohmeyer), but two conflicting views about the actual consequences of the events in question (cf. Michael and Müller). The tone still remains warm; the readers are called 'brothers' ('*adelphoi*'), the term which will be used five times more for them (though predominantly in letter C: 3[1,13,17]; 4[1,8]) and which is a hallmark of the relationship between those who are 'in Christ'.

1[13] If we have correctly determined the meaning of 'affairs' in v. 12 it is understandable that they cause some stir particularly in the

---

[1] Cf. O. ROLLER, *op. cit.*, pp. 65 and 467; Rom .1[13]; 1 Thess. 4[13]; Rom. 11[25]; 1 Cor. 10[1]; etc. In some of these instances the expression is also followed by '*adelphoi*'.

governor's palace (*'en tō praitōriō*) and throughout the city (*'en tois loipois pasin'*).[1] What must have been most perplexing to these people was the reason for the apostle's protracted silence. Had his imprisonment not lasted for such a long time that it had been possible to organise a collection for him at Philippi? Paul then explains that it is the circumstance of being 'in Christ' (cf. *ad* 1[1]) and his faithfulness to the Cross which in the first place forced him into suffering (cf. 1[29]; 3[10]) and eventually to contemplate martyrdom (cf. Lohmeyer). Up to the present time, indeed, his motives have passed unnoticed by the world, but now after the revelation he has made, it is clear (*'phanerous'*) to everyone that the reason for his imprisonment (*'tous desmous mou'*) is 'in Christ'. The *'en Christō'* cannot therefore be exclusively linked with *'phanerous genesthai'*, 'my bonds have gained in Christ real public notice' (Benoit; cf. Calvin, de Boor, Freidrich, Gnilka . . .). The real meaning of such an assertion is hard to see unless it is realised, in the terms of our hypothesis, that the self-revelation which the apostle has just made is no betrayal but is 'in Christ'. Likewise, one must not suppose with Dibelius that this notoriety 'serves Christ' but rather recognise with most commentators that 'in Christ' qualifies both the verb and its subject. But this qualification does not relate so much to the reasons for Paul's arrest as to the reasons for his acceptance of arrest.

A 'praetorium' was originally a general's tent, head-quarters of a camp, then the praetorian troops and their barracks (cf. Dibelius, Gnilka, and Lightfoot pp. 99–104). The meaning given to the word here depends on the view which is adopted as to the place of origin of the letter. Those who choose Rome think of the Imperial Palace (Patristic exegesis by and large) or of the Praetorian Guard (cf. Acts 28). But in the New Testament the word exclusively denotes the residence of provincial governors (Mt. 27[27] and par.; Jn. 18[28,33]; 19[9]; Acts 23[35]). So Lohmeyer refers to Felix and Festus at Caesarea; T. W. Manson (*BJRL*, 23, 1939, p. 193) and Matter to Gallio's tribunal at Corinth; and those who hold an Ephesian hypothesis naturally regard it as an allusion to the residence of the governor of that city, in connection with which inscriptions can be cited which indicate that praetors stayed there (cf. Dibelius).

1[14] The apostle's initiative has not only had good results outside the Christian community but also in its midst among 'brethren who have been enheartened in the Lord' by his imprisonment. The expression 'in the Lord' normally with Paul qualifies ethical actions: 'One becomes in the Lord what he already is in Christ' (M. Bouttier, *En Christ*, pp. 54–61, cf. F. Neugebauer, *In Christus*, pp. 130–49). It could here refer either to 'brethren' (Dibelius, Lohmeyer) or to

---

[1] It is hard to appreciate why almost all translators render the *'hōste'* here by 'so that', the meaning of which is far from obvious. The conjunction should be understood in its less frequent explicatory sense of 'that is to say' or even 'to the extent that'.

'confidence' ('*pepoithotas*'; most commentators). The parallels of Gal. 5[10] and 2 Thess. 3[12] support the second possibility, though in these two instances the object of confidence is not the Lord ('*en kuriō*' is only the manner) but is introduced by the prepositions '*epi*' (7 times in the New Testament) or '*eis*'. Similarly, the dative '*desmois*' ('bonds') certainly cannot be the object of the confidence; Phm. 21 cannot be taken as a decisive parallel.[1] The perfect of the verb '*peithō*' must then be given its original meaning of 'persuaded', 'convinced'—'brethren persuaded (convinced) in the Lord by my bonds'.[2] The apostle's imprisonment and sufferings have strengthened the conviction, the faith, of his brethren, and this strengthening has occurred through the initiative and under the guidance of him who is Lord of the church and of all else (cf. 2[9–11]).

The 'majority' ('*hoi pleiones*'; 'majority' not 'more', cf. B–D §244.3) of these brethren have experienced as the result of recent events a renewal of ardour ('*perissoterōs tolman*') in the preaching of the Word.[3] But the emphasis lies on '*aphobōs*', 'fearlessly', and in terms of the traditional interpretation it could be asked by what magic the imprisonment of their leader could have freed these evangelists from their fear (cf. T. W. Manson, *BJRL*, 23, 1939, pp. 185–93). By this approach one is driven willy-nilly to an understanding of the text like Lohmeyer's: the mystique of martyrdom in the Christian community is such that the prospect of a fatal outcome for the apostle provides an impulse to yet bolder evangelism. But there is no trace of any such mystique in our epistle, and we prefer to think that it is, on the contrary, the announcement of imminent freedom for the apostle which has encouraged Christian preaching.

1[15] Among those who have been encouraged by the apostle's imprisonment and have now begun to preach with renewed vigour two opposed groups must be distinguished (vv. 15–17); the one in favour of the apostle's initiative and the other on the contrary unfavourable. Vv. 15ff now fit perfectly into the argument as we have just expounded it so that there is no need to follow Barth, Dibelius and Gnilka in regarding the verses as a parenthesis of doubtful meaning.

---

[1] In the NT the object of confidence is elsewhere indicated twice by the infinitive, three times by '*hoti*' and twice by '*en*'.

[2] So the perfect has its full force of an act commencing in the past and with continuing effects, and it is thus distinguished from the main verb 'to dare': *already* convinced they *now* continue to dare. Further, the dative '*tois desmois*' might be taken in a temporal sense, 'convinced during the time of my bonds', the apostle now enjoying freer conditions. In fact, if the dative of instrument interpretation which we have given is not accepted it would no doubt be best to take it prepositionally: 'in connection with my imprisonment', 'so far as my imprisonment is concerned'.

[3] '*Ho logos tou theou, ho logos tou kuriou, ho logos*' are equivalent expressions for the totality of the Christian message; they are the object of various verbs ('*didaskein*'; '*katanggellein*', '*euanggelizesthai*', etc.); and are found with '*lalein*' in Acts 4[29–31]; 11[19]; 13[46]; etc. Cf. KITTEL, art. '*legō*', *TWNT*, IV, 1942, pp. 100–40 (pp. 115ff) (ET IV, pp. 100–41, and 114ff).

There is no lack of suggestions as to the identity of the hostile group, but one can be confident, with the majority of commentators, that what separated these people from Paul did not really stem from doctrine or Paul would have treated them more severely (cf. 3^{2ff}) and would not have said that they 'proclaimed Christ'. We must therefore reject the views of some of the Greek Fathers who see them as pagan agitators, as well as Lohmeyer's idea that they are Judaeo-Christians from Caesarea. For still more obvious reasons (e.g. of tone) we must not accept the confusing of the group in 1^{15ff} with that of 3^{2ff} (for Lightfoot, Judaeo-Christians; for W. Schmithals, gnostics; cf. *Paulus und die Gnostiker*, p. 54).

Must we then accept an opposition resting merely upon matters of personal rivalry (Barth, Beare, Müller, Vincent, etc.)?—and it can be said in this connection that such things often plagued Christian communities in those days, notably that of Rome itself (O. Cullmann, *Peter. Disciple—Apostle—Martyr*, ET 1953, pp. 104–9). This is the judicious standpoint, though a little facile. And so attempts to probe more deeply are to be welcomed with interest.

So T. W. Manson (*BJRL*, 23, 1939, p. 194) and Matter refer to the parties indicated in 1 Cor. 1–4, and G. S. Duncan (*St Paul's Ephesian Ministry*, pp. 271–75) thinks of Judaeo-Christians of Alexandria closer to Apollos than to Paul; and there is T. Hawthorn's suggestion ('Philippians 1^{12-15}', *ET*, 62, 1950–51, p. 316f) taken up by F. C. Synge in his commentary which makes not Paul but the authorities responsible for his imprisonment (Synge: the Jews) the target for the attitude of disparagement shown here. Or again, there is J. Munck's thesis (*Paul and the Salvation of Mankind*, ET 1959, pp. 323–35) accepted by C. Spicq (*Agapè*, II, 1959, p. 244f) according to which we may be concerned here with Judaisers who hardly knew how to regard the fact of the apostle's imprisonment and who found in him a hindrance to the Christian cause (cf. also Jewett, *NT*, 12, 1970, p. 364f).

This is obviously an interesting idea since it allows us to accept the authenticity of preaching which nonetheless was directed against the apostle; yet it does not completely fit either the larger context of the whole letter nor the exact meaning of 'preaching Christ' (*'ton Christon kērussousin'*). For the apostle to 'preach Christ' means one thing only, to proclaim his death and resurrection.[1] So again it would seem that we are justified in thinking of a preaching which, on the basis of the Cross itself, could reproach the apostle for the steps he has taken to secure his imminent release.

But are such attitudes as innocent as they seem? Paul has his doubts, and he exposes here a spirit of denigration, of 'malevolence'

[1] For Paul the subject of preaching is Christ (2 Cor. 1^9; 11^4; 2 Tim. 3^{16}; cf. Rom. 10^{14f}), that is, Christ crucified (1 Cor. 1^{23}; cf. 1^{21}; 2^4; Gal. 5^{11}) and risen (1 Cor. $15^{11, 12, 14}$), and now Lord (2 Cor. 4^5). With the verb '*kērussein*' we have 'the Gospel' (Gal. 2^{22}; Col. 1^{23}; 1 Thess. 2^9; cf. 2 Tim. 4^2) and 'the word of faith' (Rom. 10^8). Here '*Christon kērussein*' takes up the '*logon lalein*' of v. 14 and becomes '*Christon katanggellein*' in v. 16.

('*phthonos*'), and of 'strife', 'contention' or 'rivalry' ('*eris*')—two terms often occurring in the lists of 'vices' which he gives as well as in contemporary Judaism (cf. Gnilka; Lohmeyer; C. Spicq, *Agapè*, II, p. 246f). The brethren who remain faithful to the apostle show on the contrary good dispositions and a spirit of 'understanding and collaboration' ('*eudokia*'; cf. Bonnard, Dibelius, Lightfoot).

1[16–17] These verses are devoted to a still more precise definition of the motives underlying the preaching of each of the two groups to which reference has been made. Again it will be observed that there is no question of the genuineness of the preaching and that the verb 'to proclaim' (i.e. to proclaim Christ, '*katanggellousin ton Christon*'), taking up the word 'preach' in the previous verse, is the only finite verb in these verses. The one group do it out of love ('*ex agapēs*'), that is to say under the inspiration of the Spirit who up-builds the community, and the other from a concern for faction and intrigue ('*ex eritheias*').[1] Elsewhere these two moral attitudes appear in a stereotyped form and are found in the lists in Gal. 5[20f]; 1 Tim. 6[11] and 2 Cor. 11[20], and even with reference to the situation at Philippi itself in **2**[1–3].

But the action of the two groups is sustained by what the one party know ('*eidotes*') and the others 'imagine' ('*oiomenoi*'). The former know that by procuring his appearance before the tribunal Paul will be defending ('*apologia*') the Gospel. The term '*apologia*' most often means 'defence', 'plea' in court (cf. Acts 22[1]; 1 Cor. 9[1]; 1 Tim. 4[16]). The application of the word to the Gospel, which occurs only here and at **1**[7], therefore denotes that by making his own personal defence the apostle proposes to offer a defence of the Gospel also (cf. v. 13). The verb '*keimai*' could simply mean 'I am here, in this situation, so that . . .', unless it is taken with the sharper meaning of 'I am appointed, put here (by God) so that . . .' (Benoit, Bonnard, Huby, Michael). In any case, the traditional view by which it is the imprisonment of the apostle itself which 'pleads' in favour of the Gospel seems to lack any evidence for its support.

While the first group 'know', the second 'imagine rightly' though their judgement is not pure ('*ouch hagnōs*'), i.e. is not free from ulterior motives. It is, indeed, more natural to attach the adverb directly to the participle 'imagine' rather than to the main verb (Ewald). Most commentaries, following Nestle's text, make it a kind of absolute ('not sincerely') which is inelegant. The verb '*oiomai*' has a wide range of meaning—'to think, suppose, suspect, believe, imagine, etc.' The traditional interpretation understands the phrase as: 'they imagine (by their attacks) they will increase my sufferings'. But this comes to grief on the double objection of the parallelism with '*eidotes*' ('knowing') and the precise meaning of '*thlipsis*'. Never in the New Testament, especially in Paul, does it have the psycholo-

---

[1] The two expressions must be taken as qualifying the main verb, rather than with the pronouns '*hoi*' (against Vincent).

gical meaning of 'mental difficulty, pain' (except perhaps in Jas. 1²⁷), but it denotes quite definitely the eschatological 'afflictions' initiated by the Cross which mark the last days (Schlier, art. 'thlibō, etc.', *TWNT*, III, 1938, pp. 139–48 (ET III, pp. 139–48). Here lies the interest of the interpretation given by T. Hawthorn (*ExpT*, 62, 1950–51, p. 316f) and F. C. Synge: 'rightly supposing that affliction may spring from (be provoked by) my imprisonment'; but unfortunately it comes up against the difficulty that '*egeirein*' is a transitive verb requiring a direct object in the accusative. So a mediating solution must be adopted, half way between the traditional one and that of Hawthorn and Synge: the apostle's opponents want 'to add an affliction to his imprisonment', i.e. they think that he should launch into a series of tribulations ('*thlipsis*') which should bring him still closer to the Crucified and Risen One. (cf. vv. 21ff).

1¹⁸ The general idea of the verse presents little problem. What counts for Paul is not the attitude of one group or the other towards himself but the fact that the Gospel is proclaimed. The thought continues, therefore, coherent and vigorous; his actions have been for the sake of the Gospel and the fact that his stand has not been ineffective in that regard fills him with joy ('*en toutō chairō*; cf. *ad* 1⁵). He recognises a sort of objective power in the message of the Gospel which is independent of the messenger (Beare), and the contrast of this 'liberal' attitude to the intransigence of his other epistles has often intrigued commentators. Barth supposes some development in the apostle's thought; Lohmeyer thinks of the particular perspective given by martyrdom; and Gnilka of an awareness quickened by the imminence of the parousia. To Michael, the words just used by the apostle have gone beyond his real intention; the scheming opponents are not so far removed from him theologically but he has wanted to put them in their place. In fact, it seems to us that the reason for the recognition which the apostle gives to the validity of this adverse preaching should be sought in the particular circumstances surrounding the writing of the epistle.

As for details, is '*ti gar*' and '*plēn hoti*' to be translated 'What matter! In every way . . .' (so most commentaries) or 'What are we to think? Only that . . .' (Barth, Haupt, Müller)? The most frequent usage of the time as well as the sequence of thought itself points to the second rendering.¹ The option in fact is not, as is generally thought, between the two groups of 'brethren' who are characterised on the one hand by truth ('*eite alētheia*') and on the other by 'pretence' ('*eite prophasei*'), but, whether the view held by the second group, expressed at the end of the preceding verse, is genuine or a pretence, a kind of screen.² 'What matter . . .!' So there is no reason to take the end

¹ '*Ti gar*' is a popular exclamation found in the Bible in Job 16³ and 21⁴ (LXX); Rom. 3³; (1 Cor. 5¹²). Most often '*plēn hoti*' means 'except that'—a meaning which has embarrassed some copyists and which B–D (§449.2) has little justification for taking here as 'in any case'.

² It will be observed that the opposite of truth here is neither lie nor error.

of v. 18 as opening a new orientation of thought henceforward facing fully the spectre of death (Dibelius, Gnilka, Haupt, Müller, and Michaelis who even suggests a pause in the dictation); it is simply a reinforcement of the idea of joy (on '*alla kai*', cf. B–D §448.6). The apostle's joy is no transient thing; it will still be his tomorrow when he presents himself before his earthly judges and the day after tomorrow when he appears before the heavenly judge.

1¹⁹ Having stated the past or present consequences of his actions, Paul comes now to future consequences: he still has to appear before the tribunal (vv. 19–20) and then he will take up again his missionary work (vv. 25–26). The trial will in fact be the occasion of an important public testimony ('*en pasē parrhēsia*'), which is why he reaffirms his conviction ('*oida*', cf. '*eidotes*' and '*oiomenoi*' in vv. 16–17) of being on the right road, that namely which leads ('*apobainō*') to salvation. This salvation ('*sōtēria*') is not his liberation (cf. Ewald-Wohlenberg) but as always elsewhere with Paul, the eschatological and ultimate salvation (cf. Foerster, art. '*sōzō*, etc.', *TWNT*, VII, 1964, pp. 992–94 (ET VII, pp. 992–94)), and what leads to it ('*touto*') is not imprisonment itself, nor the preaching of the Gospel (Bonnard), nor even the general status of one called by God to himself (Gnilka), but the sequence of events which he has just set in motion and the advisability of which has been questioned. It is significant that Paul refers in this connection to a passage in Job (13¹⁶), as has been stressed particularly by Michael (cf. also Gnilka and Martin). The text corresponds exactly to that of the Septuagint and '*apobainō*' which it picks up is found nowhere else in Paul. The whole context deserves quotation:

> 'Let me have silence, and I will speak,
>   and let come on me what may.
> I will take my flesh in my teeth,
>   and put my life in my hand.
> If he slay me I will not tremble,
>   so long as I argue my case to his face.
> This moreover shall be ('*apobēsetai eis*') my salvation
>   that a godless man shall not come before him'
>   (Job 13¹³⁻¹⁶).

It is not suffering in a general sense which has led the apostle to ponder on the Book of Job (Gnilka, Michael), but more particularly the dispute even with his friends about his attitude towards it. Like Job, Paul claims to be answerable for his actions to God alone and by a kind of sequence of images, or rather their fusion, he represents his imminent appearance before the Roman governor as a figure of his appearance before the divine tribunal. The success of the former— and here Job's haughty isolation is shattered by the reality of the Christian fellowship—nevertheless depends on the prayer of the Philippians ('*dia tēs deēseōs*', cf. *ad* 1⁴) and the help of the Spirit.

'*Epichorēgia*', 'additional supply', 'aid', occurs elsewhere in the New Testament only in Eph. 4[16] but the verb '*epichorēgeō*' is found five times, in one of which it refers to the Spirit (Gal. 3[2]). But the same idea of assistance brought by the Spirit to Christians who bear witness when they appear before their judges is firmly anchored in early Christianity though it does not occur particularly in Paul (cf. Mk. 13[11]; Mt. 10[20]; Lk.12[12]). Whence also the qualification, unusual in the epistles, of the Spirit as the Spirit of Jesus Christ, i.e. the Spirit is sent by Christ so that the apostle can witness to Christ.

1[20] Paul is completely absorbed ('*kata tēn apokaradokian*') by his anticipated trial and sets his hope fully upon it ('*kai elpida mou*'). The first term belongs to late Greek and is only found elsewhere in the New Testament in Rom. 8[19] where it describes the 'longing' of all creation for the final redemption. It has a picturesque etymology: to look ('*dokein*') by turning the head ('*kara*') from ('*apo*').[1] Associated with '*elpis*' it denotes a time of uncertainty and doubt. Hope, which is mentioned here only in this epistle, indicates a patient and confident expectancy for what is to come (R. Bultmann, art. '*elpis*, etc.', *TWNT*, II, 1935, pp. 515–31 (ET II, pp. 515–33)). Paul then hopes that the events close at hand will not put him to shame ('*aischunthēsomai*'). The verb belongs to the vocabulary of the Psalms (LXX 24[3]; 68[7]; 118[80,116]; etc.) whereby the believer requests that he may not be covered with shame before his enemies.[2] Here these are quite as much 'false brethren' who challenge the apostle's actions as the judges before whom he must appear; he hopes that he is on the right road and that he will not have to repent for an error.

So much for the negative side of his expectations; but there is a positive side as well, namely the exaltation of Christ in the person of the apostle. The verb '*megalunthēnai*' also occurs in the Psalms (LXX 34[4]; 35[27]; 40[17]) though one does not have to agree with Gnilka that the antithesis 'be put to shame . . . glorify' comes directly from the Psalter. In Paul's usage it occurs again only in 2 Cor. 10[15] where he hopes to be 'magnified' in the eyes of the Corinthians. The word '*sōma*' ('body') does not have here a narrowly corporeal meaning but signifies, as elsewhere in biblical anthropology, the whole person: Christ will be magnified by the defence I make with reference to my imprisonment and the sufferings which I endured in the course of it.[3] This interpretation is confirmed by the qualifying phrase '*en pasē parrhēsia*'. '*Parrhēsia*' in classical Greek means freedom of speech, outspokenness, and so carries the idea of publicity.[4] The same

[1] Cf. G. BERTRAM, '*Apokaradokia*', *ZNW*, 49, 1958, pp. 264–70.

[2] The subject of this passive verb is none other than God himself (Friedrich).

[3] For the characteristics of the apostle's preaching and sufferings, cf. E. GÜTTGEMANS, *Der leidende Apostel und sein Herr. Studien zur paulinischen Christologie*, 1966.

[4] Cf. E. PETERSON, 'Zur Bedeutungsgeschichte von "*parrhēsia*" ' in *R. Seeberg Festschrift*, I, 1929, pp. 283–97; H. SCHLIER, art. '*parrhēsia*, etc.', *TWNT*, V, 1954, pp. 869–84; (ET V, pp. 871–86); W. C. VAN UNNIK, *De semitische achtergrond van 'parrhēsia' in het NT*, 1962.

feature is found also in the New Testament where most often it characterises '*legein*' ('to speak') or '*didaskein*' ('to teach'; cf. Mk. 8³²; Jn. 7¹³; Acts 2²⁹; Eph. 6¹⁹ᶠ; etc.). So Paul is here insisting both on the publicity of what will take place (Bonnard, Gnilka) and on the fact that he will hide none ('*en pasē*') of the reasons for his long silence or the circumstances of his imprisonment. By this Christ will be glorified—now, as always ('*hōs pantote kai nun*')! Not only does the apostle thereby show the constancy of his conduct, he also prepares the way for a further consideration. The verse actually ends with a reference to the alternatives life or death and so directly introduces the development in the following verses. But there is further a relationship between the 'now' and the mention of 'life', the 'always' and the mention of 'death'. There is nothing treasonable in his change of attitude; whether *yesterday* by *death* or *today* by *life*, his single aim has *always* been simply to glorify Christ in the most appropriate way. So we must not regard the alternatives as a sign of uncertainty as to the fate which the apostle will find in store for him. Of all the commentaries Michaelis' alone escapes this interpretation by suggesting that Paul refers to death here because he had been preoccupied by it a little before writing the epistle.

2. *The alternatives: death or continuance of apostolic work* (1²¹⁻²⁴)

(21) *For to me to live is Christ and to die is gain.* (22) *But if to live here below should still allow me fruitful work I cannot tell which to choose.* (23) *I am constrained on both sides, my desire being to depart and be with Christ, which would be much, much, the better;* (24) *but to continue here below is more expedient for you.*

DUPONT, J., '*Sun Christōi*'. *L'union avec le Christ suivant saint Paul*, Pt. I: '*Avec le Christ*' *dans la vie future*, 1952, pp. 171–87.
GIGLIOLI, A., 'Mihi enim vivere Christus est. Congettura al testo di Phil. 1.21, *RBi*, 16, 1968, pp. 305–15.
HOFFMANN, P., *Die Toten in Christus. Eine religionsgeschichtliche und exegetische Untersuchung zur paulinischen Eschatologie*, 1966, pp. 286–320.
SIBER, P., *Mit Christus leben. Eine Studie zur paulinischen Auferstehungshoffnung*, 1971, pp. 86–94.

Though the text of v. 21 is fully attested, A. Giglioli (*art. cit.*) proposes a bold emendation; for '*Christos*' ('Christ') he would read '*chrēstos*' ('profitable')—'for me to live is profitable'. In v. 22 the conditional '*ei de*' is replaced in P 46 by '*epei*', 'since'. The verse presents a punctuation problem (cf. exegesis); P 46 and B have a subjunctive '*hairēsōmai*' in place of the indicative. '*Epithumia*' is construed most easily with the simple infinitive, whence the omission of the '*eis*' before '*analusai*' in P 46, D, G in v. 23. Similarly, '*pollō gar mallon*' has seemed too difficult for some manuscripts. In v. 24 '*epimeinai*' occurs in B, 1611 as a parallel to '*analusai*', while P 46, B, *Koiné* and G add '*en*' ('in') before the dative '*tē sarki*', a reading Bonnard retains.

As we have already said, the only way to integrate these verses with their context is to appreciate that in them Paul is posing in a somewhat rhetorical vein the alternatives presented to him at the time when he took the decision to reveal his Roman citizenship, alternatives underlying the debate reflected in vv. 15ff. From this point of view the closest parallel is given by Rom. 7.7ff where the same rhetorical 'I' ('*egō*') appears. On the other hand, these verses can be construed in different ways (Gnilka; Michaelis; P. Hoffmann, *op. cit.*, p. 293) none of which is wholly convincing. Yet it is clear that the apostle's doubt does not relate to his immediate fate (acquittal or condemnation) but to the attitude to adopt and the choice to make ('*hairēsomai*'!) with respect to the future. This would also imply that the meaning of the text is being somewhat forced when it is over-exploited as source material for a reconstruction of Pauline eschatology. Not that the text is silent on this point or that the '*sun Christō einai*' ('to be with Christ') of v. 23 does not correspond to the apostle's actual thought, but he has not elaborated upon it and after all he has given up the idea for the sake of a more mundane struggle and for a place once again within human society and human affairs. The way to communion with Christ ('*sun Christō*') lies through a difficult communion with men and labour on their behalf ('*di' humas*').

1.21 'For me to live is Christ!' It is a stirring utterance and within the limits and context of Pauline theology the phrase is, so to say, not a single note but a chord (cf. Bonnard). It shows in the first place that life can have no other goal than Christ in whom is also the fulness of life (cf. Gal. 2.19ff). On this level of interpretation one can speak of mysticism and can understand why to die could be a gain, for death brings nearness to Christ (Dibelius; Calvin; Gnilka; Tillmann; P. Hoffmann, *op. cit.*, pp. 292ff). Then the verb '*to zēn*' is given a wider meaning than the preceding substantive; it includes *life* in the beyond as well. Yet even if one limits oneself to this interpretation the fundamental difference between the Greek philosophical view of death and Paul's conception must be stressed; the one rests upon the immortality of the soul and contempt for this present world while the other is uniquely and rigorously Christocentric (against J. Dupont, *op. cit.*, pp. 171–87; with Gnilka and P. Hoffmann, *op. cit.*, pp. 296–301).

But a second level of meaning is opened up by this verse, for Christ is indeed not only the Risen One but also the Crucified One and for Paul to live is therefore primarily to approach the Cross of his Master. Mysticism here is rooted in history. The approach is that of 'following' ('imitating') and of the value and importance of apostolic sufferings (2 Cor. 4.10ff), thereby approximating to Lohmeyer's thesis for whom only the possibility of martyrdom adequately explains this verse. Imprisoned, on the razor-edge between life and death, the apostle in fact identifies his life with Christ's. For this reason also death is gain, for it unites with the Cross as nothing else does that utter weakness from the midst of which will spring the power of God (2 Cor. 12⁹; Barth).

Yet we must go even further. Bonnard rightly stresses that the context is one of preaching. Now Christ for Paul is no static being but a living dynamic inescapably͵driving him to proclaim the Crucified and Risen One, so that life for the apostle can be nothing but proclaiming Christ (Bonnard, Martin, Péry). To die is then also a gain because death will give him the ultimate possibility of witnessing to Christ. It may furthermore be noted that one of the only two occasions in which Paul uses the verb '*kerdainō*' is to indicate the aim of his apostolic ministry (1 Cor. 9¹⁹ᶠᶠ) and that in our case also '*kerdos*' can be taken as parallel with the 'fruit of work' ('*karpos ergou*') in the next verse (so Michaelis, against P. Hoffmann, *op. cit.*, p. 292).

All this is 'for me', implying both an assumed 'for them'—meaning his detractors of vv. 15ff (cf. the '*gar*' indicating a strong linkage)— and the 'for you' ('*di' humas*') of v. 24. If Paul pleads for his freedom it is for no self-centred reason, rather the opposite; the simplest solution for him would have been to die. And we may note that when the verbs ('*to zēn—to apothanein*') are used here instead of the nouns ('*zōē—thanatos*') of the previous verse it is not so much because of some extension of meaning which is hard to justify (cf. above) as because the verb lays stress precisely upon the action—to die or to live—rather than upon general considerations of life and death.

1²² Whatever the precise meaning of the first part of the verse the general sense is not in doubt: there is some qualification being applied to the gain ('*kerdos*') which death entails to the point that the apostle hesitates (or has hesitated) about the line of action to take. It must be emphasised that in the active the verb '*haireō*' means 'to take into one's hands, to seize' in a very realistic way, and in the middle 'to take for oneself, to choose'. The two other instances in the New Testament (2 Thess. 2¹³; Heb. 11²⁵) simply confirm this latter meaning. It is therefore highly unlikely that Paul would have used the verb to speak about events which did not depend upon himself. Traditional exegesis does not do justice to the text by taking it as 'to hope' or 'to desire', nor is Gnilka convincing when he supposes that the apostle's choice is made before God, nor Lohmeyer who speaks of a wholly inward choice.

The same is true of the verb '*gnōrizō*' which is usually rendered by 'I do not know (what to choose)'. Such a rendering is not excluded, though in all 26 of its New Testament occurrences (18 in Paul) it means 'to make known, to declare' and does not signify 'to know' inwardly (cf. Beare, Vincent). So Lohmeyer thinks of a revelation, or rather the absence of any revelation made to Paul at this time. In our interpretation of the chapter in its entirety we take it, then, that the apostle had nothing 'from the Lord' to declare (cf. 1 Cor. 7^{10-13}) concerning the options 'to live or to die', hence the embarrassment caused him by the turmoil in the Ephesian community which his initiative had stirred up. If the first verb is taken interrogatively the translation will therefore be: 'What shall I choose? I cannot say', or 'I have nothing to declare about this matter' (B–D, §368; P. Hoffmann, *op. cit.*, p. 292; Lohmeyer). But if it is preferred to make *'ti hairēsomai'* depend upon *'gnōrizō'* (Bonnard, Dibelius, Friedrich, Staab) then it must be taken as: 'I cannot say (announce) what I shall choose.'

Why the hesitation when the apostle has just stated his interest in dying? The explanation is given by the first part of the verse, which there is no authority whatever for taking as a later gloss (against Michael), though the elliptical form of the sentence leaves several possibilities open. Some would make *'touto* etc.' depend upon *'ei'*, as does Lightfoot: 'But what if my living in the flesh will bear fruit, etc.' (cf. Lohmeyer). But it is preferable to regard *'touto moi karpos ergou'* ('this is for me a fruit of work') as the principal clause and to take it as 'if I should live, this will be . . .' (Friedrich, Staab), or as 'if to live in the flesh is fruitful for work . . .' (Bonnard; Dibelius; Gnilka; P. Hoffmann, *op. cit.*, p. 292). The latter seems more in harmony with the context. 'In the flesh' simply means 'here below', without any pejorative suggestion or allusion to sin (cf. Gal. 2^{20}; 2 Cor. 10^3; Phm. 16; A. Sand, *Der Begriff 'Fleisch' in den paulinischen Hauptbriefen*, 1967, pp. 165–68). The 'fruit of work' means the results (*'karpos'*, cf. Rom. 1^{13}) which the missionary activity of the apostle can still yield (*'ergon'*, cf. 1 Cor. 3^{12ff}; 9^1; Rom. 16^{10}). Here, as throughout the letter, the criterion of choice will be the progress of the Gospel.

1[23] So the apostle is 'pulled' in two directions, 'hemmed in' on both sides (Huby). The verb *'sunechō'* first means 'to hold together', 'to maintain', but then takes a variety of senses which 'together give *"sunechomai"* a dynamic or even violent suggestion which can only be precisely determined from the context' (C. Spicq, *Agapè*, II, p. 129). Indeed, it is not impossible that we should detect in this instance the nuance common in the papyri of 'judicial restraint', which appears moreover in the only other instance of Pauline usage (2 Cor. 5^{14}). Paul would then find himself 'accused' from two sides and not knowing easily to which constraint to yield.

The first form of the alternative is a 'desire to depart and to be with Christ'. Paul always uses *'epithumia'* ('desire') with a bad sense (except for 1 Thess. 2^{17}) and in this sense it must also be understood here (with Bonnard; against Gnilka). The verb *'analuō'*, 'to depart', then 'to hoist anchor' can be used in Greek as a metaphor for death (cf. J. Dupont, *op. cit.*, pp. 177–81; P. Hoffmann, *op. cit.*, p. 289).

But it can in no sense be taken as a technical term indicating the separation of soul and body. Dupont is not convincing, and he can offer parallels with '*luō*' or '*apoluō*' only and not with '*analuō*'. Paul here approaches current popular speech rather than the language of philosophers. In a vivid metaphor he wants to 'cast off from his moorings' and to depart from life.

He wants this in order to be with Christ. While it cannot be denied that Paul is here expressing his belief in a fellowship between himself and Christ after death, the form this would take and its place in Paul's total theology of death and eschatology are hard to determine and have been the subject of much discussion. For an analysis of these problems reference should be made to the excursus which follows the exegesis of this section of the letter. At all events, the possibility of death and of fellowship with Christ is represented as being (literally) 'much more, the better'. The expression is a pleonasm and over-emphatic and for this reason can only be ironical. Even J. Dupont who finds in this enthusiasm one of the chief supports for his thesis (*op. cit.*, pp. 175–77) can find but one other Greek text with triple comparatives (cf. also B–D §246). Even the strongest philosophical supporters of the immortality of the soul would not have gone as far as the apostle! By such forced praise Paul in fact condemns what he has himself stamped as a self-centred desire ('*epithumia*').

1²⁴ In opposition ('*de*') to the bombast at the end of the previous verse he now sets a single adjective—'*anangkaioteron*', 'it is more necessary'. In 1 Cor. 9¹⁶ proclaiming the Gospel is also presented as the result of necessity, though this idea has no real theological significance in Paul; most frequently it states mere fact, an inevitable result (Rom. 13⁵; 1 Cor. 7³⁷; 2 Cor. 9⁵,⁷; Phm. 14). So Paul has nothing solid to set up against his detractors, merely a deep inward conviction; hence his hesitation on their account. Nevertheless, theological reasoning is implicit: against purely personal desires ('*emoi*') he puts concern for others ('*di' humas*'). It was partly disheartening news from Philippi which led him to contemplate the need for his own presence in that city. The argument is also clearly half apologetic: 'How could you not agree with the steps I have taken since for your sakes I have acted thus!' The use of '*en sarki*' (cf. v. 21) for life here below with its weakness and difficulties, and the composite '*epimenō*' with its implication of effort and perseverance, still further suggest that the apostle's decision was no easy one to make.

Excursus 2: The expression 'to be with Christ' and Pauline Eschatology

It is necessary first to circumscribe as closely as possible the meaning of the expression 'to be with Christ' before trying to discern its place in Pauline eschatology.

1. Paul's use of the expression 'with Christ'

BONNARD, P., 'Vivre et mourir avec Jésus-Christ selon saint Paul', *RHPR*, 37, 1956, pp. 101–12.

BOUTTIER, M., *En Christ*, 1962, pp. 38–53.

DUPONT, J., '*Sun Christōi*', 1952.

GNILKA, J., *Commentary*, pp. 76–93.

GRUNDMANN, W., art. ' "*sun, meta*" with the Genitive', *TWNT*, VII, 1964, pp. 766–98 (ET VII, pp. 766–97).

HOFFMANN, P., *Die Toten in Christus*, 1966, pp. 301–20.

LARSSON, E., *Christus als Vorbild. Eine Untersuchung zu den paulinischen Tauf- und Eikontexten*, 1962, pp. 74–80.

LOHMEYER, E., '*Sun Christō*', in *Festgabe für A. Deissmann*, 1927, pp. 218–57.

SCHNACKENBURG, R., *Baptism in the Thought of St. Paul*, 1964, pp. 170–77.

SCHWEIZER, E., 'Die "Mystik" des Sterbens und Auferstehens mit Christus bei Paulus', *EvT*, 26, 1966, pp. 239–57.

SIBER, P., *Mit Christus leben*, 1971.

TANNEHILL, R., *Dying and Rising with Christ: a Study in Pauline Theology*, 1967.

The expression 'to be with Christ' occurs here only in the New Testament, but its peculiarity is merely formal. On a number of occasions Paul actually resorts to the preposition '*sun*' ('with') to indicate fellowship with the Lord, with Christ, or with Jesus.[1] To this use must be added a large number of verbs compounded with the prefix '*sun-*' the majority of which seem to be the apostle's own creation.[2] Furthermore, this usage is truly distinctive and since nothing fully comparable is to be found elsewhere whether in the LXX, in Hellenism or even in Rabbinic literature, it can be regarded as presenting us with a fully deliberate feature of Pauline thought and sensibility.

From various studies recently devoted to the subject (though not all issuing in identical conclusions) a number of convergent traits can be extracted. The preposition '*sun*' points above all to deep and personal communion (cf. J. Dupont, *op. cit.*, pp. 17ff; W. Grundmann, *art. cit.*, pp. 767ff). In the Pauline texts this communion is established at two particular junctures, at the parousia on the one hand[3] and at the time of participation in the death of Christ on the other, a

---

[1] The apostle uses the expression eight times (12, if Colossians is included): 1 Thess. 4[14, 17]; 5[10]; 1[23]; 2 Cor. 4[14]; 13[4]; Rom. 6[8]; 8[32]; Col. 2[13, 20], 3[3, 4].

[2] Among the most important notice: '*sumpaschomen*' (Rom. 8[17]); '*sunetaphēmen*' (Rom. 6[4]); '*Christō sunestaurōmai*' (Gal 2[19]); '*sunestaurōthē*' (Rom. 6[6]); '*sundoxasthōmen*' (Rom. 8,[17]); '*sunzēsomen autō*' (Rom. 6[8]); '*summorphizomenos tō thanatō autou*' (3[10]); '*summorphon tō sōmati tēs doxēs autou*' (3[21]); '*summorphous tēs eikonos*' (Rom. 8[29]); '*sungklēronomoi de Christou*' (Rom. 8[17]); etc.

[3] 1 Thess. 4[14, 17]; 5[10]; Rom. 6[8b]; 2 Cor. 4[14]; cf. 3[21]; Rom. 8[17,29].

participation indicated especially by baptism but whose effects are continuously felt in the life of the believer.[1] M. Bouttier has put it in a suggestive way: 'the expression "*sun Christō*" supports (the "*en Christō*" of the present life) at both ends and reveals to us its full extent.' The origins of the two groups of references distinguished in this way must be looked into. From this approach it is likely that the 'eschatological "*sun*" ' ought to be associated with Jewish apocalyptic, notably with Deut. 33[2] and Zech. 14[5] (J. Dupont, *op. cit.*, pp. 25–37; Lohmeyer) and the ' "*sun*" past and present' with Hellenism and the mystery religions (J. Dupont, *op. cit.*, pp. 19ff; Bonnard). But what is important is to clarify the unity or intermingling at the heart of Pauline language itself, of these two currents which in their origins are almost opposites.

The uniting link is found in the Christ event itself. It has often been shown that from the morphological point of view alone the expression 'with Christ' must not be dissociated from the whole semantic network created by Paul with the help of prepositions ('*huper*', '*dia*', '*en*', etc.) in order to give account of the reality of salvation (cf. M. Bouttier, *op. cit.*, p. 45; P. Hoffmann, *op. cit.*, p. 309f). The '*sun Christō*' thus has its precise source in the '*huper hemōn*' ('for us') of the death of Christ. It is not certain, however, even at this stage that Paul was the inventor of the formula. He could have found it within the tradition in some rudimentary form (R. Schnackenburg, *op. cit.*), associated for example with the theme of 'imitating' or 'following' (E. Larsson, *op. cit.*); but he gave it a peculiar lustre. So eschatology is rooted in the events of the Cross and the Resurrection and the eschatological community gave it special, personal, indeed emotional qualities (E. Schweizer, *art. cit.*). The 'mysticism' thereby acquired an historical dimension rooting it in the Cross of time past and projecting it into the future of a Kingdom still to come. From this very rootage it lost any triumphalist character, for although fellowship with Christ effectively transcends death it nonetheless bears the stamp of death (P. Hoffmann, *op. cit.*, p. 305f).

2. The expression 'with Christ' in **1**[23] *and in Pauline Eschatology*

In addition to works referred to above the following should be noted:

BAIRD, W., 'Pauline Eschatology in Hermeneutical Perspective', *NTS*, 17, 1971, pp. 314–27.
COLLANGE, J. F., *Enigmes*, pp. 170–243.
CULLMANN, O., 'Immortalité de l'âme ou résurrection des morts? Le témoignage du NT', *VC*, 10, 1956, pp. 58–78.

---

[1] Rom. 6[1f]; 8[17a]; Gal. 2[19]; 3[10]; 2 Cor. 13[4]. One cannot really speak of a 'sacramental "*sun*" ' established uniquely at baptism. Baptism is but one of the points, albeit a privileged point, of fellowship with the event of the Cross which itself precedes and surpasses it (cf. P. BONNARD, *art. cit.*, p. 111; M. BOUTTIER, *op. cit.*, p. 48f).

FEUILLET, A., 'Mort du Christ et mort du chrétien d'après les épîtres
    pauliniennes', *RB*, 66, 1959, pp. 481–513.
GRUNDMANN, W., 'Überlieferung und Eigenaussage im eschatolo-
    gischen Denken des Apostels Paulus', *NTS*, 8, 1961–62, pp.
    12–26.
MENOUD, P. H., *Le sort des trépassés d'après le NT*[2], 1966.

The expression in 1^{23} falls perfectly into place in the general context we have just outlined. But it raises also a particular problem,
namely, the question of a state intermediary between death and
resurrection. 'To be with Christ' is directly linked here with death
and it is impossible to believe with Michaelis that it is associated only
with the parousia. Yet although Paul expresses a belief in communion with Christ *at the time of* and *after* death he never speculates
about it and a less embellished affirmation of it than his could hardly
be imagined. So it would be as well not to betray him and put words
into his mouth which he did not consciously want to say. Views,
therefore, like those well illustrated by J. Dupont, who would see
here a Hellenisation of Pauline thought and fusion with a doctrine
of the immortality of the soul, are to be rejected. Such views gain
most support from a general theory about the development of
Pauline eschatology (see our *Enigmes*, pp. 171–74) as very Jewish
and apocalyptic in *1 Thessalonians* and still in *1 Corinthians* and then
slowly Hellenised as a result of experiences which brought the apostle
to the verge of death and which may have made him reconsider the
matter from a new angle. If that were so 2 Cor. 5^{1-10} would mark a
transitional stage, Jewish and Hellenistic conceptions being there
closely interwoven, and *Philippians* (1^{23}) would seal the ultimate outcome of the development with Paul entirely adopting there the Greek
hope of immortality of the soul. The tendency is for this view to be
increasingly abandoned (cf. W. Baird, *art. cit.*; there are further
retractions by Staab and A. Feuillet, *art. cit.*). It has long been seen
that the perspective of the parousia is far from absent from our
epistle (1^{10}; 2^{16}; $3^{10,21}$) or from the Epistle to the Romans which followed the Second Epistle to the Corinthians. The idea of develop-
ment is further nullified by the consideration that our epistle, which
dates from an Ephesian captivity, is very close in date to *1 Thessalonians* and *1 Corinthians*. As for the texts themselves, we have just
seen that the problems raised by 1^{23} owe nothing to Hellenism, while
we have shown elsewhere (*op. cit.*) that the same is true of 2 Cor.
5^{1-10} in which the outlook is essentially Christological.

But although the Hellenistic thesis cannot be given credence in its
elaboration of the subtle theme of being with Christ the same
reserve must be shown towards too Judaistic an approach. Of course
a dual hope of the coming of apocalyptic events on the one hand and
the establishment of a state intermediate between death and resurrection on the other is perfectly well attested both in Jewish apocalyptic and in Rabbinic literature (cf. P. Hoffmann, *op. cit.*, pp. 317ff;

Gnilka, pp. 88ff). It is furthermore probable that this double hope was not without some influence in early Christianity, and it will be noticed so far as our passage is concerned that Paul seems to be referring to a notion familiar to his readers upon which he felt no need to elaborate. Yet both the general context provided by 1 Thess. 4^1; 1 Cor. 15 and 2 Cor. 5 with the semantic web woven by the prepositions used for expressing the impact of Christ, as well as the particular argument of this chapter, demonstrate that the apostle's point of departure is exclusively Christocentric.

In 1^{23} one might even speak of 'Cross-centredness' inasmuch as it could be asked whether 'to be with Christ' does not mean primarily 'to die in bearing witness to the death of Christ' (Péry). The apostle is then not so much interested in giving details of what life after death can be like as in the present conditions which will permit participation in it.[1] 'To die' and 'to be with Christ' are therefore in large measure synonymous. Life with Christ after death is no problem for the apostle; it flows like a pure spring from the victory of Easter (cf. Rom. 8^{31-39}). What is important is to be in harmony with this victory and to share in it, and this is something which is in Paul's own hands; everything else rests with God. So 1^{21ff} is not dominated by the idea of dwelling in heaven, which is merely mentioned incidentally, but by the actual conditions for conformity with the work of Christ and fidelity to his Word.

3. Anticipation of reunion (1^{25-26})

(25) *Convinced of this, I know that for the sake of your progress and the joy of your faith I shall remain and continue with you all,* (26) *and my return amongst you will give you an opportunity to glory abundantly in Christ Jesus.*

At the beginning of v. 25 the comma can be placed either before or after '*oida*'. With Luther and the RSV we prefer the former. Immediately after '*oida*' P. Ewald suggests reading '*ho ti*' instead of '*hoti*' to remove the apparent contradiction between these verses and v. 20; the attempt is legitimate, its success doubtful. Then the *Koiné* reads '*sumparamenō*' for '*paramenō*', no doubt because the former often means 'to remain in life along with' (Lohmeyer).

How can these verses be understood within the context of traditional hypotheses about the author's circumstances? How can someone who has just been affirming the utter uncertainty of his fate now convincingly and without more ado make plans for the future?

---

[1] The perspective is the same when Paul comes to speak of 'paradise' in 2 Cor. 12^{1ff} and when he says of the dead that they 'sleep in Christ' (1 Thess. 4^{13ff}). No exact information can be extracted from the verb '*koimasthai*' ('to be asleep'), which was a current euphemism for death (P. HOFFMANN, *op. cit.*, pp. 186–206). The exact information comes from the '*en Christō*' (1 Thess. 4^{16}).

Dibelius contrasts theoretical possibility (v. 20) with concrete plans (v. 25); Lohmeyer takes up Bengel's exegesis which Lightfoot and Vincent have already opposed, and speaks of a prophetic revelation; while the majority of commentators, along with Bonnard and Gnilka, think of a kind of inward dialogue which commences at v. 20 and issues here in a statement of optimistic faith. But it is obvious that all these interpretations do violence to the plain meaning of the text (cf. Michaelis).

In fact Paul is elaborating the '*di*' *humas*' ('for your sakes') at the end of the previous verse. The final argument which has sparked off his decision as to what to choose ('*hairēsomai*', v. 22) has been the state of the community at Philippi and the necessity ('*anangkaioteron*') for his presence there. In the verses which follow (1²⁷ᶠᶠ) he will warn against a number of deviations which have appeared at Philippi. Our particular verses provide then a transition to the exhortation of the second part of the letter (1²⁷–2¹⁸); they also crown the first part which has been devoted to the apostle's circumstances and framed within the two occurrences of '*prokopē*' ('progress'; vv. 12 and 25). The steps taken by the apostle signify progress for the Gospel in relation to pagans (vv. 13, 20), the Christians at Ephesus (vv. 14ff) and those at Philippi (vv. 25–26).

1²⁵ The stress does not fall then so much upon the fact that Paul will remain ('*menō*'), which would have been very clumsily expressed, but upon the conviction which he has ('*pepoithōs*', '*oida*') that this is in the best interests of the Philippians. '*Touto*' refers essentially to what has gone before (B–D §290; with Dibelius, Gnilka, Müller; against Bonnard, Lohmeyer), in which case the phrase should doubtless be construed: 'Convinced of this (i.e. that my presence is more useful) I know that for the sake of progress, etc.' The verb '*oida*' ('I know') expresses therefore the same kind of conviction as in v. 19. Further, the verb '*paramenō*' is not merely an artistic variant for the simple '*menō*'; it has a deeper meaning than the latter and means also 'to stand fast'—to stand fast before the judges whom he must confront and in face of his Christian detractors; to stand fast because it is the faith ('*pistis*') of all ('*pasin*', cf. *ad* 1¹) the Philippians which is at stake, as 1²⁷,²⁹ will go on to show and, later, the whole of **3**. So, as in v. 12, the attitude of the apostle will have led to the advancement ('*prokopē*') of the Gospel, the faith. The word '*chara*' ('joy') is a mark of his tact; joy alone can dominate his relations with his readers (cf. *ad* 1⁴).

1²⁶ The apostle has never had in mind anything but the well-being of others and he hopes that his arrival at Philippi will be an occasion when his readers will 'glory in Jesus Christ'. The stress is on '*en Christō* (cf. *ad* 1¹) which reappears in 2¹ and particularly in 2⁵ᶠᶠ. The striking parallel in 3³—'we who glory (boast ourselves) in Christ Jesus and have no confidence in the flesh'—shows that the Philippians were tempted to other kinds of glorification. Man has no rights before God (cf. 2^{16}) except through the work of Christ and by resting on that alone; in this world's eyes such dependence is indicative of a sort of weakness and impoverishment (cf. 2 Cor. 12^9; Gal. 6^{14}; R. Bultmann, art. '*kauchaomai*, etc.' *TWNT*, III, 1942, pp. 646–54 (ET III, pp. 646–54)). The apostle shows that he is convinced that 'in Christ' his readers possess this right already, so it is all the more necessary that they accept it more consciously and really follow out its consequences ('*perisseuē*').

THIRD PART

The Situation of the Philippians (1^{27}–2^{18})

When he has given news of his own situation Paul turns, as vv. 24b–26 have already foreshadowed, to the community at Philippi. It too has its problems—adversaries ('*antikeimenoi*', 1^{28}) troubling it and its unity threatened by the rivalries to which it is a prey (1^{27}; 2^{1ff}).

One is accustomed to not seeing any link between the two types of difficulties encountered by the Philippian community, although the reference to adversaries occurs within appeals for unity and the transition from 1^{30} to 2^1 is simply given in the form of a consequence ('*oun*', 'therefore'). But traditional interpretations, whatever form they take, give no genuine place to vv. 28b–29 within the passage vv. 27–30. The problem can only be resolved by regarding 1^{27}–2^{18} as a response to one and the same set of circumstances.

The analogies between this section of the epistle and 3 are also striking. In both there are references to humility (2^{2ff} and 3^{1ff}), to suffering (1^{29f} and 3^{10}), to a future glory (2^{10f} and $3^{10f,21}$), to progress in the Christian life (2^{12ff} and $3^{12f,20}$). In both are figures of speech drawn from the running-track (2^{16} and 3^{12ff}) and from combat (1^{29f}) and the community is called to unity (1^{27f}; 2^{2f} and 3^{16}) and to imitation (1^{30} and 3^{17}). The basis of these exhortations is the event of the Cross and Resurrection (2^{6ff} and $3^{10,18ff}$). These correspondences have often been highlighted by those who support the unity of the epistle, and we have already given the reasons which compel us not to follow them on this point, namely, that along with the similarities are striking differences in tone and in the details of the polemic. So, with W. Schmithals (*Paulus und die Gnostiker*, pp. 53f, 71), we regard 1^{27}–2^{18} and 3^{1ff} as treating the same crisis but at different stages. At the point we have reached the apostle still thinks that a strong appeal to the unitedness, steadfastness and Christian conscience of his readers will be sufficient to make them face up to things.

An outline sketch of the adversaries has already been given in the Introduction (*supra*, pp. 12ff). Allied to the false apostles who are disparaged in *2 Corinthians*, these itinerant Jewish Christians supported their preaching by an appeal to a series of superior qualities due to their Jewish origin or to more or less exotic spiritual phenomena. They thereby introduced a kind of rivalry within the community which was unfaithful not only to the fraternal spirit which should reign there but also to the humility of the Cross which was its origin. Hence the apostle's exhortation, which at this stage is still calm and serene.

1. Appeal to strive together unitedly: 1^{27-30}
   The community must defend itself. For this it must remain truly united. The Christian life is a strife which is not without its suffering.
2. Appeal to unity in humility: 2^{1-4}
3. The basis of the Christian life: 2^{5-11}
   The Christian life is a communal life rooted in the event of the Cross which alone leads to glory.
4. The dynamic of the Christian life: 2^{12-18}
   Its rootage in the Christ-event produces a practical obedience which is expressed in an outgoing drive—the Word must be carried to the world in the hope of the coming Kingdom.

1. *Appeal to strive together unitedly* (1^{27-30})

(27) *In any event, let your behaviour to one another be worthy of the Gospel of Christ; let me hear it said of you, while I am absent, and let me see for myself when I come to you, that you stand firm in one Spirit, striving together for the faith of the Gospel* (28) *and in no way afraid of your opponents. What is for them a sign of perdition is in fact your salvation, and it comes from God,* (29) *namely, that you have been graciously allowed* (*to live*) *for Christ, which not only means believing in him but also suffering for him,* (30) *sharing in the same struggle in which you have seen me engaged and which you know I still share.*

The variants which occur are of no significance. But it is surprising that the genitive '*humōn*' in v. 28b has been changed to a dative ('*humin*': Koiné *al*; '*hēmin*': C*, D*, G, *al*), a sign of the real difficulty of the presence of the genitive in view of the dative '*autois*' at the beginning of the verse.

The verses do not show any particular strophic pattern (against Lohmeyer and Michaelis) but on the contrary a rather maladroit construction due to the fact that the apostle is now beginning to introduce a fresh subject. The theme is that the life of a Christian community must be a struggle, a striving ('*stēkete*', v. 27b; '*sunathlountes*', v. 27b; '*antikeimenōn*', v. 28a; '*agōna*', v. 30).[1] There again

[1] Cf. V. C. Pfitzner, *Paul and the Agon Motif*, 1967, pp. 109–29.

the goal and guide of the strife are the advancement of the Gospel of
Christ (the word occurs twice). Since this Gospel is the Gospel of
Christ (v. 27) it involves some element of suffering and of difficulties
(v. 29f) and it shifts a man's centre of concern from himself turning
him to Christ, to other people, and to the future (v. 28). In this sense
also it is a gospel of faith (this word also occurs twice), of grace
(*'echaristhē'* v. 29) and of the gift of God (*'touto apo theou'*, v. 28b).
As an active power, it demands a unity and solidarity (v. 27) whose
origin is the Spirit (v. 27b).

1[27] With *'monon'*, 'only', a new subject commences (Barth) the
importance of which is emphasised: 'the one essential thing' (cf.
Gal. 1[23]; 2[10]; 3[2]; Bonnard, Heinzelmann, Gnilka). The adverb
puts a certain restriction on what has just been said (Haupt, Vincent)
shown in the incidental alternatives, 'whether . . . or . . .' (*'eite . . .
eite'*). Not that Paul is voicing here any uncertainty about his
immediate fate, but rather that his readers do not need to wait for his
arrival to start making the effort which the life of their community
demands.[1] This is what the verb *'politeuomai'* signifies. Its primary
meaning is 'to discharge your obligations as a citizen', 'to live as a
citizen', a meaning which Scott and R. R. Brewer retain here ('The
meaning of *Politeuesthe* in Phil. 1.27', *JBL*, 76, 1954, pp. 76–83); but
in Hellenistic Judaism it differs little from *'peripateō'*, 'to live one's
life', whence Bauer (Arndt-Gingrich *Lexicon*), Barth, de Boor,
Dibelius, Strathmann (art. *'polis'*, etc.', *TWNT*, VI, 1959, p. 534 (ET
VI, p. 534)) give it this meaning here. Actually, it is not certain that
even in Hellenistic Judaism *'peripateō* and *'politeuomai'* can be
entirely synonymous (cf. Gnilka) and the fact that Paul precisely
does not use the first of these verbs here although it is often on his
pen predisposes us, with the majority of exegetes, towards a more
specific meaning. The context shows clearly that there is no question
of relationships with the city or the state, nor of individual conduct
but rather of community life, so that Bonnard is right to take it as
'live a community life worthy of the Gospel'; and v. 27a then
appears as the theme of the whole section **1**[27]**–2**[18] (Lohmeyer,
Michael).

   This community life must have as its rule (*'axiōs'*, cf. Rom. 16[2];
Eph. 4[1]; Col. 1[10]; 1 Thess. 2[12]) the Gospel of Christ. So the apostle's
basic preoccupation remains the same. Just as all his own actions are
determined with reference to the Gospel so must it be with his
readers (cf. *ad* **1**[5]). The qualification 'of Christ', although it occurs
elsewhere also (Rom. 15[19]; 1 Cor. 9[12]; 2 Cor. 2[12]; etc.), in the
present context and in view of **1**[29f] and **2**[5-11] can mean only one thing,
that the Gospel exhibits a 'glory' attributable not to itself but to

---

[1] The phrase is ill constructed; it should have been something like: *'eite
elthōn kai idōn humas eite apōn kai akouōn ta peri humōn, mathō'* (Dibelius,
Haupt, Gnilka). In the present case the stress is more on the hypothesis of
absence (Michael, Vincent) which points to the urgency of the Philippians' task
(cf. *ad* **2**[12, 19ff]).

Christ, and by that very fact becomes effective, through struggles and sufferings, in the steady achievement of real progress, especially in brotherly community life.

For this to be so it is necessary first of all to 'stand firm' ('*stēkete*, cf. 4¹) in the face of attacks made upon the Gospel. And firmness presupposes 'a single spirit'. Does this refer to man's spirit (Lohmeyer; Michaelis; Müller; Schweizer, art. '*pneuma*', *TWNT*, VI, 1959, p. 433 (ET VI, p. 435)) or to the Holy Spirit (Bonnard; Ewald-Wohlenburg; Gnilka; Martin)? It is not certain that the two senses are mutually exclusive (Scott, Michael) but since the chief point at issue is the basis of the community and its action the theological sense seems preferable. Moreover, the '*mia psuchē*' ('one mind') which follows should not be taken in an assimilative sense (1 Thess. 5²³; Heb. 4¹²) but on the contrary as making a distinction, the statement about '*stēkete*' being elaborated by two participles, '*sunathlountes*' and '*mē pturomenoi*'. Also in 4¹ and 1 Thess. 3⁸ '*stēkete*' has '*en kuriō*' as indirect object, and, in the present epistle, '*pneuma*' is only used (except for 4²³) in a theological sense. So our verse leads on to 2¹ and 3³ where we can divine that, as will happen in the case of Corinth (2 Cor. 11⁴), 'another Spirit' than that of the Gospel may be at work among the Philippians causing trouble and dissension.

The general principle of 'standing firm in one Spirit' has two aspects, expounded by the two participles which follow, one active ('contending'), the other passive ('not fearing'). Rare in classical Greek, the verb '*sunathleō*' is found again in the New Testament only at 4³, and this shows the importance Paul gives it in his exhortations to the Philippians. We have seen already how the ideas of fellowship and community undergird the apostle's entire thought in this letter, shown notably in the repeated use of verbs in '*sun-*' (cf. *ad* 1⁷).[1] Here, however, it is rather a case of struggle, of combat; and it is the faith ('*pistis*') which is threatened. So it cannot be taken as 'strive *through* the faith' (Bonnard, de Boor), but rather as 'strive *for* the faith' (Beare, Gnilka, Heizelmann), for the whole context is polemical, especially the reiteration in v. 29 of the verb '*pisteuō*' ('to believe'). The issue is that of the faith which the opponents who are about to be mentioned are nullifying by proclaiming a message which is not founded upon pure grace but upon self-glorification, so at one blow destroying all brotherly communion. The qualification 'of the Gospel', leading back to the central theme of the letter, can mean 'the faith which the Gospel gives' (Bonnard, Lohmeyer, Vincent) or 'the faith which is the Gospel' (Dibelius) or 'faith in the Gospel' (Michaelis). One would like to take it as 'the Gospel of faith'.

1²⁸ Steadfastness in the Spirit makes striving possible and banishes

[1] The prefix does not therefore refer to '*tē pistei*', 'struggle with the faith' (against Ewald-Wohlenberg, Lohmeyer, Vincent); it strengthens the '*mia psuchē*' ('with one soul').

fear ('*pturō*', here only in the New Testament), the fear aroused by adversaries ('*antikeimenoi*'). The verb '*antikeisthai*' is used six times by the apostle but in such varying contexts that they throw no light on our verse. The most one can say, with Bonnard, is that 'the New Testament regards the church as always confronted with opposition which shows itself in highly diverse ways'. In this instance it is not a question of persecutors (Lohmeyer), or simply of enemies whether Jewish or pagan making all kinds of trouble for the community at Philippi (most commentaries) but more precisely of itinerant Jewish-Christian preachers whom Paul takes to task more violently in 3[2ff]. Examination of the second part of the verse gives support to this view.

The next few words actually present a problem. They are usually taken as meaning either that the steadfastness of the Philippians (Dibelius, Gnilka, Lohmeyer, Michael; cf. 2 Thess. 1[5]) or the opposition they are encountering (Bonnard, Calvin) is a sign of salvation for them but of destruction for their adversaries. It is then hard to see how the sentence is structured to the end of v. 30, so that Westcott and Hort even suggested putting vv. 28b–29 into parentheses and attaching v. 30 directly to v. 28a. The thought, moreover, seems to be expressed very elliptically, even if, with most commentaries, appeal is made to a prophetic discernment which can detect divine signs in events. Moreover, account must be taken of the difference between the dative '*autois*' and the genitive '*humōn*', a distinction we have seen perplex more than one scribe. We therefore propose the interpretation: 'what ('*hētis*', feminine by attraction to '*endeixis*') is for them ('*autois*') a sign of perdition is your ('*humōn*') salvation.' The '*hētis*', an indefinite relative pronoun often used to introduce sentences of a general kind (cf. Mt. 5[39,41] etc.), is explained by the phrase opening with '*hoti*' (v. 29): 'what is . . . namely, that it is necessary to suffer.' The adversaries set little store by any weakness or suffering, which for Paul is a mark of the Cross; these they take as a sign of perdition in comparison with the glorious tokens of salvation which they themselves offer. But, the apostle explains, it is precisely situations of difficulty, tokens of a salvation to come, which are 'of God' ('*apo theou*'). One could presume, indeed,—and analysis of **3** supports it—that the apostle and his opponents do not give the same meanings to the terms '*apōleia*'—'*sōtēria*'; for Paul the pair signify processes *on the way to being realised* which have not yet reached their goal, while for his opponents they represent qualities already actualised. It is therefore quite intelligible that in their reckoning 'weakness' can be nothing but the antithesis of salvation.

1[29] Salvation is graciously bestowed ('*echaristhē*') and the grace is reflected in humility, obedience, and suffering for Christ's sake ('*to huper Christou*'). That this elliptical expression is found nowhere else in the New Testament but 2 Cor. 12[10] is very eloquent of the meaning which must be given to it. Doubtless belonging to the cluster of expressions traditionally arising from the '*huper hēmōn*' ('*peri*', '*anti*') with reference to the death of Christ (cf. *Excursus 2*, §1), the phrase embodies a suggestion of hardship and suffering; but Paul feels the need to dot all the i's. If the Philippians have thought that the faith ('*pisteuein*') which the Gospel demands 'for Christ's sake' is merely some intellectual or emotional adherence they have not understood the Gospel; put within the orbit of the Cross faith becomes embodied and effective rather in suffering. The polemical force of this may be deduced also from the fact that Paul does not normally use the verb 'to suffer'.

1³⁰ The Philippians are well aware that the Gospel can always be depicted as a conflict, leading those who proclaim it along difficult paths, for they have shared Paul's trials at Philippi (Acts 16²²ᶠᶠ; cf. 1 Thess. 2²) and since then have always had a part in the numerous difficulties which the apostle has encountered along his way (4¹⁵ᶠᶠ) the last of which has perhaps not been the least.

2. *Appeal to unity in humility* (2¹⁻⁴)

(1) *If therefore there is any consolation in Christ, if any solace in love, if any fellowship in the Spirit, if there is any deep affection and sympathy between us* (2) *make my joy complete—be moved by the same aspirations, the same love, striving with one mind to a single goal.* (3) *Act neither from factious squabbling nor vainglory, but humbly regard others as superior to yourselves;* (4) *and let each have an eye not to his own endowments but to those of others!*

BARCLAY, W., 'Great Themes of the New Testament: Phil. 2.1–11', *ExpT*, 70, 1958–59, pp. 4–7 and 40–4.
SPICQ, C., *Agapè*, II, 1959, pp. 252–65.

The manuscripts provide a number of variants. The two most important relate to the indefinite adjective '*tis*' ('*ti*') in v. 1 and the two '*hekastoi*' in v. 4. The difficulty in v. 1 arises from the fact that all manuscripts (except a few minuscules) read '*tis*' before '*splangchna*', which calls for the grammatical correction to '*ti*' (eventually to the '*tina*' attested by Chrysostom). By over-zealous harmonisation the (correct) '*ti*' in front of '*paramuthion*' has then become a '*tis*' (D*, L, 33), regarded as an indeclinable particle. B–D (§137/2, 2) takes the opposite view and suggests reading an indeclinable '*ti*' throughout, but that involves too great an alteration of the text and it would be better to take the fourth '*tis*' ('*ti*') as a lapse on Paul's part or even as very early dittography due to the 's' of '*splangchna*' (Michaelis; cf. Dibelius). In v. 4 the variants relate to the two plurals '*hekastoi*' which the *Koiné* changes to the more widely current singular form. The singular certainly occurs, though on the first occurrence only, in P 46,ℵ, C, D, which may suggest that this is the more original reading—singular, then plural. The tendency to uniformity has led some manuscripts to give a plural in the first occurrence as well (Gnilka). It is not impossible that the second '*hekastoi*' should be attached to v. 5 (ℵ*, A, C, *al*). Other variants are less important, and we note merely that in v. 2 א*, A, C, I, read '*auto*' instead of '*hen*', so repeating the same two words as before, and that in v. 4 some manuscripts have tried to make the phrase less cumbersome by replacing the participle with an indicative or an imperative.

It must not be said that after having spoken of external dangers threatening the community Paul now speaks of dangers which threaten from within (Bonnard, Gnilka, Heizelmann). On the contrary, these verses continue and deepen what Paul has just said about the threat represented by his opponent preachers: unity of action must rest on unity of intention. Hence there are a number of words with psychological connotations connected with the verb '*phroneō*' which occurs three times (including v. 5). For the same reason the link between 1²⁷⁻³⁰ and 2¹ᶠᶠ is clearly marked by an '*oun*' ('therefore') and some words also are found in both of the sections ('*pneuma*', '*psuchē*', '*agapē*', etc.). Furthermore, these verses are strongly tinctured by the hymn which Paul is going to quote from v. 6 onwards. The hymn is not introduced just by chance; 2¹⁻⁵ is a sort of 'overture' to it, and hence there are a number of identical words and the 'in Christ' occurs twice, in vv. 1 and 5.[1] If the Christological hymn is a cultic gem associated notably with baptism or the Lord's Supper, Paul's intention here, particularly in v. 1, is clear enough: what the 'false apostles' are recommending to you is not the Christian experience in which you are living, or should be living, because this involves love, fellowship in the Spirit, etc., and is an existence 'in Christ'. Now to be 'in Christ' means . . .

2¹ As a consequence of the foregoing ('*oun*') this verse can hardly be understood in any other way than 'If you have experienced all this . . . make my joy complete' (Hendriksen, Huby, Synge). The experience was undergone both in the cult and in the relations established between the apostle and the Christians of Philippi. The same style of argument also occurs in 4⁸. The '*paraklēsis*' at the beginning of the verse should not then be taken in the sense of 'exhortation',[2] but of 'consolation'[3] which is by far the most frequent meaning with Paul. And indeed in a general way 2¹ should not be regarded as a particularly solemn exhortation (against Benoit, Beare, etc.) but on the contrary as a kind of 'non-exhortation', the main verb before the '*hina*' of v. 2 not even being expressed; Paul is taking every precaution to avoid the appearance of giving orders. The 'consolation'

---

[1] But there is no need, with Lohmeyer and Gnilka, to view this passage as a little poem with a definite structure.

[2] Against Benoit, Beare, Gnilka, Michaelis, Staab, Vincent.

[3] With BARCLAY (*art. cit.*, p. 40), Bonnard, Calvin, Jones, Lohmeyer, Médebielle. But the statements introduced by '*ei*' should not, however, be taken as Barclay and Médebielle do as hypothetical—'if you should wish to give me some consolation . . . act thus . . .'

is what comes from the fellowship and community of Christians, especially in their coming together in worship and in what has recently been shown by the Philippians' gesture to the apostle (Calvin, Michael). The consolation is 'in Christ', that is 'it flows from the Christ-event and should reign in a community which is in Christ' (F. Neugebauer, *In Christus*, 1961, p. 105).

In the same way the 'solace afforded by love' has reference both to the communal reality of worship and to the assistance the Philippians have sent to Paul which in 1^{91} he ranks as an 'act of love'. The matter is even plainer in the case of 'fellowship of the Spirit'; the polemical context allows us to conclude that the Holy Spirit is meant and not merely mutual harmony (cf. 1^{27}); the Spirit is primarily a creator of fellowship and not of more or less abnormal phenomena which destroy fellowship (cf. 1 Cor. 12ff). Moreover, this fellowship ('*koinōnia*') is what unites the Philippians with Paul through their 'share in the Gospel' ($1^{5,7}$). He adds a reminder that the bond which unites Christians to each other—and he himself has just had experience of it in relation to the Philippians—is something really deep, something 'visceral'. '*Splangchna*' always denotes with Paul a deep affection, particularly such as binds him to the churches he has founded.[2] The word clearly relates to 1^{8} and to Paul's tender feeling for the Philippians. This is emphasised by the '*kai oiktirmoi*' which shows the strength of the relationship (Col. 3^{12}), and indicates that the affection uniting Christians rests upon God's compassion for men ('*oiktirmoi*'). This latter word corresponds, in fact, to the preceding '*en Christō*' and '*pneumatos*' and signifies essentially in the Bible God's numerous acts of compassion.[3]

2^{2} Although the Philippians have already done much to give Paul joy (cf. *ad* 1^{4}), the state of their community does not cease to be a matter of concern. Hence the tactful expression 'make my joy complete'. This requires[4] 'a unity of intention or of active disposition' (Bonnard). We have already in 1^{7} observed the difficulty of finding a simple rendering for the verb '*phroneō*'; it signifies an intention which is being achieved by definite acts. The intention here is conceived as underlying the life of the community, as is not infrequent in Paul (Rom. 12^{16}; 15^{2}; 2 Cor. 13^{11}; 4^{2}). One cannot agree with Gnilka that it is a matter of a banal motif lacking clear meaning. Rather, we must observe with Lohmeyer that 10 of the 23 Pauline instances of the word occur in this epistle, and link it with the '*ton auton agōna*' ('the

---

[1] The sequence '*paramuthion*(-*thia*)—*paraklēsis*' is virtually stereotyped in Paul: 1 Cor. 14^{3}; 1 Thess. 2^{12}; 5^{14}.

[2] Cf. Köster, art. '*splangchnon*, etc.' TWENT, VII, 1964, p. 556 (ET VII, p. 555f).

[3] Cf. Rom. 12^{1}; 2 Cor. 1^{3}; LXX 2 Kgs. 24^{14}; 1 Chr. 21^{13}; etc. Both words '*splangchna*' and '*oiktirmoi*' are used also in the lists of virtues, cf. S. WIBBING, *Die Tugend und Lasterkataloge*, 1959, p. 105.

[4] '*Hina*' does not then depend upon '*plērōsate*' but upon a verb which is understood: 'I beg you that . . .' (cf. B–D §392).

same struggle') of 1^{30}. Heresy has as its consequence the dissolution of the unity of the Philippian community.

This unity shows itself chiefly in love ('*agapē*') which, according to the context, is a turning of attention from the self to others; it is then directed to a single aim ('*to hen*'), namely to the 'accomplishment of a single mission' (Bonnard) and 'with one mind' ('*sumpsuchoi*'). It is better to attach this adjective to '*to hen phronountes*' rather than to take it as unattached (with Gnilka, Haupt, Lohmeyer, Müller, Vincent). The word is found only here in the New Testament, but obviously it should be associated with the '*mia psuchē sunathlountes*' ('striving with one mind') of 1^{27} and with words compounded with '*sun-*' in which our epistle is particularly rich. The meaning of the text would not be overstretched if we took it as 'advance with single heart into the battle'.

2^3 What Paul understands by unity ('*to auto phronein*') is made more explicit first by two negative statements ('*mēden . . . mēde*') and then by a positive argument ('*alla*') with a verb to be understood such as 'do'. So the dangers besetting the Philippian community are here defined; they are named as intrigue or factious squabbling and vainglory. The former ('*eritheia*') has a very general force with Paul since it is met with in the lists of vices in 2 Cor. 12^{20} and Gal. 5^{20}; but it should be observed that these letters were written to churches which we know were encountering difficulties akin to those at Philippi (cf. also *ad* 1^{15}). But reference to '*kenodoxia*' ('vainglory') is the more significant. It occurs here only in the New Testament, though '*kenodoxos*' is found in Gal. 5^{26} where it is also provided with a good definition: 'Do not seek a vain glory ("*mē ginōmetha kenodoxoi*") by provoking one another'. On the other hand, the simple '*doxa*' ('glory') occurs six times in our epistle; on four occasions it relates entirely to God (1^{11}; 2^{11}; $4^{19,20}$), once to the future world (3^{21}), and lastly it is used polemically to disparage those who put their glory in shameful and earthly things (3^{19}). If furthermore it is remembered that '*doxa*' is a key word in the polemics which echo in 2 *Corinthians* (cf. ch. 3f) then the introduction of the terms '*doxa-kenodoxia*' in *Philippians* in a similar context is easily understood: glory does not pertain to the Christian at the present time, for then it would be '*kenodoxia*', a vain glory which destroys the whole communal spirit by the rivalry and jealousy it introduces.

Christians, on the contrary, should display humility ('*tapeinophrosunē*'). The assonance '*phroneō—tapeinophrosunē*' should be observed; it is a matter of '*phronein*' humbly ('*tapeinos*'). In fact for the Greeks humility was far from being a virtue; it was associated with a slave's condition (cf. Gnilka). It is only in the Old Testament that it is viewed as a quality in relationship with God. At Qumran also it inspired the life of the community (1 QS 2.24; 4.3; 5.23, 25). It is noteworthy that Paul uses cognates of '*tapeinoō*' only in 2 *Corinthians* and *Philippians*, except for Col. $2^{18,23}$.

Humility consists in regarding others as superior to oneself. It is not a matter of superiority on a spiritual or moral level but of the simple fact that the Christian should live his life in such a way that his ultimate concern is the other man, *he* is paramount (Rom. 13¹; 1 Pet. 2¹³; cf. Barth).

2⁴ 'Take account of others' can also mean do not have regard to one's own spiritual endowments but to those of others. With Bonnard and Martin, it is this restricted meaning which must be given to '*ta*' ('things') having due regard to the context and to the usage of the verb '*skopeō*' which always implies a down to earth idea of seeing. If this is so it is not merely a general recommendation 'do not seek your own concerns but also those of others' (Gnilka), but more precisely do not over-value the more or less spirit-inspired manifestations in which some people glory. The plural '*hekastoi*' which is used could well allude not to the attitude of individuals but to that of groups or factions.

3. *The basis of the Christian life* (2⁵⁻¹¹)

(5) *Behave in this way among yourselves; for this is how it was in the case of Jesus Christ:*

*

(6) *Being in the form of God*
He did not profit from his equality with God,
(7) *But divested himself*
Taking the form of a slave,

*

Coming into existence as a man
And regarded as a man
(8) *He humbled himself*
Becoming obedient to death,

***

The death of the Cross.

*

(9) *So God has raised him on high*
And given to him the Name
Which is above every Name,
(10) *That at the name of Jesus*

*

Every knee should bow
In heaven, on earth and in the abyss,
(11) *And that every tongue should confess*
That Jesus Christ is Lord

*

To the glory of God the Father.

Excursus 3: The Christological Hymn

The mass of studies of this hymn is considerable, and at this point only those which provide amply bibliographical references are mentioned.

FEUILLET, A., 'L'hymne christologique de l'épître aux Philippiens (2.6–11)', *RB*, 72, 1965, pp. 352–80; 481–507.

HENRY, P., art. 'Kénose', *SDB*, V, 1950, cols. 7–161 (a monument of erudition and of clarity).

KÄSEMANN, E., 'Kritische Analyse von Phil. 2.5–11', in *Exegetische Versuche und Besinnungen*, I, 1960, pp. 51–95.

LOHMEYER, E., *Kyrios Jesus. Eine Untersuchung zu Phil. 2. 5–11*, 1928.

MARTIN, R. P., *Carmen Christi. Philippians 2.5–11 in Recent Interpretation and in the Setting of Early Christian Worship*, 1967.

SANDERS, J. T., *The New Testament Christological Hymns*, 1971.

SCHMAUCH, W., *Complément au commentaire de Lohmeyer*, 1964, pp. 19–34.

The text is certain; variants are few and unimportant. In v. 5 the *Koiné* (as also P 46, D, G . . .) strengthens the link with the preceding verses by a *'gar'* and reads the passive imperative *'phroneisthō'* instead of the active. In v. 7, P 46 and some Church Fathers preferred the singular *'anthrōpou'* to the genitive plural *'anthrōpōn'*, no doubt because it paralleled the expression which followed. The *Koiné* again (with D, G) notices in v. 9 that the 'name' referred to is not actually stated and thus suppresses the definite article. Finally, in v. 11 some manuscripts (A, C, *Koiné*, D, G) correct the aorist subjunctive to a future indicative and so give the sentence an entirely eschatological slant in accordance with the text of Isa. 45[23].

The hymn we have now reached presents a daunting aspect, not only by reason of the genuine exegetical difficulties it contains but also by the impressive mass of studies which it has provoked, so that one has some scruples about adding to what may already seem more than enough. Yet such is the fascinatingly enigmatic nature of this gem of early Christian faith that it still has not yielded up all its secrets. We shall very briefly summarise the issues under debate, and then enunciate certain methodological principles which though at first glance they may seem obvious have nevertheless often been neglected at the cost of leading interpretation astray into what seem to us to be various impasses.

The departure point for current exegesis is marked by E. Lohmeyer's rich study *Kyrios Jesus*, in which the author lays particular emphasis upon the rhythm and structure of the passage, boldly deciding on the reading on the basis of the form and the source. He thereby deduces that Paul was quoting an already existing Christological hymn. A number of awkward features in the Greek text and the weight which such a 'traditional' poem would carry for Paul and his correspondents suggests an Aramaic original coming perhaps from the church of Jerusalem; its *Sitz im Leben* may have been the Eucharistic liturgy (pp. 65ff). So far as origin is concerned, Lohmeyer would find it in the Iranian-Jewish myth of the Son of Man, strongly influenced by the figure of the Servant of the Lord in Isaiah (pp. 68ff).

Reference will be made to all the main points of this study, either in confirmation or criticism. Thus, even if there is general agreement that we have here an already existing passage, opinions vary as to its form and structure. Likewise the problem of authorship is far from being settled. Paul still has staunch supporters, while those who deny that he composed the poem can be divided into those who champion an Aramaic origin and those who prefer a Graeco-Hellenistic source. The issue is closely linked with that of determining the soil from which the hymn sprang—was it heterodox Judaism, Hellenistic Gnosticism, reflection strictly limited to the Old Testament or a reaction against some political circumstances of the time? Nor has the determination of the *Sitz im Leben* produced unanimity—was it the Eucharist, baptism or hymnology?

To these questions of an exegetical and historical kind are to be added others of a more dogmatic nature about the pre-existence of Christ, 'kenosis', and the ethical example Paul would give to Christians by evoking the humble, obedient figure of the Son of God.

We shall try to find a way through the complicated labyrinth by following the three-stranded Ariadne-thread, namely:

1. The hymn must not be understood in terms of one or other of its sections alone but as comprising a unity.
2. The hymn must be understood primarily as a Christian hymn.
3. The hymn must be understood as having been inserted by Paul at a definitely chosen place in his letter to the Philippians.

1. The hymn must be understood in its own terms and as a whole

The problem

There is a great risk of isolating some particular word or expression and as a result of researches often of baffling erudition to foist upon it a meaning which no longer makes it possible to integrate it correctly into the context of the hymn itself. Thus, to take but one example, there is the notorious '*morphē theou*' ('form of God') at the beginning of v. 6. It has often been alleged that it can only be a synonym for '*eikōn theou*' ('image of God') and that one should see in it an allusion to Gen. 1[26] and to the Pauline doctrine of two Adams. But this ingenious suggestion comes to grief on the fact that within the hymn itself '*morphē theou*' corresponds to '*morphē doulou*' ('in the form of a slave', v. 7b) for which an equivalence with '*eikōn*' makes no sense. How, moreover, could one envisage that the true Man (v. 6a) should become incarnate (v. 7)? It is therefore in the framework of the '*theos–doulos*' antithesis that the above expressions must be understood and not in that of the opposition of the two Adams.

A similar danger occurs on the level of the hymn as a whole. A glance at the studies devoted to it is enough to show that the sections devoted to vv. 6–8 are much more weighty than those to vv. 9–11, the reasons for which are in no sense discreditable in themselves; but the lack of balance all too easily leads to a regarding of the two parts thus created as though they were two sections entirely separate from each other. We therefore conclude that any interpretation of one part of the hymn which fails to do justice to the other is misleading. This drives us to a consideration of the actual structure of the hymn.

The structure of the hymn

CERFAUX, L., 'L'hymne au Christ—Serviteur de Dieu (Phil. 2.6–11 = Isa. 52.13–53.12)', in *Recueil L. Cerfaux*, II, 1954, pp. 425–37.
COPPENS, J., 'Une nouvelle structuration de l'hymne christologique de l'épître aux Philippiens', *ETL*, 43, 1967, pp. 197–202.
DEICHGRAEBER, R., *Gotteshymnus und Christushymnus in der frühen Christenheit*, 1967, p. 122.
FEUILLET, A., *art. cit.*, *RB*, 72, 1965, pp. 499ff.
GNILKA, J., *Commentary*, p. 136f.
HÉRING, J., *Le Royaume de Dieu et sa venue*, 1959, p. 159f.
JEREMIAS, J., 'Zur Gedankenführung in den paulinischen Briefen', in *Studia Paulina in honorem J. de Zwaan*, 1953, pp. 152ff.
LAMARCHE, P., *Christ vivant*, 1966, pp. 36–41.
LOHMEYER, E., *Kyrios Jesus*, 1928, p. 5f.
MARTIN, R. P., *Carmen Christi*, pp. 24–41.
MICHEL, O., 'Zur Exegese von Phil. 2.5–11', in *Theologie als Glaubenswagnis. Festschrift für K. Heim zum 80. Geburtstag*, 1954, pp. 79–95.
SANDERS, J. T., *op. cit.*, pp. 9–12.
SCHMAUCH, W., *op. cit.*, p. 21–3.
STRECKER, G., 'Redaktion und Tradition im Christus-Hymnus. Phil. 2.6–11', *ZNW*, 55, 1964, pp. 63–78.

The various solutions proposed for this problem derive from two broad patterns—that of Lohemyer or that of Cerfaux-Jeremias.

Lohmeyer detects six strophes of three lines each, the first three describing the abasement of the Son of Man (vv. 6–8) and the last three his exaltation (vv. 9–11). Lohmeyer further regards v. 8c ('even the death of the cross') as a genuinely Pauline addition to the already existing hymn. This analysis of his is reproduced with varying nuances by P. Benoit, Dibelius, Héring, Beare, Bonnard and Lamarche. We quote below Benoit's rendering from the English edition of the Jerusalem Bible:[1]

[1] This translation obviously derives from Lohmeyer only in form. Among slight divergencies it may be observed that Lohmeyer put v. 8c into brackets; in v. 9b the first mention of the name is transferred to the following lines as is the reference to the heavens in v. 10b.

(6) His state was divine,
   yet he did not cling
   to his equality with God
(7) but emptied himself
   to assume the condition of a slave,
   and to become as men are;
(8) and being as all men are,
   he was humbler yet,
   even to accepting death,
   death on a cross.
(9) But God raised him high
   and gave him the name
   which is above all other names
(10) so that all beings
    in the heavens, on earth and in the underworld,
    should bend the knee at the name of Jesus
(11) and that every tongue should acclaim
    Jesus Christ as Lord,
    to the glory of God the Father.

Jeremias criticises this scheme for doing violence to the syntax of
the hymn: only strophes 3 and 6 end completed sentences. He proposes a composition in three strophes of four lines each, structured
according to the *parallelismus membrorum* of Hebrew poetry. These
three strophes treat respectively the pre-existence, the earthly life
and the heavenly life of Christ. But to meet the demands of this
scheme not only the mention of the Cross in v. 8 but also that of
heavenly, earthly and infernal beings in v. 10 and the final 'to the
glory of God the Father' (v. 11) must be taken as Pauline additions
to the original hymn. R. Deichgräber, J. Coppens, G. Friedrich,
O. Michel, J. T. Sanders and R. P. Martin more or less concur with
these suggestions, though the last named does not adhere to the
division into three strophes but thinks of the hymn as formed from
six small units of two lines each, for use antiphonally in worship.
Gnilka's suggestion should also be associated with this type of
structure, since he separates off '*hos en morphē theou huparchōn*'
(v. 6a) as a kind of title to the hymn which then comprises five small
units of two lines each.
   There is one type of suggestion which ought to be eliminated at the
outset, namely the possibility of various additions to the original
hymn detected by one scholar or another. Let us say at once that we
agree with Dibelius, Cerfaux, Michaelis and Lamarche in seeing no
evidence for them. One gets the impression that Jeremias has only
removed vv. 10c and 11c in order to have a third strophe of four
lines comparable with the two previous ones, although these two
lines are essential to the meaning of the whole hymn. Likewise the
reference to the Cross is central and can perfectly well be retained in
a number of viable schemes. One can only hesitate at seeing G.

Strecker, followed by A. Feuillet (*art. cit.*), take the whole of v. 8 ('he humbled himself, etc.') as a Pauline addition while retaining vv. 10c and 11c, retrieved from Jeremias, as part of the original hymn. This game could be played for a long time! So in the absence of decisive criteria we take the hymn as we have it in front of us in its entirety.

These preliminaries settled, we must agree with Lohmeyer that the hymn has a twofold structure. Indeed, the pattern 'abasement—exaltation' leaps to the eye. Further, for the whole first part (vv. 6–8) Christ alone is the subject and his action is stressed by the double *'heauton'* ('himself', vv. 7a, 8a), while the second part (vv. 9–11) speaks only of God's action. In vv. 6–8 the 'hero' appears anonymously but vv. 9–11 revolve round the Name conferred upon him.

Yet Jeremias has grasped the structure of the first part of the hymn better than Lohmeyer. It is marked, in fact, by a number of answering expressions—*'morphē theou'* (v. 6a), *'morphē doulou'* (v. 7b); *'genomenos'* (v. 7c), *'genomenos'* (v. 8b)—so that one is led to think of two strophes framed by these two pairs (vv. 6a—7b; 7c—8b). The two first lines of the first strophe have the word 'God', and the two first of the second the word 'man'; the third line of each strophe has the main verb of the sentence qualified on each occasion by 'himself' (*'heauton'*), and the last line states the result of the action with emphasis on its humble and degrading character.

The same structure is clearly discernible in the second part of the hymn, but it is less obvious for reasons which spring from the origin of the poem which will shortly be mentioned. A first strophe of four lines (vv. 9–10a) can easily be detected which speak of God's action and revolve around the Name (*'onoma'* three times) and a second strophe also of four lines giving the response of the whole of creation to this divine activity (vv. 10b—11b). The two strophes end by reference to the identity of him who in the first part was anonymous, namely, Jesus. This verse division must not be blamed for breaking through the final clause introduced by *'hina'* in v. 10a because it simply emphasises the proclamation of the Name which itself is the subject of this confession of faith; and in any case there is some lack of homogeneity between vv. 10a and 10bc because these latter lines are merely a quotation from Isa. 45[23].

There remain v. 8c ('the death of the Cross') and v. 11c ('to the glory of God the Father'). Under no condition ought they to be deleted from the hymn, for indeed they mark the two climaxes. And if with R. P. Martin the hymn can be regarded as having an antiphonal structure it should be understood that in these two final lines the two sets of voices come together in unison.

This, then, is the layout which emerges:

I. A.   6. *'hos en morphē theou huparchōn
           ouch harpagmon hēgēsato to einai isa theō*

7. *alla heauton ekenōsen*
   morphēn doulou labōn

                     *

B.   *en homoiōmati anthrōpōn genomenos*
       kai schēmati heuretheis hōs anthrōpos

8. *etapeinōsen heauton*
   genomenos hupēkoos mechri thanatou

                     *

    thanatou de staurou.

                     ***

II. A. 9. *dio kai ho theos auton huperupsōsen*
       kai echarisato autō to onoma
       to huper pan onoma
   10. *hina en tō onomati Iēsou*

                     *

B.   *pan gonu kampsē*
       epouraniōn kai epigeiōn kai katachthoniōn
  11. *kai pasa glōssa exomologēsētai*
       hoti kurios Iēsous Christos

                     *

    eis doxan theou patros.'

Consequences

This way of construing the hymn leads, within each section, to a number of important conclusions; but it is necessary to recognise at once that we have here a drama with two protagonists, God and Jesus. The theme of the drama is none other than the Lordship of creation. And this leads us to the second of the methodological rules which we have enunciated:

2. The hymn is essentially a Christian hymn

No one doubts that the hymn is a Christian one; but we are laying stress on the word 'essentially' because many studies seem to look at the matter the other way round by envisaging a pre-existent plan or even actual draft which the writer of the hymn has simply 'Christianised'. So Gnilka regards vv. 6–7 as comprising originally an independent poem, while Bonnard talks of 'an adaptation by Paul of a hymn which originally spoke of the appearance of a heavenly Man in Jewish Christian terms. It was Paul who may first have given it a Christian interpretation.'

The question of sources

BAKKEN, N. K., 'The new humanity: Christ and the modern age', *Interpretation*, 22, 1968, pp. 71–82.
BORNHAEUSER, K., *Jesus Imperator Mundi*, 1938, pp. 21–4.
BORNKAMM, G., 'Zum Verständnis des Christus-Hymnus Phil.

2.6–11', in *Studien zu Antike und Urchistentum. Gesammelte Aufsätze*, II, 1959, pp. 177–87.

CERFAUX, L., *art. cit.*, *Receueil L. Cerfaux*, II, 1954, pp. 425–37.

COPPENS, J., 'Phil. 2.7 and Is. 53.12', *ETL*, 41, 1965, pp. 147–50.

CULLMANN, O., *The Christology of the New Testament*, ET 1959, pp. 177ff.

DUPONT, J., 'Jésus-Christ dans son abaissement et son exaltation d'après Phil. 2.6–11', *RSR*, 37, 1950, pp. 500–14.

EHRHARDT, A. A. T., 'Jesus and Alexander the Great', *JTS*, 46, 1945, pp. 45–51.

FEUILLET, A., *art. cit.*, *RB*, 72, 1965.

— *Le Christ Sagesse de Dieu d'après les épîtres pauliniennes*, 1966, pp. 340–49.

FURNESS, J. M., 'Behind the Philippian Hymn', *ExpT*, 79, 1967–68, pp. 178–82.

GEORGI, D., 'Der vorpaulinische Hymnus Phil. 2.6–11', in *Zeit und Geschichte (Dankesgabe an R. Bultmann zum 80. Geburtstag)*, 1964, pp. 263–93.

HENRY, P., art. 'Kénose', *SDB*, V, 1950, cols. 38–56.

HÉRING, J., 'Kyrios Anthropos', *RHPR*, 16, 1936, pp. 196–209.

— *Le Royaume de Dieu et sa venue²*, 1959, pp. 159–64.

JEREMIAS, J. art. '*Pais theou*', *TWNT*, V, 1954, pp. 676–713 (ET V, pp. 677–717).

— 'Zu Phil. 2.7; "*heauton ekenōsen*" ', *NT*, VI, 1963, pp. 182–88.

KÄSEMANN, E., 'Kritische Analyse . . .', in *Exegetische Versuche und Besinnungen*, I, 1960, pp. 51–95.

KNOX, W. L., 'The "Divine-Hero" Christology in the NT', *HTR*, 41, 1948, pp. 229–49.

KRINETZKI, L., 'Der Einfluss von Jes. 52.13–53.12 par. auf Phil. 2.6–11', *ThQ*, 139, 1959, pp. 157–93, 291–336.

LAMARCHE, P., *Christ vivant*, 1966, pp. 36–41.

LOHMEYER, E., *Kyrios Jesus*, pp. 13ff, 68ff.

REY, B., *Créés dans le Christ Jésus*, 1966, pp. 77–86.

ROMANIUK, K., 'De Themate Ebed Yahve in soteriologia Sancti Pauli', *CBQ*, 22, 1961, pp. 14–25.

SANDERS, J. T., *The New Testament Christological Hymns*, 1971.

SCHWEIZER, E., *Erniedrigung und Erhöhung bei Jesus und seinen Nachfolgern²*, 1962, p. 100f.

VOEGTLE, A., 'Der Menschensohn und die paulinische Christologie', in *Studiorum Paulinorum Congressus Internationalis Catholicus 1961*, I, 1963, pp. 199–218.

The source of the hymn has been variously attributed to heterodox Judaism, Iranian religion (Lohmeyer), Greek epic tradition (Beare, Ehrhardt, Knox), or to political circumstances of the time (Bornhäuser). Gnosticism has also been suggested, regarded either as of Hellenistic origin (Käsemann, Bultmann 'school', Friedrich, Beare, Dibelius) or of Jewish origin (Gnilka, J. T. Sanders). But the kind of view most favoured by scholars today is one which seeks to root the hymn in the Old Testament. Thus, E. Schweizer fastens upon the righteous man of the Old Testament who is abased and then exalted; Krinetzki, Cerfaux, Jeremias, Romaniuk, Coppens and Furness return basically to the Servant Songs of Isaiah; while Bonnard, Cullmann, Héring and Rey think particularly of the figure of Adam and the Pauline doctrine of two Adams. These two last views are also often associated (Bonnard, Cullmann, Feuillet, Lamarche). D. Georgi tries to link the hymn with the wisdom tradition and speculations about wisdom (cf. also A. Feuillet, *Le Christ Sagesse de Dieu*).

None of these approaches is short of a rich supply of supporting evidence, yet none has won general acceptance. So we have Georgi (pp. 263ff) challenging Käsemann's thesis, and not without sound arguments; Bornkamm and Dupont are hesitant about an Isaianic reference; the same Bornkamm and Vögtle emphasise the difficulties about the identification with Adam, and so it goes on. In our judgement, this points to the fact that none of the views listed above is able to give account of the hymn in its entirety. The evidence is inescapable that it is impossible to pass directly from the hymn or from this or that expression within it to one or other Old Testament prototype *and to retain the Christian context* of the hymn. No one doubts that Christianity was the melting-pot which produced a fusing of all kinds of influences the traces of which are *indirectly* revealed by our hymn. But it is not just a matter of traces, and the alloy which comes from the crucible has a character *sui generis*; the hymn is not primarily a Christianised copy of prior speculations; it is an original and profound reflection on *the Church's confession of faith* and on its implications for traditional *theology* using, of course, intellectual and religious material which the author may have had at his disposal. It remains to attempt a more detailed account of the genesis of these reflections.

The rootage in tradition

CULLMANN, O., *The Earliest Christian Confessions*, ET 1949.
KRAMER, W., *Christos-Kyrios-Gottessohn Untersuchung zu Gebrauch und Bedeutung der christologischen Bezeichnungen bei Paulus und den vorpaulinischen Gemeinden*, 1963, pp. 61–80.
NEUFELD, V. H., *The Earliest Christian Confessions*, 1963.

The fine study by J. T. Sanders which has just been mentioned is an example of the careful placing of the Christological hymns of the New Testament within a Christian context, though unfortunately we cannot say that his treatment of 2^{6-11} has been convincing. We have reservations about setting within the same framework passages as diverse as this one, Col. 1^{15-20}; 1 Tim. 3^{16}; 1 Pet. $3,^{18-22}$; Heb. 1^3 and the Prologue to St John's Gospel. The writer also passes too quickly into comparative religion studies. The quest must rather be in a different direction.

Now our hymn offers at least one secure reference point which can hardly count as a vulnerable target, namely the confessional acclaim of Jesus as Lord in v. 11. W. Kramer and V. H. Neufeld, following Cullmann and basing themselves on a study of Rom. 10[9]; 1 Cor. 12[3]; 2[11]; (and 1 Cor. 8[6]), have shown in effect that *'kurios Iēsous (Christos)'* was one of the basic confessions *('(ex)-homologeō')*—if not *the* one—of the Pauline churches. By it the church acknowledges that he who was Jesus of Nazareth is now Lord both of the church and of the whole universe, whatever further varied implications his Lordship may have. Our particular passage, by its reference to the kneeling and confessing with acclamation by every tongue implies that the recognition of Christ's Lordship related to some actual and definite element in worship.

The development

It must also be said that a considerable part of the Christological thought of the New Testament rests on what at first were brief confessions of faith. There is certainly no possibility of tracing a linear development, but so far as we are concerned the following observations may be made:

(1) that mention of the 'Name' (*'onoma'*) often seems linked with a confession of Lordship, as in 1 Cor. 5[4f]; 6[11]; cf. 1[10,13,15] (cf. W. Kramer, *op. cit.*, pp. 71–6); while Heb. 13[15] has *'onoma'* and *'homologeō'*;

(2) that a number of antithetical pairs seem to have been developed from the fundamental antithesis contained in the expression *'kurios Iēsous'*, e.g. *'ho katabas/ho anabas'* (Eph. 4[10]); *'ho apothanōn/egertheis'* (Rom. 8[34]); *'ho genomenos/ho horistheis'* (Rom. 1[3f]); *'kata sarka/kata pneuma'* (*ibid*);

(3) and that while the confession was basically related to Jesus it very soon tried to bring God in, as we find in 1 Cor. 8[5-6]; 1 Tim. 2[5]; 6[13f]; 2 Tim. 4[1f].

The problem of authorship

Daniélou, J., *Théologie du judéo-christianisme*, 1958, pp. 199–215.

Deichgraeber, R., *Gotteshymnus und Christushymnus . . .*, 1967, p. 119.

Delling, G., *'Monos theos'*, TLZ, 77, 52, pp. 469–76.

Gibbs, J. G., *Creation and Redemption*, 1971, pp. 73–94.

Longenecker, R. N., 'Early Christological motifs', NTS, 14, 1967–68, pp. 526–45.

Our opinion is therefore that the hymn came into being by someone reflecting upon the confession which he was led to make within the setting of the community and which constituted the centre of his faith and his life. The New Testament context to which reference has been made shows that very early on (how could it be otherwise?) the question was raised about the relationship between the Lord Christ and the God from whom he took, along with the Name (Yahweh = '*kurios*'!), the function of sole and almighty Lordship. Given the structures of the Old Testament and Jewish monotheistic context, expressed particularly by the 'Name', it is understandable that Christianity could not escape this problem. This is supported also by the Christological use of the noun '*Onoma*', (Daniélou, Longenecker) shown by a study of early Christian literature. Deichgräber notes furthermore that the hymn strongly resembles Ex. 15 and Jg. 5 except that Jesus takes the place of Yahweh. Finally, it must be remembered that the basic affirmation of Jewish monotheism ('*heis theos*') is also associated with a confessional proclamation of faith, in this case the Shema (Dt. 6⁴; Delling).

We have observed that the hymn involves only the two figures of God and Christ, and that the theme of the drama it describes concerns their Lordship over creation. This receives expression from v. 6, and J. G. Gibbs is right to refer to this passage in studying the relation between creation and redemption in the New Testament. From this angle the basic contrasts between the first part where Christ is the subject and the second where God takes this place is easily comprehended, as is the significance of the quotation from Isa. 45²³ in vv. 10–11 where dominion over all peoples, in the Old Testament an exclusive attribute of Yahweh himself, is transferred to Christ. This also is the reason why the hymn both opens and closes with a reference to God (vv. 6a, 11c), because the confession of Jesus as Lord in no way detracts from the glory of God but on the contrary belongs to his benevolent purpose, issues from his free decision (vv. 9ff) and is to his glory because it reveals his Fatherhood (v. 11c). The solution to this—which at first sight appears like squaring the circle—the author of the hymn reveals in the obedience and humility of Jesus of Nazareth, in his abasement and in his death upon the Cross. Even further, consideration of the life of this 'man' leads the hymn 'higher still' into taking account of the pre-existence of Christ. This explains why the first part of the hymn is more clearly structured than the second, for there the writer wields the pen freely in his own hands while in the second he is involved in the defined situation of cultic confession and also the quotation of Isa. 45. Finally, it must not be forgotten that the Younger Pliny in writing to Trajan depicts the Christians as singing hymns to Christ *as a God* ('*quasi Deo*'; Letters, X, 96, 7).

The 'Sitz im Leben'

DEICHGRAEBER, R., *Gotteshymnus und Christushymnus* . . ., 1967, p. 132f.

DELLING, G., *Worship in the NT*, 1962.

GAMBER, K., 'Der Christushymnus im Philipperbrief in Liturgiegeschichtlicher Sicht', *Bibl.*, 51, 1970, pp. 369–76.

JERVELL, J., *Imago Dei. Gen. 1.26f im Spätjudentum, in der Gnosis und in den paulinischen Briefen*, 1960, pp. 205ff.

LARSSON, E., *Christus als Vorbild. Eine Untersuchung zu den paulinischen Tauf- und Eikon-texten*, 1962, pp. 230ff.

LIGIER, L., 'L'hymne christologique de Phil. 2.6–11, la liturgie eucharistique et la bénédiction synagogale *nishmat kol hat'*, in *Studiorum Paulinorum Congressus Internationalis Catholicus*, 1961, II, 1963, pp. 65–74.

There is no profit in pursuing further the cultic setting of the hymn. Some scholars are content with this general placing (Deichgräber, Martin), while others favour more particularly a baptismal or a Eucharistic context. Certainly, baptism would be a good setting for the movement *katabasis/anabasis* (Käsemann, Jervell, Larsson), but the Last Supper would account better for the ideas of incarnation and humiliation, the reference to death on the Cross and the final joy and triumph of vv. 9–11 (L. Cerfaux, *art. cit.*, p. 437; E. Lohmeyer, *op. cit*, pp. 65ff). Indeed, it is unnecessary to draw a sharp distinction between these three options since in practice they were often associated together. In favour of the Eucharistic view it may, however, be noted that the rhythm of the hymn fully corresponds with that of the Hallel Psalms (Gamber) and that in the Jewish benediction used at the celebration of the Passover there occur both stress on the Name, the gesture of adoration derived from Isa. 45^{25} and the statement of a strict monotheism (Ligier). What is truly important is the prominence of '*en Christō*' in vv. 1 and 5. The very basis of the Christian community is that it lives through worship in which it is built up in '*agapē*' ('love'; 1 Cor. 12ff) because then it is grafted into the stock of Christ, that is to say receives the gift of himself made in the incarnation, his death and the victory of Easter.

Authorship

FURNESS, J. M., 'The authorship of Phil. 2.6–11', *ExpT*, 70, 1958–59, pp. 240–43.

GNILKA, J., *Commentary*, pp. 131ff.

MARTIN, R. P., *Carmen Christi*, 1967, pp. 42–62 and 297–309.

SCHWEIZER, E., *Erniedrigung und Erhöhung*[2], 1962, p. 93, n. 373.

The identity of the author of the hymn is still very much discussed. Although the majority of scholars come down in favour of a non-Pauline origin,[1] those who attribute its composition to Paul himself are by no means silenced.[2] Of course, an acknowledgment of the prior existence of the verses does not necessarily involve a denial that they are authentically Pauline, in that Paul himself could well have written them for use on some particular occasion quite apart

[1] Beare, Bonnard, Gnilka, Friedrich, Lohmeyer; Bornkamm, Cullmann, Georgi, Jeremias, Käsemann, Martin, Schweizer, G. Strecker (*art.* and *op. cit.*).
[2] Dibelius, Michaelis, Scott; Cerfaux, Furness, P. Henry (*art. cit.*).

from his letter to the Philippians. It must be granted that some of the terms are foreign to the apostle's vocabulary;[1] but do we not elsewhere find texts of indisputable authenticity which are also sprinkled with rare words? And is not one whole section of the vocabulary altogether Pauline?—'*huparchein*'; '*doulos*'; '*homoiōma*'; etc. While it is true that the Christology which the hymn reflects is not specifically that of the apostle to the gentiles and makes no mention of the resurrection or of Christ's death 'for us', it is equally true that given the precise problem which the author is facing it would have been hard for him to bring in these particular ideas.

Doubt is therefore legitimate. It must also be granted that the author of the hymn had very pronounced Jewish attachments. The quotation of Isa. 45 in v. 10, the whole matter of the Name and of the implication for monotheism of using the title Lord for Jesus, the kinship of our verses with the synagogue liturgy (L. Ligier, *art. cit.*), all point to the author as a one-time Jew. But this should not be taken so far as to suggest an Aramaic or Hebrew original of which 2[6-11] was merely a translation, an hypothesis advanced by E. Lohmeyer (*op. cit.*, p. 9), given definite shape by R. P. Martin (*op. cit.*, pp. 40ff), but opposed by R. Deichgräber (*op. cit.*, pp. 126ff) who gathers eight expressions or turns of speech among others difficult to imagine as translations of a Semitic original.

It would seem clear also that the author is Greek in language and culture. Indeed the confession '*kurios Iēsous*' appears to have been developed particularly within Hellenistic Christianity, churches of Jewish origin preferring the formula '*Christos Iēsous*'. Moreover, the use of the double name '*Iēsous Christos*' (v. 11) suggests that the second term has lost its primary meaning of 'Messiah' and is now only regarded as a personal name, and this would be especially understandable in a Greek community.

Then should the origin of the hymn be attributed to the bilingual community at Antioch, the importance of which is so well known in the ministry of Paul (J. Héring, *Le Royaume de Dieu*, 1959, p. 160f)— unless we should think of the Hellenists mentioned in Acts 7 who are believed to have been Judaeo-Christians whose language was Greek? At all events, their link with Paul has been canvassed by G. Bornkamm who believes that the church of Damascus, the cradle of Paulinism, had its origin with them (*Paul*, ET 1971, pp. 23ff). Yet it must be said that Stephen's speech in Acts 7 bears little trace of Christological speculation.

If a definite name has to be chosen Paul's own would seem the most suitable, for in addition to the qualities of both Jew and Hellenist the author must have possessed a genius which is not at everyone's disposal. As well from the literary as from the theological point of view 2[6-11] concentrates into an exceedingly concise poem considerable theological substance and is the work of a master. If,

[1] '*Harpagmon hēgeisthai*'; '*kenoun*'; '*tapeinoun*'; '*huperupsoun*'; '*morphē*;' *schema*'.

furthermore, regard is paid to the fact that this passage comes to us only interwoven within a Pauline context—and how fully interwoven it is with the thread of the argument!—and that the coming of Christ in the flesh (Rom. 1³; 8³; Gal. 4⁴), the specific reference to the Cross (v. 8) and the rigorous theocentrism (vv. 9a, 11c) are also authentic Pauline themes, then it would be ungracious to deny to the apostle the authorship of a hymn which perhaps reflects preoccupations of his youth to which the theologian of the epistles was less partial.

The pre-existence of Christ

FEUILLET, A., 'L'hymne christologique', *RB*, 72, 1965, pp. 499ff.

GEWIESS, J., 'Zum altkirchlichen Verständnis der Kenosisstelle (Phil. 2.5–11)', *ThQ*, 120, 1948, pp. 463–87.

JEREMIAS, J., 'Zu Phil. 2.7; "*heauton ekenōsen*" ', *NT*, 6, 1963, pp. 182–88.

LOOFS, F., 'Das altkirchliche Zeugnis gegen die herrschende Auffassung der Kenosisstelle—Phil. 2.5 bis 11', *Theologische Studien und Kritiken*, 100, 1927–28, pp. 1–102.

PETAVEL-OLLIF, E., 'La kénose après la transfiguration. Etude exégétique sur Phil. 2.5–11', *RTP*, 29, 1896, pp. 138–64.

TALBERT, C. H., 'The problem of pre-existence in Phil. 2.6–11', *JBL*, 86, 1967, pp. 141–53.

BENOIT, P., 'Préexistence et incarnation' *RB*, 77, 1970, pp. 5–29.

CULLMANN, O., *The Christology of the New Testament*, ET 1959, pp. 247ff.

HAHN, F., *The Titles of Jesus in Christology*, 1969, p. 304f.

KRAMER, W., *Christos, Kyrios, Gottessohn*, pp. 108ff.

SCHNACKENBURG, R., *Das Johannesevangelium*, I, 1965, pp. 290–302.

SCHWEIZER, E., 'Zur Herkunft der Präexistenzvorstellung bei Paulus', in *Neotestamentica*, 1963, pp. 105–9.

That the hymn takes cognisance of the pre-existence of Christ does not strike everyone as obvious. The Lutheran exegetical tradition, for instance, holds that the historical Jesus alone is being referred to. F. Loofs tried to show how this view was rooted in Patristic exegesis, but the results of his investigation have been challenged by J. Gewiess. It was nevertheless on the same lines that Petavel-Ollif was working in his suggestive study which appeared in 1896 where he applied the 'kenosis' of v. 7 to the descent of Christ towards the Cross following the Transfiguration. Without being as definite as this the more recent studies by Jeremias, Feuillet and Talbert who derive the reference to Christ's death from the same verse, equally deny that there is any question of pre-existence in the hymn.

In fact, the construction as well as the purpose of the hymn exclude the adoption of this kind of interpretation. Yet even if a reference to pre-existence is hardly in doubt it must not be given an exaggerated importance so far as this passage is concerned. 2⁶⁻¹¹ does

not occur in isolation and the belief in pre-existence is found elsewhere in the New Testament, notably in Paul.[1] Now it can be
appreciated that, for the New Testament as a whole, the affirmation
of Christ's pre-existence appears at the same time as a direct consequence of confessing him to be '*Kurios*' (Cullmann) and as a reflection upon the mystery of Jesus, his relationship with God and his
work (Benoit). The ultimate theological and philosophical basis from
which such reflections spring has a kind of dual aspect like a dip-
tych (Schnackenburg). On the other hand there is a specifically
Jewish current of thought linking certain entities or qualities with
God (the Name of the Messiah, the Throne of Glory, Wisdom, etc.)
which henceforward take on an eternal character; and on the other,
there is a gnostic current, deeply anthropological, for which the idea
of pre-existence arises from belief about the origin of man. It is
obvious that the hymn is connected with the former, as are all Paul's
references to the pre-existence of Christ, references which seem
strongly impregnated with wisdom theology (Schweizer). The first
part of the hymn certainly carries a number of terms which have
parallels in gnosticism (Gnilka, Käsemann, Sanders)[2] but it can
then only be remarked how gnostic thought emerges crippled in the
Christian application of it; this application may use gnostic terms but
challenges the system by applying these terms to a series of ridiculous
historical events.

3. The place of the hymn in the Epistle to the Philippians

The interpretation of the hymn just given accords perfectly with its
place in the epistle. The apostle is not so much trying to give his
readers a pattern of the exemplary attitude which they should follow
—for then why vv. 9–11? It must be remembered that Paul found
himself confronting a community in danger of disintegration because
of the competitive spirit creeping in among the members and he
reminds them of their foundation and of what builds them up as a
community, namely the confession of faith which they make when
they assemble together. This confession acknowledges but one Lordship, that of God and of Christ; how then can Christians aspire to
any superiority of one over another? The confession gives glory to
God alone, how then can Christians display vainglory, '*kenodoxia*'
(v. 3)?

Furthermore, this confession-proclamation rests upon a series of
definite historical acts—acts of abasement and of self-giving even
unto death. How could Christians forget it? The humiliation and the
incredible exaltation of Christ teach us that the only way to glory lies
through suffering and renunciation.

2[5] By concluding the exhortation of vv. 1–4 and introducing the
hymn, vv. 6–11, this verse has essentially a transitional nature

[1] Cf. Rom. 1[3f]; 8[3]; Gal. 4[4]; 1 Cor. 10[4]; 2 Cor. 8[9].
[2] Cf. *C. Herm.* 1.12, 14, 15; *The Song of the Pearl* 1.23f; *Odes Sol.* 7.3ff.

(Gnilka), and so with Lohmeyer two parts of the sentence must be distinguished. The first is a fresh appeal to '*phronein*' (vv. 2, 3), rounding off what has gone before:[1] 'Do this!'; 'Act as I have just said!'. Thus the '*en humin*' can only have a communal reference, 'Behave in this way among yourselves' (so the majority of commentaries, against Hendriksen, Lightfoot, Vincent).

Then the second half of the sentence means, 'For ('*kai*') this is how it was in the case of Jesus Christ'. Ancient exegesis took the '*en Christō*' in the ethical sense:[2] 'Have the same attitude among yourselves as Jesus Christ had'. But such an interpretation does not correspond to the parallel with the communal '*en humin*' which precedes nor agree with the second part of the hymn (vv. 9–11)— Christ cannot serve as an example in so far as his Lordship is concerned. So it has to be understood as 'Behave in the way in which those who are in Christ behave', whatever nuance is given to the same expression elsewhere.[3] This then is the sense which has to be accepted here. The Christians of Philippi are being referred to the community experience which is the basis of their existence (cf. *ad* 2[1]), namely the confession of Christ as Lord and of God as Father, which makes them servants (cf. *ad* 1[1]) and brothers. However, the ethical interpretation[4] must not be totally abandoned. The first part of the hymn also indicates the series of historical events which form the basis of the Lordship of Christ; so an indelible and irreversible character has been stamped upon history with its new direction as Christians affirm, the mark, namely, of humility and self-sacrifice. Hence the race to honours and precedence threatening the Philippian community stands condemned on two counts: 'in Christ' there is but one Lord, one who is crowned with glory; and this Lord shows that only renunciation and sacrifice can invoke the grace which alone exalts and leads to the goal—though there is nothing automatic about this; nothing in the first part of the hymn leads us to anticipate God's action in the second.

The hymn, commencing at this point, comprises therefore two parts identical in structure. The first describes a voluntary self-abnegation on the part of the hero and the second his exaltation to Lordship through the grace of God alone. To mark the antithesis these headings will serve:

I. vv. 6–8: God alone is Lord
II. vv. 9–11: Jesus is Lord

[1] '*Touto*' refers back to what precedes, cf. B–D §290.3.
[2] And still today Hendriksen, Lohmeyer, Michael, Staab; A. SCHULZ, *Nachfolgen und Nachahmen*, 1962, p. 273f.
[3] Barth, Dibelius, Bonnard, Gnilka, Huby; E. KÄSEMANN, *art. cit.*, p. 91; NEUGEBAUER, *In Christus*, 1961, p. 106.
[4] Cf. H. D. BETZ, *Nachfolge und Nachahmung Jesu Christi im NT*, 1967, pp. 162–67; G. STRECKER, *art. cit.*, p. 66f and R. DEICHGRÄBER, *Gotteshymnus*, 1967, pp. 188–96. There are no grounds for assuming a verb to follow the '*en Christō*' (against Barth, Dibelius, Käsemann).

Vv. 6–8 are composed of two equal strophes with the addition of an *envoi* referring to the Cross. Each strophe is framed by a key word, '*morphē*' in the first case, '*genomenos*' in the second. In each case the third line contains the main verb of the sentence, which is qualified by the reflexive personal pronoun 'himself'. In the first two lines of the first strophe the word 'God' occurs, and of the second 'man'. Thus there is described the humiliation, in all respects voluntary, which leads One who was in a divine 'state' to the annihilation of death, and this humiliation took place through the incarnation.

2⁶ The relative pronoun opening the hymn is typical of the literary genre (cf. Col. 1¹⁵; 1 Tim. 3¹⁶; Heb. 1³), so there is no need to postulate an original '*kurios*' or '*Iēsous*' for which Paul had substituted the pronoun. To name the hero at the start would be nonsensical having regard to the issue discussed in the hymn (cf. R. Deichgräber, *op. cit.*, p. 124). We thus at once run up against the mysterious meaning of the expression 'form of God ('*morphē theou*'), the form 'in' which ('*en*') the hero was found.

BEHM, J., art. '*morphē*', *TWNT*, IV, 1942, pp. 750–60 (ET IV, pp. 750–59).
DUPONT, J., 'Jésus-Christ dans son abaissement . . .' *RSR*, 37, 1950, pp. 502–4.
FEUILLET, A., 'L'hymne christologique . . .', *RB*, 72, 1965, pp. 368ff.
HENRY, P., 'Kénose', *SDB*, V, 1950, cols. 56–135.
HÉRING, J., 'Kyrios Anthropos', *RHPR*, 16, 1936, p. 207f.
— *Le Royaume de Dieu*², 1959, p. 161f.
JERVELL, J., *Imago Dei*, 1960, pp. 277ff.
KÄSEMANN, E., *Exegetische Versuche*, 1960, p. 67.
KRINETZKI, L., 'Der Einfluss von Is. 52.13–53.12', *ThQ*, 139, 1959, p. 164–68.
LARSSON, E., *Christus als Vorbild*, 1962, pp. 237ff.
LIGHTFOOT, J. B., *Commentary*, pp. 127–33.
LOOF, A., 'Une ancienne exégèse de Phil. 2.6–11 dans la ketàbà demasquàtà (livre des Degrés)', in *Studiorum Paulinorum Congressus Internationalis Catholicus 1961*, II, 1963, pp. 523–33.
MARTIN, R. P., *Carmen Christi*, pp. 99–133.
WALLACE, D. H., 'A note on morphé', *ThZ*, 22, 1966, pp. 19–25.

Should '*morphē*' be understood as 'essence', 'condition', 'glory', 'image', or as 'form of existence' ('*Daseinsweise*')? The first interpretation, which confuses '*ousia*' and '*morphē*', was widely current in patristic exegesis and has been taken up by Lightfoot and, to some degree, by Scott. It wins little acceptance today, although it has in its favour—apart from the philosophical use of the term by Plato and Aristotle, which is of no great significance—the antithesis of '*schēma/morphē*' which throws into relief the idea of an underlying reality for the '*morphē*' which is often set over-against a superficial appearance ('*schēma*'). So Michaelis seems to have little justification for taking the two terms as synonyms and translating the '*morphē*' here as 'external form'.

In reaction against this 'essentialist' interpretation and in order to take account of the parallelism with v. 7b, '*morphē*' has next been understood as 'condition', a mark of position or 'status', and not of being (Benoit, Bonnard, Dupont, Huby); but the opinion comes to grief over the absence of this meaning for '*morphē*' in Greek, in spite of E. Schweizer's attempt to prove the contrary (*Erniedringung und Erhöhung*[2], 1962, p. 96, n. 383). Furthermore, it would constitute a clear ambiguity in the interpretation of the hymn as a whole. Nevertheless, along the same lines J. Behm takes '*morphē*' as the equivalent of '*doxa*' ('glory'), a token of the power and authority with which the pre-existent Christ was invested. This interpretation gains support from Jer. 17[5] and it has been adopted by Krinetzki and Staab among others, but against it is the fact that the equivalence of '*morphē*' and '*doxa*' never occurs clearly. So very many scholars prefer to equate '*morphē*' not with '*doxa*' but with '*eikōn*' ('image'), in which case the idea would be that Christ is regarded as the 'second Adam' (cf. Rom. 5), the first Adam also, according to Gen. 1[26], being regarded as an 'image of God'.

This suggestion was introduced into current exegesis by J. Héring in 1936 and received important support from R. P. Martin (pp. 102–120).[1] But it has quite rightly been challenged by D. H. Wallace; it comes to grief fundamentally on the fact that this meaning of '*morphē*' certainly cannot be adopted for the second occurrence of the word in v. 7b. There therefore remains the interpretation of those who, with Käsemann, associate the hymn with gnostic texts, particularly with the *Corpus Hermeticum*. Then '*morphē*' is translated as '*Daseinsweise*', 'form of existence' and there is a refusal to distinguish between fundamental essence and appearance.[2]

The outcome of all this is that from the start any interpretation of the first occurrence of '*morphē*' which will not apply to the second (v. 7b) must be rejected. This then excludes the Adamic interpretation, the reference to Adam being in addition clearly alien to the purport of the hymn. And it must be said that although '*morphē*', '*doxa*' and '*eikōn*' are often related they are never confused but always retain their own shades of meaning, so that it must be assumed that the writer knew what he was doing when he used one term in preference to the others.

Why, then, '*morphē*'? Because the word indicates a most profound and genuine identity, as early exegesis rightly divined, yet one which

[1] It has been upheld also by O. CULLMANN, *Christology*, ET pp. 177ff; A. FEUILLET, *RB*, 72, 1965, pp. 365–80; P. LAMARCHE, *Christ vivant*, pp. 32ff; E. LARSSON, *op. cit.*, pp. 237ff. A. Loof demonstrated also the antiquity of this view. Feuillet mentions the names of d'Estius (1631), Dom Calmet, etc.

[2] Those who take '*morphē*' in this sense include Dibelius; Gnilka; BORNKAMM, 'Zum Verständnis . . .', p. 180; BULTMANN, *Theology* . . ., ET p. 193; J. JERVELL, *op. cit.*, pp. 277ff (with reference to gnostic speculations about Adam).

was *hidden*, not manifest. We have the same contrast in Josephus
(*Contra Apionem*, II. 22) between the 'form and greatness of the
invisible God' ('*morphēn de kai megethos*') and the 'works and acts of
grace' through which he is manifested. The same characteristics of
the word are found also in the use Paul makes of compounds of
'*morphoō*' ('to form'; Rom. 12^2; 8^{29}; 2 Cor. 3^{18}; Gal.
4^{19}; 3^{10}),
which express all the mystery of a relationship whose depth and
reality cannot be doubted. The author of the hymn has therefore
quite deliberately refrained from using '*doxa*' or '*eikōn*' whose
Christological slant was different. He means to say that Christ was
God though the entire world was unaware of this because he was not
exercising divine Lordship.

This is also expressed by the verb '*huparchō*'. Frequent in the
whole New Testament just as it is with Paul, it signifies a condition of
existence which in this case stands in opposition to the active force of
the verbs which will follow. Although truly God, Christ was nevertheless passively so. When he moved into action 'He did not profit
from his equality with God'.

Everything relevant has been said about the meaning of '*harpagmos*'.

BOUYER, L., '*Harpagmos*', *RSR*, 39, 1951, pp. 281–88.
FOERSTER, W., art. '*Harpagmos*', *TWNT*, I, 1933, pp. 472–74 (ET I,
    pp. 472–74).
FURNESS, J. M., '*Harpagmos . . . heauton ekenōsen*', *ExpT*, 69,
    1957–58, p. 93f.
GEWIESS, J., 'Die Philipperbriefstelle 2.6b', in *Neutestamentliche
    Aufsätze* (*Festschr. für J. Schmid*), 1963, pp. 69–85.
GRIFFITHS, D. R., ' "*Harpagmos*" and "*heauton ekenōsen*" in Phil.
    2,6–7', *ExpT*, 69, 1957–58, pp. 237–39.
HOOVER, R. W., 'The harpagmos enigma: a philological solution',
    HTR, 64, 1971, pp. 95–119.
KATTENBUSCH, F., ' "*Harpagmon*" ? "*Arpagmon*"! Phil. 2.6—Ein
    Beitrag zur paulinischen Christologie', *Theologische Studien und
    Kritiken*, 104, 1932, pp. 372–420.
LIGHTFOOT, J. B., *Commentary*, pp. 133–37.
MARTIN, R. P., *Carmen Christi*, pp. 134–64.
REICKE, B., 'Unité chrétienne et diaconie; Phil. 2.1–11', in *Neotesta-
    mentica et Patristica. Freundesgabe O. Cullmann*, 1962, pp.
    203–12 (p. 209).
ROBINSON, D. W. D., ' "*Harpagmos*": the deliverance Jesus refused ?',
    ExpT, 80, 1968–69, pp. 253–54.
TRUDINGER, P., ' "*Harpagmos*" and the Christological significance
    of the Ascension', *ExpT*, 79, 1967–68, p. 279.
VOKES, P. E., ' "*Harpagmos*" in Phil. 2.5–11', in *Studia Evangelica*,
    II (ed. F. L. Cross), 1964, pp. 670–75.

Very rare in classical Greek and here only in biblical Greek, '*harpagmos*' always has an active force, 'act of seizing', 'robbery': 'he did not regard equality with God as robbery . . .'—but of what? The lack of an object has often troubled scholars. So there are only a few, such as Furness, Vokes and Robinson, who still hold to this interpretation. They see this sentence as referring either to the temptation of Jesus in the wilderness or to Gethsemane from whence he could have been taken directly to heaven without passing through death. Trudinger takes it as meaning that Christ refused to ascend to God by way of mystical raptures ('*harpagmos*').

But most scholars favour a passive and admittedly exceptional interpretation of the word as 'a thing seized', 'a prey', 'booty'. In this case Greek words ending in '*-mos*' and in '*-ma*' are being taken as synonyms, and '*harpagmos*' would only be equivalent to the much better attested '*harpagma*' meaning 'booty', 'prize'. If this is so, are we to regard divine equality as a prize already in Christ's possession but to which he did not wish to cling ('*res rapta*')[1] or, on the contrary, as something he did not possess yet did not want to seize by force ('*res rapienda*')?[2] The latter view clearly permits reference to Adam as a antetype and to Gen. 3^5 ('*esesthe hōs theoi*', 'you shall be as gods') or to Satan (cf. Isa. 14^{12f}; Michaelis).[3] The theological reflections to which these alternatives can lead are also obvious: was the pre-existent Christ God or was he not? But is it actually necessary to distinguish between *res rapta* and *res rapienda*? Some doubt this and rely rather on the 'popular' meaning which the expression '*harpagmon hēgeisthai*' could take of 'to regard something as a windfall, an unexpected asset' (Henry; Lohmeyer, pp. 20–29; Martin, pp. 143ff). Bonnard explains it thus: 'Contrary to what has often been thought, there is no radical difference between these two interpretations . . . Christ, who enjoyed divine status did not regard this status (which was his possession) as grounds for taking advantage of God and so attaining equality with him.'

Beyond the philological disputes and researches the essential question to be raised about this is why in a hymn so brief there is reference to a refusal about which we seem to hear nothing elsewhere. A reply to this basic question is to be found nowhere other than in the hymn itself. If nothing were known otherwise about the meaning of '*harpagmos*' the general trend of these verses would inevitably lead to the interpretation that Christ did not exercise the powers of Lordship pertaining to his equality with God, he did not show himself as Lord, he did not profit in a egoistic or despotic way from what he was. Such a view is further strengthened if attention is paid to the direct

[1] Beare, Dibelius, Friedrich, Gnilka, Lightfoot, Müller; Bornkamm, Käsemann, Jervell, Larsson (*art.* and *op. cit.*).
[2] Michael, Michaelis, Staab; Bouyer, Cullmann, Feuillet, Gewiess, Héring, Lamarche, Lohmeyer (*art.* and *op. cit.*).
[3] Others also see an allusion either to the Servant of the Lord and to Isa. 53^{12} or 49^{24f} (L. CERFAUX, *art. cit.*, pp. 430ff; J. M. FURNESS, *art. cit.*, p. 181f) or to Wisdom (7^{11}–14^{27}; 10^{13f}; D. GEORGI, 'Der vorpaulinische Hymnus', p. 277f).

(1988

parallelism between v. 6b and v. 7d which are respectively the second lines of the strophes of the first part of the hymn. In v. 7d it is not so much a matter of the reality of Christ's humanity (v. 7c) but of the way in which it is *manifested*, the way in which it has been perceived (*'heuretheis'*) by God and by the created order. And this is also the subject of v. 6b—the way in which Christ has been perceived by God and by creation, but this time in his divine state.

Philology in fact allows no other interpretation. On this point the most detailed study is by R. W. Hoover who in conclusion (p. 118) translates the verse: 'He did not regard the fact of equality with God as something he could use to his own advantage'. In fact, the active force of the word which alone is attested should carry most weight in the interpretation to be given to the phrase. Furthermore, in Jas. 1[2] and 2 Pet. 2[13] the expression *'hēgeisthai ti'* means 'to regard as an opportunity for', and certainly this is how Paul takes it when, in clear anticipation of the quotation which will follow, he twice uses the verb *'hēgeisthai'* in vv. 3 and 4: 'In humility, regard others as superior to yourselves'. Christ himself did not consider equality with God as an opportunity to assert himself in the eyes of others (B. Reicke, *art. cit.*).

Analysis of the expression 'to be equal with God' further confirms our interpretation. What it says is of course not fundamentally different from what is meant in v. 6a, that identity with God is full and complete. But as Gewiess, Lohmeyer and Michaelis have rightly shown, there is a shift of emphasis. Use of a neuter plural functioning adverbially (*'isa'*; cf. B–D §434.1) rather than the adjective itself (*'isos'*) gives the expression a more legal air. It is a matter of the equality of two powers, two functions. Christ did not use the power which was in his own possession to 'put his hand' on all creation.

2[7ab] With the verb *'kenoō'* ('to empty') we come to the term by which the theories known as kenotic gain their chief support; of these we shall speak later. The phrase is striking by its concise and unusual nature; indeed, no convincing parallel is to be found in the whole of Greek literature.

FURNESS, J. M., ' "*Harpagmos . . . heauton ekenōsen*" ', *ExpT*, 69, 1957–58, p. 93f.
GRIFFITHS, D. R., ' "*Harpagmos*" and "*heauton ekenōsen*" in Phil. 2.6–7', *ExpT*, 69, 1957–58, pp. 237–39 .
JEREMIAS, J., art. *'Pais'*, *TWNT*, V, 1954, pp. 653–713 (ET V, pp. 654–717).
— 'Zu Phil. 2.7: "*Heauton ekenōsen*" ', *NT*, 6, 1963, pp. 182–88.
MARTIN, R. P., *Carmen Christi*, pp. 165–96.
WARREN, W., 'On "*heauton ekenōsen*" ', *JTS*, 12, 1911, pp. 461–63.

Once again, the singularity of the phrase has led to a search for parallels or analogues. So in 1911 W. Warren (cf. Furness and

Griffiths) was already detecting an allusion to Isa. 53[12]: 'he poured out his soul to death' ('*he'erāh lammāweth naphshô* = LXX: '*paredothē eis thanaton hē psuchē autou*'). This suggestion has been energetically championed by Jeremias who argues from the frequent rendering of the Hebrew ''*ārāh*' by the Greek '*ekkenoun*', of '*nephesh*' by the reflexive pronoun '*heauton*', and from the fact that in Ps. 141[8] the phrase 'do not pour out my soul' ('''*al-te'ar naphshî*'') also expresses abandonment to death.[1] Consequently, in 2[7a] there ought to be seen a reference to the death of Jesus on the Cross and not to the incarnation.

But as G. Bornkamm (*art. cit.*, p. 180) and R. Deichgräber (*op. cit.*, p. 123f) have rightly urged, the argument goes too far. It would gain in strength if it were proved that the word '*doulos*' ('slave') in the following line corresponded to Isaiah's Servant of Yahweh. But the parallelism with v. 6a in fact makes this correspondence very unlikely. The verb in question must therefore be understood along the lines already laid down for v. 6: Christ has not wished to exercise any arbitrary authority but by an act of his own free consent ('*heauton*') emptied himself of his power (Hendriksen, Müller), depriving himself of the exercise of the powers of Lordship.

But why '*kenoō*'? Because Paul several times uses this verb in the passive meaning 'to make vain, useless' (Rom. 4[14]; 1 Cor. 1[17]; 2 Cor. 9[3]). The passive has disappeared in this instance and the stress is rightly placed upon the subject's own freedom, but the meaning is similar: by depriving himself of the exercise of his Lordship Christ made himself 'empty', 'ineffective'. Yet there is perhaps a further reason which explains the use of '*kenoō*' here, namely, an implicit antithesis to 'fulness' ('*plērōma*'). Whatever the source or precise meaning of this truly Pauline concept, Paul certainly links it with Christ and does so quite rightly, in the extent to which Christ exercises dominion whether over all creation or merely over the church (Col. 1[19]; 2[9]; Eph. 1[23]; 3[19]).[2] So there is no need to linger over the fact that such language was probably borrowed from gnostic systems; so far as the hymn is concerned these systems are shattered and their fragments (i.e. words) given a place in a new system which transforms them. In short, what is said here is that Christ remains God but that he renounces the exercise of the power of God; he emptied himself of the fulness of this power.

The last line of this first strophe repeats the same idea: 'He took the form of a slave'. The word '*doulos*' here certainly unites the semi-honorific meaning which it has in the Old Testament where the servant is usually the representative of his master, and the more pejorative Greek sense of slave. The incarnation is both humiliation

---

[1] Jeremias is followed by L. KRINETZKI (*art. cit*), A. FEUILLET (*art. cit.*, pp. 357ff), P. LAMARCHE (*op. cit.*, p. 40) and Scott.

[2] On this topic cf. P. BENOIT, *Exégèse et théologie*, II, 1961, pp. 138–53; G. DELLING, art. '*plērēs*, etc.', *TWNT*, VI, 1959, pp. 283–309 (ET VI, pp. 283–311); A. FEUILLET, *Le Christ Sagesse de Dieu*, 1966, pp. 228–38 and 275–319; H. SCHLIER, *Der Brief an die Epheser*, 1963, pp. 96–9.

and mission. But it would be going too far to see any clear allusion here either to Isaiah's Servant of Yahweh or to the pessimistic gnostic notion that the human condition is slavery. The term '*doulos*' stands, rather, in opposition to an implicit '*kurios*', rendered by '*theos*' in v. 6a. Likewise the aorist participle '*labōn*' is opposed to the static '*huparchōn*' (v. 6a).[1] As for 'form' ('*morphē*') which occurs again, it expresses as in v. 6a both the mystery and the reality of a profound relationship.

2[7] and the kenosis of Christ

BARTH, K., *Church Dogmatics*, IV Pt. I, ET 1956, pp. 180ff.
DAWE, D. G., 'A fresh look at the kenotic Christologies' *SJT*, 15, 1962, pp. 337–49.
FAIRWEATHER, E. G., 'The "kenotic" Christology', appendix to Beare's *Commentary*, 1959, pp. 159–74.
HENRY, P., art. 'Kénose', *SDB*, V. 1950, cols. 136–61.
MARTIN, R. P., *Carmen Christi*, pp. 66–8.
TAYLOR, V., *The Person of Christ in NT Teaching,* 1959, pp. 260–76.
THOMAS, T. A., 'The kenosis question', *EvQ*, 42, 1970, pp. 142–51.

By the term 'kenoticism' is meant a dogmatic position which originated in Germany in the second half of last century, though in a more or less disguised form it is found throughout the history of theology (Fairweather, Henry). As expounded in the 19th century it affirmed that at the incarnation Christ divested himself of the 'relative' attributes of deity, omniscience, omnipresence and omnipotence, but retained the 'essential attributes' of holiness, love and righteousness. K. Barth in particular has reacted violently to this view; in his opinion to tamper with anything relating to the divinity of Christ is to call in question the reality of salvation itself. For Barth kenosis could only mean this: 'As God, therefore, (without ceasing to be God) he could be known only to himself, but unknown as such in the world and for the world. His divine majesty could be in this alien form. It could be a hidden majesty . . . He had the freedom for this condescension, for this concealment of his Godhead. He had it and he made use of it in the power and not with any loss, not with any diminution or alteration of his Godhead' (*op. cit.*, p. 180).

Dawe reaches a similar conclusion that the traditional alteration of attributes should be reversed. Our hymn then demonstrates one thing only: 'Kenosis says that God is of such a nature that the acceptance of the limitations of a human life does not make him unlike himself. Kenosis is a way of saying that in his revelation God is free for us, i.e. he is free to be our God without ceasing to be God the Lord' (*art. cit.*, p. 348).

---

[1] Those who find an allusion to Isa. 53[12] in v. 7a stress the anteriority of the action usually implied by the aorist participle in relation to the principal verb: Christ would die upon the Cross (v. 7a) *after* having taken the form of a servant (v. 7b). But this feature of aorist participles is not a general rule (B–D §339).

There is in fact little difficulty in showing that the terms of this polemic are quite alien to the issues of the hymn itself (Thomas), and Henry is doubtless right when he suggests that the inspiration for kenoticism springs from 'a predeliction for an idealistic type of philosophy, expressing itself more readily in psychological categories than in terms of being and tending to identify personality with self-consciousness.' It remains to be seen whether every doctrine of the incarnation is not led, in one way or another, to speak of a limitation of divinity, a kenosis (Taylor). By claiming that in order to become man Christ renounced the exercise of Lordship our hymn takes up the Barthian stance: 'his divine majesty could be in this alien form. It could be a hidden majesty.' But is anything fundamentally different being said when one speaks of the surrender of omnipotence, omniscience and omnipresence?

2^{cd} The second strophe of the hymn is also carefully structured and on a plan very like that of the first. Just as the first was framed by two '*morphē*' the second is delimited by two '*genomenos*' ('became'). The antithesis of the two verses is also clear, the first dealing with the quasi-ontological phase of pre-existence and the second with becoming and existence. This existence means human existence, and the two '*anthrōpos*' of vv. 7c and 7d correspond to the twofold '*theos*' of vv. 6a and 6b. But the true link between these two phases in the mystery of Christ and what marks the identity and continuity through all the changes is the voluntary self-abasement, humility and obedience expressed in the third line of each of the verses where the main verb occurs associated with the reflexive pronoun 'himself'.

The hymn now states that the service and the mission to which Christ devotes himself is the human plight. But it is not possible to take the participle '*genomenos*' in the sense of 'was born' (i.e. as a man; against Beare) particularly because of parallelism with the same participle in v. 8a. The word essentially stands over-against the immobility of what appertains 'in God' ('*huparchōn*'; v. 6a), while also bearing a certain traditional flavour (cf. Rom. 1³; Gal. 4⁴; Jn. 1¹⁴). The coming into existence is accomplished in the 'likeness' of men. Here '*homoiōma*' signifies identity; Christ identifies himself with humanity (cf. J. Schneider, art. '*homoios*' and cognates, *TWNT*, V, 1954, pp. 186–98 (ET V, pp. 186–99)). The word is found in the New Testament only with Paul which is a not unimportant indication in favour of Pauline authorship of the hymn (cf. Rom. 8³). In association with the '*schēma*' which follows, '*homoiōma*' implies a more profound, essential identity; indeed it is simply the '*morphē doulou*' which is here taken up again but with more sharpness and precision; the reality of Christ's humanity is beyond question, yet without any occasion being given for speculation about the mystery of 'two natures'. The stress, however, placed upon this reality which is expressed by the three successive terms '*morphē*', '*homoiōma*' and '*schēma*', while Christ's divine identity calls for but a single noun, '*morphē*', shows that at that time it was easier to believe in the deity of the 'Lord' than in his genuine and complete humanity. Paul therefore sets himself here against all gnostic temptations in theology, and far from speculating about the Danielic Son of Man (O. Michel, *art. cit.*, pp. 90ff) his mind is wholly set to understand and expound the human and historic fact denoted by the name 'Jesus of Nazareth'.

The second line of the strophe, with '*schēmati*', marks a kind of step forward in relation to the first. Having become man, Christ has also been judged to be man; his outward appearance and manner have been those of a man (cf. J. Schneider, art. '*schēma*', *TWNT*, VII, 1964, pp. 954–59 (ET VII, pp. 954–58)). Why this apparently repetitive insistence? Not only to avoid any risk of docetism but particularly to keep to the central theme of the hymn, which is not simply a general account of the Incarnation. With v. 7d God and the Creation, the other actors in the drama, are in fact reintroduced (cf. the *passive* participle '*heuretheis*')—not only has Christ become man but it is as such, and not as a Lord or tyrant in disguise, that he has comported himself and been esteemed. Thus the leading idea of the whole hymn re-emerges and it was noticeably the same progression in the first verse which led from the self-subsistence of the Pre-existent (v. 6a) to the conditions of his manifestation as such (v. 6b). Once again, it is quite out of place to want to see here speculation about the Son of Man, as does E. Lohmeyer, the more so as the construction with '*hōs*' ('as') is far from being an Aramaism representing '*kebarnash*', 'as a Son of Man' (*Kyrios Jesus*, 1928, pp. 38ff).

2[8] We have already shown that there can be no question for a moment of following G. Strecker (*ZNW*, 55, 1964, pp. 63–78) and A. Feuillet (*RB*, 72, 1965, pp. 499ff) in thinking that v. 8 could not have belonged to the original hymn. Even Gnilka is unjustified in detecting here a vocabulary which is more biblical than vv. 6–7 and in drawing conclusions about different 'sources'. Verse 8 is the essential focus of interest for those who hold to a so-called ethical interpretation of the hymn or to supporters of an Isaianic interpretation who relate it to Isa. 53. In expounding v. 5 we have already treated the first of these interpretations. The second one, supported notably by Cerfaux, Jeremias, Krinetzki and Romaniuk, is an attempt to answer the question why precisely *these* terms were used to describe the final humiliation of Christ. While it is true that '*tapeinōsis*' ('humility') occurs in Isa. 53[8] in connection with the killing of the Servant, the same does not hold for '*hupēkoos*', and more especially in the other direction the idea of a sacrifice for sins which is fundamental in Isaiah does not appear in the hymn. On the other hand, it should be observed that in the New Testament words of the '*tapeinos*' family are often used in opposition to what is proud and exalted[1] and that Paul uses them particularly in his polemic against the 'super-apostles' of Corinth. Likewise in classical Greek '*hupakouō*' pertains to the

[1] Lk. 1[52]; Rom. 12[16]; Jas. 1[9]; Mt. 23[12]; 2 Cor. 11[7]; 4[12].

condition of a slave. The reason for the use of the two words is to be sought nowhere else than in the antithesis which they express to lordly power, which is the dominant theme of the hymn.

The ultimate outcome of kenosis, of humility and obedience, is death. There is no speculation in the hymn about its meaning or value, it is simply mentioned as the exact opposite of life and divine Lordship. It is quite possible that death is referred to here as part of a three stage cosmology—heaven, earth, abyss (cf. v. 10)—through each of which in succession Christ would have passed (Lohmeyer); but it seems more likely that we should see here primarily a reference to the historical event which took place on Golgotha. This is further emphasised by the last line of this first part of the hymn (v. 8c; intensive, explicative *'de'*) which was perhaps said in unison by the whole congregation. For it is the Cross indeed, opening an abyss of nothingness under the feet of the disciples, and the extraordinary plenitude with which the resurrection suddenly fills this abyss, that is the source of all Christological reflection—this, and no theoretical or abstract speculation.

2⁹ With v. 9 we reach the second part of the hymn which we have entitled Jesus Christ as Lord. To the night of the Cross succeeded the morning of Easter Day; to the solitary Lordship of God was added now that of Jesus Christ—not in virtue of any logical entailment (Lohmeyer thinks of the law *'per aspera ad astra'*) but by pure grace (v. 9: *'echarisato'*); not as an attack on God's power but to the glory of his fatherhood (v. 11c). So the supreme subject of this second part will be God, as over-against the first part of the drama which brought into play only the action of Christ. Otherwise, we find the same structure in vv. 9–11 as in vv. 6–8, namely two strophes of four lines each crowned by the final doxology. The first strophe revolves around the Name (*'onoma'*) which God sovereignly confers upon Christ and although it is not expressly said the name is that of Kyrios-Yahweh; and with it is therefore bestowed upon Jesus power over all things. The second strophe expresses the attitude of the whole of creation to this new order of things: it kneels and confesses that 'Jesus Christ is Lord' (v. 11b), in accordance with the prophecy of Isa. 45²³ and the confession of the church in worship. The two verses each end with the name *'Iēsous'*, in harmony with the well determined attitude of the worshipping congregation. Even the marked grammatical caesura between the two verses only throws into stronger relief the *Sitz im Leben* of the hymn. At the very moment when for the first time the name of the hero was proclaimed the congregation responded to the announcement by kneeling and making its confession of faith.

The *'dio kai'* ('this is why') which opens v. 9 does not then indicate the reward (Michaelis) or the outcome of some law (Lohmeyer) but the gracious sovereign act of God (Barth). Enough has already probably been said about the meaning and the importance of the

Name in the hymn for there to be no need to return to it here. It is familiar that to the ancient world a name revealed the inner being of what was named. In the Old Testament the Name of God was the subject of revelation (Ex. 3) and was characterised by its exclusiveness: 'Hear, O Israel, Yahweh our God is the only Yahweh!' (Dt. 6⁴). Both these aspects are given a stronger suggestion of sovereignty in the LXX translation of 'Yahweh' by '*kurios*': God reveals himself as Lord and his Lordship is exclusive (cf. Bietenhard, art. '*onoma*, etc.', *TWNT*, V, 1954, pp. 242–83 (ET V, pp. 242–83)). So early Christian faith was not able to escape the problem which its own confession of Jesus as Lord raised in the face of the strict monotheism of the Old Testament. By using a verb dear to Paul ('*charizomai*') the hymn replies that this confession is no more than the outcome of the free grace of God who, by investing with Power one who had turned his back on it (vv. 6–8), was only revealing his fatherhood (v. 11c).

The verb '*huperupsoō*' (to 'super-exalt') must not then be taken in a comparative sense as though the status now attained by Christ was superior to his pre-existent one (Bonnard, Dibelius, Ewald, Cullmann; J. Héring, *op. cit.*). Both the context and deep lexicographical study[1] prevent its being taken as anything but a superlative: nothing is higher than Christ who is truly placed over ('*huper*') all things (cf. again the '*huper*' in v. 9c).[2] Though it is true that the verb '*hupsoō*' is not found elsewhere in Paul, his taste for compounds with '*huper*' is well known (19 out of the 28 instances in the N.T.).

2¹⁰ The result and the goal ('*hina*'; Bonnard, Gnilka) of God's sovereign act consists in the submission and confession of the church and of the whole creation. It is, indeed, arbitrary to draw a line here between Lordship over the church and Lordship over the cosmos so as to lay the stress on the latter (against Beare, Bonnard, Friedrich; Bornkamm, p. 183; Käsemann, p. 85; Martin, pp. 249–55). Granted the cultic *Sitz im Leben* of the hymn, it is evident that the congregation shared in the proclamation and the kneeling called for by it; and it must further be noticed that the church regarded itself as the firstfruits of the New Creation and its confession and submission have a universal significance. It is no matter of indifference that the Name invoked should be that of *Jesus*, the man—the real man—of whom the first part of the hymn speaks, who had shared all the vicissitudes of man in an historical setting. Consequently the church's faith does not appear as something speculative, however perfect that might be, but as a response to a definite historic intervention, that of Jesus of Nazareth.

[1] Cf. G. DELLING, 'Zum steigernden Gebrauch von Komposita mit '*huper*" bei Paulus', *NT*, 11, 1969, pp. 127–53.
[2] Beare, Friedrich, Medebielle, G. Bornkamm, E. Käsemann, *art. cit.*; BERTRAM, art. '*hupsos* etc.', *TWNT*, VIII, 1969, pp. 600–19 (p. 607), (ET VIII, pp. 602–20 (p. 608f)).

The quotation of Isa. 45²³ is significant.¹ The verse in fact stresses both the universality of salvation and its exclusive nature. Paul, who uses the verse again in Rom. 14¹¹ (though in connection with God), is therefore taking a very deliberate step when he uses it of Christ, a step which summarises the issue which the whole hymn is about, namely the reconciling of the Lordship of God with that of Jesus. They are in fact identical and proceed from the same benevolent plan of God. This is also why the faith proclaimed by the early church must be characterised by its universalism and, over-against the multiplicity of pagan cults, by its exclusiveness. It is this, again, which the three classes of creatures invoked at the end of the verse indicate: nothing whatever in the created order, visible or invisible, can put a limit on the Lordship of Christ (cf. J. G. Gibbs, *Creation and Redemption*, 1971, p. 74f).

2¹¹ The hymn finally ends with the revelation awaited from its very beginning and which was at the heart of early Christian faith. The simple form of the verb '*homologeō*' often in the New Testament introduces a confession of faith as traditionally received (Rom. 10⁹; Jn. 9²²; 1 Jn. 4¹⁵; etc.). The compound form '*exomologeō*' essentially indicates either public praise or a confession of sin.² Here it points to the public and liturgical character of the confession which acclaims Jesus in the same way that crowds acclaim earthly monarchs (Lightfoot; Michaelis). So there is no need to be held up by the tense of the verb as either future indicative or aorist subjunctive (see introductory text critical comments); we are dealing with an action which is in course of development, illustrated for the present by the confession of the church but to be fully manifested at the end of time.³

'Jesus Christ is Lord' means in the first instance that Christ is the same 'Lord' as the 'Lord' of the Old Testament and that henceforward he surpasses all '*kurioi*' who by one title or another lay claim to power. So we find mingled here nuances of the word Lord which are characteristic of both the Old Testament and Hellenism.⁴ Now this Lord is also the man Jesus, who has suffered the extremes of abasement, humility and death. It is precisely these features which resolve the conflict of authority which might have arisen between God and his Son. Confession of the Lordship of Christ can only be the fruit of an historical process, in spite of the fact that in origin Jesus was 'in the form of God'.

For this reason his Lordship is 'to the glory of God the Father'.

---

¹ LXX: '*emoi kampsei pan gonu kai exomologēsetai pasa glōssa tō theō*'.
² Cf. MICHEL, art. '*homologeō*, *TWNT*, V, 1954. pp. 199–220 (ET V, 199–220); V. H. NEUFELD, *Early Christian Confessions*, 1963, pp. 13–33.
³ R. P. MARTIN, *op. cit.*, pp. 266–70; E. SCHWEIZER, *Erniedringung und Erhöhung*, ² 1962, p. 98.
⁴ Cf. L. CERFAUX, *Recueil*, I, 1954, pp. 3–188; O. CULLMANN, *Christology*, ET 1959, pp. 193–237; F. HAHN, *The Titles of Jesus in Christology*, ET 1969, pp. 68–135; QUELL-FOERSTER, art. '*kurios*, etc.', *TWNT*, III, 1938, pp. 1038–98 (ET III, pp. 1039–98).

One should not then follow Vincent in linking this last line with *'exomologēsētai'* as though it was the confession which was to the glory of God, nor suppose with Michaelis that v. 11c simply depends on the *'hina'* of v. 10. But in all strictness, as W. Thüsing has rightly seen when he adduces the parallel in Rom. 15[7ff] (*Per Christum in Deum*, 1965, pp. 46–60), the Lordship of Christ leads to the glory of God. And if it is true that this is a specifically Pauline trait (Jeremias, Thüsing) nothing prevents us from believing that it belonged to the original hymn. On the contrary, it focusses the whole issue yet again, so that the hymn which opened with a reference to God and highlights his sovereign action could end only with a second reference to him. The Lordship of Christ is therefore within the ambit of the divine glory and far from masking it actually reveals it, and this ultimate revelation is founded on the Fatherhood of God. The true glory of God is to be Father; the Father of Christ in the first place, but also through him of the entire creation. It is clear that although it cannot be said that the appellation Father for God originated entirely with Jesus, it is nonetheless true that it held an important place in his preaching (cf. J. Jeremias, *New Testament Theology*, I, 1971, pp. 61–8; Schrenk, art. *'pater,* etc', *TWNT*, V, 1954, pp. 946–1024 (ET V, pp. 945–1022)). From this angle again the hymn then looks specifically, not to say exclusively, 'Christian' and there is no need to look elsewhere for the origin of the terms it uses (against Lohmeyer). In particular the hymn shows us that history could have consisted of relationships merely of power (v. 6b: *'harpagmos'*) whereas it culminates with the revelation of a fatherhood inspiring confidence and love.

4. *Appeal for communal harmony* (2[12–18])

(12) *So then, my beloved, you who have always acted with obedience, turn to good account the salvation which is yours in a spirit of respect and humility, not only in view of my return but even more from this very moment, although I am absent.* (13) *For it is God who promotes among you the will and the action for good relationships.* (14) *Do everything without arguing and disputing;* (15) *become irreproachable and pure, blameless children of God in the midst of a perverse and erring generation, where you shine as lights in the world,* (16) *bearers of a word of life; it will be to my glory in the day of Christ, that I have not run or laboured in vain.* (17) *In so far as it is like a libation completing the sacrifice and service of your faith (this running and labouring of mine) I rejoice, and I rejoice along with all of you.* (18) *In the same way, do you all rejoice, and rejoice along with me.*

DENIS, M. A., 'La fonction apostolique et la liturgie nouvelle en Esprit. Etude thématique des métaphores pauliniennes du culte nouveau', *RSPT*, 42, 1958, pp. 617–56.

Didier, G., *Le désintéressement du chrétien*, 1955.

Eichholz, *G.*, 'Bewahren und Bewähren des Evangeliums: der Leitfaden von Phil. 1–2', in *Hören und Handeln. Festschrift für E.
Wolf* (ed. H. Goldwitzer and H. Traub), 1962, pp. 85–105.

Glombitza, O., 'Mit Furcht und Zittern. Zum Verständnis von Phil.
2.12', *NT*, 3, 1959, pp. 100–106.

The text is assured and the variants of no consequence. We may observe
however that B, 33, 1241 and some versions suppress the '*hōs*' in v. 12,
so lightening an overloaded sentence. In v. 15 the *Koiné*, D, G read '*amō-
mēta*' for its synonym '*amōma*' no doubt under the influence of Dt. 32[5];
and P 46, A, D* and G replaced the '*genesthe*' by a form of the verb 'to
be', namely, '*ēte*'.

In approaching this passage the actual situation of those to whom
it is addressed must not be lost from sight. It is because the community at Philippi was a prey to dissensions and rivalries that the
apostle had judged it necessary to introduce the hymn of vv. 6–11,
though not primarily as a guide for imitation (cf. *ad* 2[5]). It is in the
face of the same situation that he now exhorts his readers to act with
'respect and humility' (v. 12), 'in good harmony' (v. 13) and 'without
murmuring and disputing' (v. 14). In this way they will 'turn to good
account' ('*katergazesthe*') the 'salvation' ('*sōtēria*') which has just
been so magnificently described to them (v. 12) in the Christ-drama.
There are no reasons for speaking here of a 'fresh departure' (Barth,
Michaelis), nor for raising the question whether vv. 12–18 belong
directly with 1[27ff] before the Christological hymn (Dibelius, Ewald,
Staab, Tillmann) or on the other hand take up again the major theme
of the hymn which is obedience (Bonnard, Martin, Vincent).

2[12] There is no appeal here to 'achieve salvation' and it is pointless to
imagine with Dibelius that Paul is using a Jewish maxim. The
demand is to carry it through, to 'make fruitful' (notice the force of
the prefix '*kata-*' upon the basic '*energeō*' which is used of the
divine action in the following verse) what has already been given.
The totality of actions presented in vv. 6–11 are summarised here as
'salvation'. Both the context and the plural '*heautōn*' ('the salvation
of all of you') also show that the word has not only an individual
sense but denotes above all a reality which is both wider and communal (Bonnard, Gnilka, Martin, Michael; G. Didier, *op. cit.*, p.
150). It is incumbent on the community to live out this reality—and
that requires both 'obedience' ('*kathōs pantote hupēkousate*') and
'respect and humility' ('*meta phobou kai tromou*').
   The first of these characteristics does not primarily mean obedience
to the apostle (Barth, Dibelius, Gnilka), nor to the authoritative
figures of the community (Bonnard) but as often with Paul (Rom.
1[5]; 15[18]; 16[19], etc.) to the faith itself as expressed in day to day
attitudes and here as it issues from the work of Christ ('*hupēkoos*',

v. 8; Lohmeyer). The second characteristic is less easily determined. O. Glombitza (*art. cit.*) has even suggested connecting the negative '*mē*' at the beginning of the verse with the verb '*katergazesthe*' and translating, 'Work at your salvation *without* fear or trembling!' But such a construction seems forced and there is no evidence elsewhere that the Philippians had been subject to 'complexes' from which Paul may have wanted to free them. Far from it! Yet Glombitza is right to stress that the expression '*phobos kai tromos*' does not apply in Paul's usage to the relation of man to God but of man to his fellow men (1 Cor. 2³; 2 Cor. 7⁵; Eph. 6⁵). So we are still dealing strictly with communal life at Philippi (Barth, Bonnard). Furthermore, for the apostle the phrase has a much attenuated force and means something like 'humbly', 'respectfully' (G. Eichholz, *art. cit.*, p. 103).

As throughout this part of the letter Paul shows himself extremely cautious in the comments made to his readers about their behaviour; his criticisms appear in an amicable light; so he does not hesitate to address them as '*agapētoi*', 'beloved', an appellation which will occur again in 4¹. He is also insistent on a point which is not usually sufficiently stressed: 'not only in view of my return, but even more from this very moment'. It seems actually hardly likely that the '*parousia*' should here mean Paul's past presence at Philippi (against Bonnard and Michaelis); the parallelism with 1²⁷ and the matters which will arise in 2¹⁹ᶠᶠ show rather that the forthcoming arrival of the apostle is meant (Lohmeyer). Consequently the particle '*hōs*', which has blemished some manuscripts and which can only be an encumbrance if it is given its usual comparative force, must be taken in its acceptable though less frequent meaning of 'with a view to', 'in view of'. It is not fear of the big, bad wolf—i.e. the apostle, who, of course, does not know just when he will return to Philippi—which should be the motive for good feeling among the Philippians. This motive lies elsewhere as the following verse shows.

2¹³ Understanding of this verse has been too much influenced by Catholic/Protestant polemics about synergism and grace. 'Here is the real artillery to topple every lofty fortress', says Calvin, opening a discussion of free will. What in fact must be sought is the point of contact between v. 13 and v. 12. Barth seems to make the text say more than it intends when he says that humility alone can reign among Christians because everything which takes place within them is not their own work but God's. On our view the linkage occurs rather through the allusion to the presence and absence of the apostle. 'You do not need to wait for my arrival to reform your community life (says Paul) because ("*gar*") it is God himself, not I, who presides over this.' Once again, '*en humin*' must be taken with reference to the community ('among you') and not individualistically ('within you')—with Beare, Bonnard, Gnilka, Martin; against Michaelis and Vincent. Further, '*eudokia*' should not here be given the meaning it usually has in the Bible of 'God's good pleasure' (against the majority of commentaries). This would involve giving the unacceptable meaning of 'in conformity with' to the preposition '*huper*' ('*eudokias*'), a meaning so alien to it that B–D (§231.2) feel obliged to attach '*huper tēs eudokias*' to the following sentence, which only raises more problems than it solves. The only interpretation which really takes account both of the context and grammatical rigour is the one which gives '*eudokia*' its anthropological meaning of 'good understanding' (Ewald-Wohlenberg, Tillmann; Arndt-Gingrich *Lexicon*, *loc. cit.*). This is also its meaning in **1**[15] the only other place where it occurs in the epistle (cf. Rom. 10[1]; 2 Thess. 1[11]).

Having said this it remains true that the verse gives God a dominant place at the very heart of human activity; he it is who 'energises' ('*ho energōn*') the action of man ('*to energein*') and even motivates it ('*to thelein*'). But it must be noticed that Paul does not state this truth in a *restrictive* sense as though putting a bridle upon human freedom, but rather with a *positive, out-going* meaning; henceforward no obstacle can any longer shackle the efforts of men 'directed at mutual good will' since God himself is at work in these efforts. Divine action does not curtail human action but rather provokes a reaction which it supports. The '*energein*' of God provokes the '*katergazein*' of man (v. 12); the salvation *already* achieved is *still* to be actualised.

2[14] There is continuity between v. 13 and v. 14, so that it is not clear why Gnilka and Michaelis want to start a new paragraph here. The purport is clear: 'Oh that the Philippians would stop arguing!' The four New Testament instances of '*gonggusmos*' concern the attitude of men to each other (cf. K. H. Rengstorf, art. '*gongguzō*, etc.' *TWNT*, I, 1933, pp. 727–37 (ET I, pp. 728–37)), so it should not be taken here as an attitude towards God (against Beare, Gnilka). Likewise the '*dialogismoi*' which the Philippians should avoid are not doubts or denials (Lohmeyer) but, as always in Paul, unhealthy speculations; and in this instance we shall think of the empty arguments in which the false apostles at Philippi may have indulged.

2[15–16a] The 'good appearance' of the Christian community is linked also with its objective. It is not a question of a closed society, living by itself and for itself; the church exists only as a function of its purpose and this purpose determines the form of the church. It is this purpose which the apostle now calls to mind, resorting no doubt to a traditional theme. The wording in fact is not at all Pauline; the quotation (elaborated!) from Dt. 32[5] seems to be the result of reflection which is not apparent here, and the mention of the 'world' ('*en kosmō*') forms a pleonasm with the '*en hois*' which introduces the relative clause. The fact remains that the purpose of the church appears here as 'holding up the light to a world of darkness in the perspective of a judgement to come'. That the statement is polemical is not to be excluded. To adversaries proud of their Jewish descent (3[2ff]) Paul gives a reminder that even Scripture itself admits that these people are 'perverse and crooked' (Dt. 32[5]) and that it is right for the church to keep away from them; and adversaries claiming to be radiant with their ecstasies (cf. 2 Cor. 3) are reminded by the apostle that the only 'illumination' of value is of the order of preaching ('*logon zōēs epechontes*') and of uprightness ('*amemptoi kai akeraioi*').

The irreproachability ('*amemptos*') which is demanded here ('*genēsthe*') is surprisingly enough condemned in 3[6]. That is because the perspective is different. It is to be understood that the ethical is not a prior requirement but a consequence; no 'salvation' can be founded upon it, yet it flows like a spring from a 'salvation' already given which has still to diffuse itself. Because of this diffusion it is necessary also to be '*akeraios*', uncontaminated, intact, pure.[1] The transformation undergone by the text of Dt. 32[5] here quoted is significant for the position of the early church in relation to Israel. The text says in effect: 'Although they (the Israelites) have corrupted themselves, no fault attaches to him (God); the shame is his children's, a perverse and crooked race' (LXX: '*hēmartosan ouk autō tekna mōmēta, genea skolia kai diestrammenē*'). So then the church takes over from Israel the privilege of being God's 'child', but a child 'without reproach' ('*amōma*'), not a bad, blameworthy child ('*mōmēta*'), and robbed of this privilege nothing remains for Israel but to melt away into the 'perverse and straying' mass of the world's ('*en kosmō*') humanity. These two latter adjectives both suggest something twisted, astray; they are both used elsewhere to qualify '*genea*' in Acts 2[40] ('*skolia*') and Mt. 17[17] ('*diestrammenē*').

In Judaism Adam or certain great rabbis were regarded as light-bearers (Billerbeck, I, p. 236f); here it is the duty[2] of Christians to bear light to the world. The noun '*phōstēr*' simply means 'light' or 'that which gives light' and there is no need to regard it as a metaphor referring to the stars. The word and the idea itself is found only here in Paul, who however explains its meaning immediately: the light is a word and the word conveys life. Conversely, the life can *only* be conveyed by that word.

2[16b] The final argument directed at convincing the Philippians of the necessity for a community life 'in Christ' is the apostle's fate in the 'day of Christ' (cf. *ad* 1[9]). Will they allow him to have 'run and laboured in vain'? The figure of the race is found a number of times in the epistles either for the Christian life in general (Gal. 5[7]; 3[12ff]; (Rom. 9[16])) or for the apostolic ministry in particular (1 Cor. 9[24ff];

---

[1] The word is only found again with Paul in Rom. 16[19] where he is grappling with adversaries akin to those he combats here.

[2] '*Phainesthe*' could be either an imperative (Michaelis) or an indicative (Bonnard, Gnilka, Lohmeyer).

Gal. 2²; 2¹⁶; 2 Thess. 3¹).¹ The verb 'kopiaō' itself is used by Paul of the pains and sufferings which go with apostolic activity.² It is symptomatic how, in defining his ministry, the apostle does not have recourse to a vocabulary associated with honour, dignity or 'glory' but on the contrary to words denoting effort and difficulties. Yet honour itself does come; not from the apostle himself or from his office but from others—from those who will be his 'pride in the Day of Christ'. The word 'kauchēma' therefore bears a meaning here which borders upon joy (G. Didier, op. cit., p. 152).

2¹⁷ Everything in this verse seems to be an allusion to the imminent martyrdom of the apostle and Lohmeyer appropriately finds it one of the strongest supports for his theory. Likewise Bonnard affirms: 'Even if Paul has to die and be offered as a sacrifice ('spendomai') he will rejoice with the Philippians because he will be united with them in a single offering to God, the apostle offering his life and the Philippians their faith'. Michaelis, T. W. Manson (BJRL, 23, 1939, p. 184f) and A. M. Denis (RSPT, 42, 1958, pp. 630–45) seem quite isolated when they think that Paul is referring only to the general difficulties of the apostolate.

And yet is it not surprising, this single note of joy sounded in connection with the supposed martyrdom? At most, we might imagine an exhortation to joy; it is difficult to think of joy coming as a matter of course ('sungchairō pasin humin'). We can hardly suppose, with Lohmeyer, that the Philippians themselves were also suffering persecution and rejoiced at seeing the apostle join them in martyrdom. Gnilka and Haupt try to avoid the difficulty by attaching 'epi tē thusia' to 'chairō' and not to 'spendomai': 'Even if I suffer martyrdom I rejoice because of the sacrifice of your faith'. But this disrupts the sacrificial metaphor which unites 'spendomai' ('to pour a libation') and 'thusia' ('sacrifice'). Moreover, a few verses further on (v. 24) Paul reiterates his hope of soon being with the Philippians.

Can one be quite sure that the verb 'spendomai' denotes a killing? The detailed study by A. M. Denis gives grounds for doubting it. In the active voice the verb means 'to make a religious offering of a liquid' or simply 'to pour out'. In the middle voice the meaning is 'to pour libations one for another', i.e. 'to make a treaty', 'to seal an agreement on certain terms' ('epi' with the dative). A libation accompanied most sacrifices in the Greek world and in the Jewish cultus it concluded the entire liturgy, rounding off the daily sacrifices. Never in the Greek Bible nor in the Hellenistic world is this word used for libations of blood (='haimassein').

The link which may hold vv. 16 and 17 together is still to be determined. Barth and Lohmeyer make v. 17 start a new paragraph

---

¹ Cf. V. C. Pfitzner, Paul and the Agon Mitif, 1967; O. Bauernfeind, art. 'trechō, etc.', TWNT, VIII, 1969, pp. 225–35 (ET VIII, pp. 226–35).
² A. v. Harnack, '"Kopos (kopian, hoi kopiōntes)" im frühchristlichen Sprachgebrauch', ZNW, 27, 1928, pp. 1–10.

(2¹⁷-3¹ᵃ) which links more directly with 1²⁶ than with what immediately precedes. Why, then, the conjunction 'but' ('*alla*')?
Gnilka does not explain it either when he thinks that the allusion to the
apostle's sufferings in v. 16 means the ultimate suffering which still
awaits him. Actually, Paul has just asked himself whether his sufferings for the community at Philippi do not risk being in vain
(v. 16). But he does not want to end on so pessimistic a note so he
adds that to the degree in which his sufferings have set a seal on the
sacrifice of faith of the Philippians—just as a libation completes a
sacrifice—there is every reason to rejoice: 'But ('*alla*') if it is ('*ei kai*'
is here restrictive rather than concessive, cf. 2 Cor. 5¹⁶) over the
sacrifice of your faith that I suffer, then I do so with joy'. Here as
elsewhere in the epistle joy does not arise from some peculiar
mystique of martyrdom but is the mark of a community ('*sungchairō
pasin humin*') which lives for the advancement of the Gospel (1¹²⁻¹⁸).

Faith ('*pistis*') is precisely what the apostle intends to reawaken at
Philippi (cf. 1²⁹ and 3²ᶠᶠ), and if here it is qualified by 'sacrifice'
('*thusia*') and 'liturgy' ('*leitourgia*') that is because these are the signs
by which it is manifest and which so lamentably fail to appear among
his correspondents. This is clear with reference to the spirit of sacrifice (cf. Eph. 5²; Rom. 12¹), but it is so too for '*leitourgia*', which
means not the service of worship but public service (cf. Strathmann,
art. '*leitourgeō*, etc.', *TWNT*, IV, 1942, pp. 221–38 (ET IV, pp.
215–31)). It is also not impossible that Paul is alluding to the material
aid which the Philippians have sent to him in prison (for '*thusia*' cf.
ad 4¹⁸; for '*leitourgia*' cf. Rom. 13⁶; 15²⁷; 2 Cor. 9¹²; 2²⁵⁻³⁰). The
apostle therefore concludes this section of his letter dealing with the
condition of the Christian community at Philippi with a reminder
that beyond any defects and unfaithfulness it is in conformity with
the 'faith of the Gospel' (1²⁷), and this at least prevents him from
regarding his sufferings as useless and compels him to rejoice and he
would wish that all of them might do so with him.

2¹⁸ This is again stressed in v. 18, where '*to de auto*' means 'in the
same way' (so most commentaries) rather than 'for the same reason'
(Vincent). Without going as far as Beare who takes the '*chairete*' as
'farewell' it should be observed that the accumulation of appeals for
rejoicing is indicative that a letter is reaching its conclusion.

FOURTH PART

The immediate future: $2^{19}-3^{1a}+4^{2-7}+(4^{21-23})$

After dealing with his own circumstances (1^{12-26}) and then those of the community at Philippi ($1^{27}-2^{18}$) the apostle ends his letter, as he so often does, by touching upon particular matters relating to the immediate future. This brings him to speaking of companions who are with him (2^{19-30}) or are at Philippi (4^{2ff}). Reference to this web of human concerns, to people of whom otherwise we know next to nothing, throws more light than a long treatise on the reality of the Christian fellowship at that time ('*sungkoinōnoi*': 1^7; 4^{14}), in which we encounter the richness but also all the problems of a typical human society. The apostle recognises and accepts the richness and does not evade the problems; he lives in no idealistic realm which has lost its grip on human affairs. He does not disguise the difficulties but he views them in a serene and brotherly spirit arising from the light which the Gospel sheds over all things, preventing any obstacle from assuming an undue importance. In a conquering spirit he faces up to the difficulties so that joy yet again shines through this last section of the letter (2^{28f}; 3^{1a}; 4^4).

For the analysis of the letter to which we were led reference should be made to the Introduction §2, but in the Commentary we follow the traditional order of the verses. Originally, this section was arranged as follows:

1. The mission of Timothy (2^{19-24})
2. The return of Epaphroditus ($2^{25}-3^{1a}$)
3. Final exhortations (4^{2-7})
4. Greetings and blessing (4^{21-23})

1. *The mission of Timothy* (2^{19-24})

(19) *I hope in the Lord Jesus soon to send Timothy to you, that I also may be reassured by having news of you.* (20) *He is the only one who truly shares my preoccupations and can legitimately deal with your affairs.* (21) *For all seek their own interests and not those of Jesus Christ.* (22) *You know that he has approved himself and that by my side he has served the cause of the Gospel like a son with his father.* (23) *So I hope to send him as soon as I see my situation clearly,* (24) *confident also in the Lord that I myself shall soon rejoin you.*

In v. 21 the form 'Jesus Christ' is better attested than the more archaic

'Christ Jesus' (B, the *Koiné*). In v. 23, C and the *Koiné* have the non-aspirate form '*apidō*' for '*aphidō*', and in v. 24 A and C complete the phrase by adding '*pros humas*'.

We now encounter Timothy again, who appeared in 1^1 as co-author of the letter. His appearance at that point left a doubt whether his authority was unanimously accepted at Philippi and the present passage confirms this. Paul takes every precaution by insisting that Timothy is 'one of the best', although this does not prevent him promising in the end to come himself. This shows again the gravity of the situation at Philippi which Timothy, whatever his ability otherwise, will find it difficult to tackle. The somewhat spineless character of Timothy is apparent also from 1 Cor. 16^{10}; 2 Tim. 1^{6ff}; 1 Tim. 4^{12}. There is no reason at all to speak as Bonnard does of a 'definite instance of the transmission of apostolic authority to an assistant of the second generation of Christians', which presupposes the imminent death of the apostle. In fact, Paul does not know exactly when he will be freed, or the time he will need to deal with the problems of the community at Ephesus (cf. 1^{15-18}), so he prefers to lose no time and sends Timothy to Philippi as quickly as possible. It goes without saying that all these plans could much more easily mature in a Ephesian setting than a Roman one.

2^{19} The verb '*elpizō*' ('to hope') is sometimes used of the apostle's travel plans (Rom. 15^{24}; 1 Cor. 16^7; Phm. 22) which shows that there is nothing exceptional about the present situation (Michaelis). If this hope is 'in the Lord' this is no doubt to stress indirectly the importance of Timothy's mission which is thereby placed under the authority of the Lord of the church. The explicit aim of the mission is news of Philippi which could reassure the apostle; the implicit aim is doubtless the Philippians' return to 'orthodoxy'. The verb '*eupsuchō*' is rare and occurs here only in the New Testament; it is often found in funerary inscriptions where it expresses condolences, but there are no grounds for thinking that by use of it here Paul is hinting either at his own near death or at martyrdom among the Philippians. On the contrary, what is striking is the '*kagō*' ('I also') with its implication that the Philippians will be reassured by the news sent to them by the apostle concerning his own destiny. This destiny is far from being fatal and Paul, for his own part, wants *also* to be reassured about the Philippians.

2^{20} The adjective '*isopsuchos*' is rare and means literally 'of equal soul' or 'power' or 'feeling' (cf. Panagotis Christou, ' "*Isopsukos*" Phil. 2.20', *JBL*, 70, 1951, pp. 293–96). But what is the object implied? It could be interpreted as 'I have no one who shares *my* preoccupations as he does and who . . .' (Bonnard, Huby, Vincent; Panagotis Christou), or as 'I have no one among those who are equal to *him* who . . .' (Beare, Gnilka, Michael, Michaelis). The context

favours the former, as does the word-play with the preceding
'*eupsuchō*': Paul wants it to be quite clear that the decisions Timothy
may make will be his (Paul's) as well and no one should oppose the
disciple on the grounds that his master might not think as he does.
Again, it is Timothy alone who can *legitimately* ('*gnēsiōs*') deal with
the problems of the community. Commentators are too hasty who
commonly say that the adverb '*gnēsiōs*' does not have its original
sense of 'authentically', 'legitimately' here. So Bonnard, Benoit,
Michaelis and Gnilka who translate it as 'sincerely', Vincent as
'truly', and Lohmeyer who reads 'equally well'. But the father-son
simile appearing in v. 22 leaves no ambiguity: Timothy is a legitimate son, the sole authorised representative of the apostle (Lightfoot; cf. 1 Tim. 1 [2]; Tit. 1 [4]).

2 [21] The verse is not a striking illustration of the isolation in which
the apostle found himself at the end of his life, as is often said. The
'*pantes*' ('all') has a measure of exaggeration aimed at reinforcing
once more Timothy's authority. The striking analogy with v. 4 of the
same chapter (Barth) should also be noted, such that it could be
asked whether Paul is not rather alluding here to the situation at
Philippi than to that of the community at Ephesus: 'If any one
among you, whosoever he may be, questions Timothy's authority,
then be sure it will be out of self-concern and not concern for Christ'.

2 [22] Timothy, in fact, is nothing less than a son to the apostle (cf. 1
Cor. 4 [17]; 1 Tim. 1 [2,18]; 2 Tim. 1 [2]; 2 [1]). But this status has nothing
arbitrary about it; it springs from companionship ('*sun emoi*'; on
the rather clumsy structure of this phrase, cf. Dibelius and Vincent)
in service ('*douleuō*'). Here again the intention of 1 [1] re-emerges and
more especially the basic meaning of our whole chapter, that
authority can rest only upon humility and service; yet not upon any
kind of service but upon that of which the aim and content is the
Gospel ('*eis to euanggelion*'), that is to say the announcement of
God's free and mighty intervention in history through the event of
the Cross and Resurrection (cf. *ad* 1 [5]). Here again we encounter the
very theme of the letter. For there is nothing easy in serving the
Gospel; this service carries with it 'tests' ('*dokimē*') which from Rom.
5 [4] we learn are to be ranked between patience and hope.

2 [23] This takes up v. 19, making it more precise and delimiting it:
Timothy will not leave immediately; before he does so Paul must
have a clearer view of his own situation. And this (let it be said
again) not because his life is in danger and in case of mishap he
wants to have Timothy at hand (Gnilka, Lohmeyer) but because,
immersed in the legal processes which are under way, with the
delicate situation within the Ephesian community and the varying
news he may receive from other communities, the apostle cannot
make precise plans for the immediate future (Michaelis). '*Aphoraō*'

here means 'to view from a distance', 'to have in full view'; *'hōs an'*, 'as soon as', as in Rom. 15²⁴ and 1 Cor. 11³⁴. After *'hōs an exautēs' 'tēs hōras'* must be understood (cf. B–D §§12.3; 241.3).

2²⁴ The confidence the apostle shows about his own visit to Philippi is no less strong than it is for Timothy's (against Michael), so that we see clearly that the idea of imminent death was far from the apostle's mind. From **1²⁵** to **2²⁴** the thought is quite definite and his arrival at Philippi is seen as a project 'in the Lord', that is to say springing from ('in') the Lord of the church and also subject to him (Barth; Calvin; cf. *ad* **2¹⁰** and **2¹⁹**).

2. *The return of Epaphroditus* (**2²⁵–3¹ᵃ**)

(25) *But I have thought it necessary to send back to you Epaphroditus, my brother, my companion in the work and the conflict, and your envoy charged to provide for my needs.* (26) *For he was longing for you all and was distressed that you had heard of his illness.* (27) *He was ill indeed and at the brink of death; but God had mercy on him, and not on him only but on me as well that I might not have grief upon grief.* (28) *So I am sending him as quickly as possible that seeing him might make you happy and that I too might be less sorrowful.* (29) *Receive him therefore in the Lord with unmixed joy; show esteem for people like him,* (30) *because it was for the work of Christ that he came near to death, having risked his life deputising for you in the service you could not render me yourselves.*—(**3¹ᵃ**) *Finally, my brothers, rejoice in the Lord.*

D and the Alexandrine tradition add *'idein'* in v. 26 after *'epipothōn'* by analogy with Rom. 1¹¹; 1 Thess. 3⁶; 2 Tim. 1⁴. In v. 27 *'paraplēsion'* is construed with the dative rather than with the genitive (B, P); in v. 30 one hesitates between the readings *'Christou'* (P 46, B, G, *al*), *'tou Christou'* (the *Koinē*, D) and *'kuriou'* (ℵ, A, P) unless with C and Lightfoot one simply eliminates the defining genitive. However, *'paraboleusamenos'* ('he risked his life'), a rare but perfectly correct term, should be preferred to the *'parabouleusamenos'* ('he paid no regard to his life') of the Textus Receptus.

The Epaphroditus here in question had been delegated by the brethren at Philippi to bring their monetary gift to the apostle in his need. This is said clearly in **4¹⁸** and it corresponds to the *'apostolos humōn'* ('your envoy') in v. 25 and to the *'leitourgos/leitourgia'* of vv. 25 and 30. The name Epaphroditus was common in the Greek of the day and meant 'Amiable', 'Charming'. In the New Testament it occurs only here and in **4¹⁸**. The name Epaphras mentioned in Col. 1⁷; 4¹²; Phm. 23 may have had the same origin (cf. B–D §125.1) but it seems unlikely that one and the same person is meant. At this point Paul thinks it necessary to send Epaphroditus back to his own folk after the severe illness which had brought him to the brink of death. It seems unprofitable to speculate about other particular reasons which may have induced Paul to send him back; Lohmeyer suggests persecution, Gnilka the fact that he could be a substitute for Timothy who for the moment was hindered from making his way to Philippi. What is clear is that Paul saw the need to load him with praise as though to ward off certain reproaches. Would the Philippians think he had not stayed long enough with the apostle (Bonnard, Ewald-Wohlenberg, Gnilka, Friedrich)? It is quite likely that Epaphroditus was the bearer of this letter (B) otherwise it would be hard to understand what interest the news in the letter could have if Epaphroditus had already previously[1] arrived at Philippi. Finally, this paragraph takes for granted a considerable number of communications to-and-fro between Paul and Philippi[2] which points rather to an Ephesian origin for the letter.

From a more theological angle, it is striking to see Paul in another light than that of a talented polemicist. His friendliness appears here in its depth and sincerity, and just as before (cf. 2^{22}) it has been forged in the service of the Gospel, in struggles and suffering. Verse 29f lay particular stress upon this in striking contrast with the scale of values current in the community at Philippi (cf. 2^{1ff}). It is precisely in the midst of difficult situations, even life and death ones, that an authentic experience of grace occurs (v. 27)—'My grace is sufficient for you, for my power is made perfect in weakness' (2 Cor. 12^9). The only true 'liturgy', the only 'sacrifice acceptable to God and which he receives' (2^{25-30}; 4^{18}) therefore consists essentially in this struggle shoulder to shoulder on behalf of the Gospel under the perpetual threat looming over those who go forward under the shadow of the Cross so that they may also have continually the transforming experience of the reality of the Resurrection.

2^{25} The return of Epaphroditus proceeds from an inner conviction ('*anangkaion*') like those expressed in 1^{24} or 2 Cor. 9^5 where the same phrase is used, '*anangkaion hēgēsamēn*'. The aorist is doubtless an epistolary aorist, the writer putting himself in the place and time of his readers, and therefore it does not necessarily imply that Epaphroditus had already left at the time Paul was writing (for the meaning of the verb, cf. *ad* $2^{3,6}$; $3^{7,8}$).

Epaphroditus is described with five different words, the first three showing particularly how he is attached to Paul and the two last his attachment to the Philippians. First, he is 'my brother' ('*adelphos*'), which is not merely a synonym for 'Christian' (against Boor, Matter,

---

[1] Beare, Dibelius, Haupt, Heinzelmann, Lightfoot, Michael, Michaelis, Staab, Vincent.

[2] Five can be counted: the Philippians learn of Paul's imprisonment; Epaphroditus is sent; the Philippians hear of their envoy's illness; *he* hears that his friends are worrying about him; Epaphroditus is sent back. It is true that the figure could be reduced to three or four by accepting the complicated hypotheses of LIGHTFOOT (p. 37) or C. O. BUCHANAN, 'Epaphroditus' sickness and the Letter to the Philippians', *EQ*, 36, 1964, pp. 157–66.

Heinzelmann) but which shows the affection of the apostle, rooted of course in his faith (Beare, Bonnard, Gnilka, Jones, Péry). But this brotherliness was forged essentially in common work and conflict, and so we have two words commencing with '*sun-*', which is one of the familiar characteristics of this epistle (cf. *ad* 1⁷). The first of these is almost restricted in the New Testament to the Pauline vocabulary (12 out of 13 times) in which it is used of a disciple or a colleague with the idea that master and disciple are together engaged in God's great work of the Gospel (1 Cor. 3⁹; 2 Cor. 6¹; cf. Bertram, art, '*sunergos*, etc.', *TWNT*, VII, 1964, pp. 869–75 (ET VII, pp. 871–76)). The second word is a military term for those who have fought side by side, though Bauernfeind thinks that in Paul's time it had been strongly influenced by Zealotism or Pharisaism (art. '*strateuomai*, etc.', *TWNT*, VII, 1964, pp. 701–13 (ET *ibid.*)). However that may be, the Gospel is represented here as a combat which Epaphroditus has not shirked.

From the Philippian side, Epaphroditus is the envoy to the apostle ('*apostolos*' in the loose sense of 2 Cor. 8²³, with a suggestion of delegated powers; Benoit) whom they have commissioned. To meet Paul's material needs ('*chreia*', cf. 4¹⁶⁻¹⁹; Rom. 12¹³) is to do the work of a 'minister' ('*leitourgos*'). The word has very little in common with its modern application. In secular Greek words of the '*leitourgeō*' family covered a great variety of public services (cf. Strathmann, art. '*leitourgeō*, etc.' *TWNT*, IV, 1942, pp. 221–38 (ET IV, pp. 215–31)). It is only the LXX, giving priority to just one of the current meanings, that will employ it specially in the cultic realm. Paul usually keeps to a secular usage (cf. *ad* 2¹⁷), but the association twice with '*thusia*' ('sacrifice') in 2¹⁷ and 4¹⁸ clearly shows that the cultic application is not entirely absent and that Paul's use indeed reflects a theological intention which is particularly clear in Rom. 12¹ff: the worship acceptable to God is that which shows itself in the practical solidarity of those who strive for the advancement of the Gospel.

2²⁶ The cause ('*epeidē*', cf. B–D §456.3) of Epaphroditus' return lies with his illness and his homesickness to see his own folk (for '*epipotheō*' cf. *ad* 1⁸). There are no grounds for suspecting an underlying reason for his distress—the verb '*adēmonō*' is the strong one used to describe Christ's agony in Gethsemane according to Mk. 14³³ and Mt. 26³⁷—such as the difficult circumstances of the community at Philippi (Calvin, Lohmeyer, Scott), although that cannot be excluded.

2²⁷ The apostle now elaborates upon the seriousness of Epaphroditus' illness (intensive '*kai gar*') which had brought him to the brink of death (the adverbial use of '*paraplēsion*' here only in the New Testament). Lohmeyer, from his angle of martyrdom, is surprised to find that Paul does not regard death as a great blessing, but we

should be struck, as Calvin was, by the apostle's 'humanity': 'Paul
here shows a human sensitivity which puts him far beyond the harsh-
ness of the Stoics' (Calvin); his strength does not lie in any passive
acceptance but in recourse to the mercy of God (Bonnard). Moreover,
the verse gives food for thought about what is usually called 'faith
healing' (Hendriksen). Paul says nothing about resorting to any
thaumaturgic activities; he mentions neither faith nor prayer nor the
laying on of hands any more than he does the effect of medicines or
of a doctor. It goes without saying that these various procedures are
more or less taken for granted, yet what concerns the apostle is not
the healing itself but its significance. He sees it as a sovereign, merci-
ful act of God himself ('*eleēsen*'), that is to say as a concrete and
definite manifestation of the great purpose which, in Jesus Christ,
touches all aspects of history and the whole of humanity (cf. again
G. Crespy, *La guérison par la foi*, 1952). But inasmuch as these manifestations of mercy are of God they are not mechanical events taking
place of their own accord. Paul is well aware that in addition to his
imprisonment and his difficulties with the community at Ephesus he
had been prepared to endure the death of a companion and thereby
to suffer 'grief upon grief' ('*lupēn epi lupēn schō*').

2²⁸ The comparative '*spoudaioterōs*' ('more speedily') can have the
force of a superlative (B–D §244) unless 'than expected' or 'than
Timothy' is to be understood as completing the comparison. In
sending Epaphroditus back as quickly as possible (again '*epempsa*'
is an epistolary aorist, cf. v. 25) Paul wants to be consistent with the
sum total of preoccupations which have been his hitherto, namely,
to impart joy—a joy produced as much by visible proof of Epaphroditus' recovery as by the mere fact of his return.

2²⁹ᶠ Nevertheless the apostle has a foreboding that the joy may well
not be unmixed. No doubt the Philippians, accustomed to a scale of
values which we have seen denounced at the beginning of the chapter, may have been disappointed by the lack of drive or ostentation
of their envoy. But, says the apostle, it is precisely this type of person
who should be honoured (cf. Rom. 16²) and 'welcomed in the
Lord', i.e. according to the spirit of the hymn 2⁶⁻¹¹; for in the church
what in fact should induce respect and to some extent be a criterion of
authority is not concern for oneself and for one's own reputation
(2²¹) but concern for the Gospel ('*to ergon Christou*'; cf. *ad* 1⁶).
Epaphroditus has not failed in such concern even to the brink of
death. The Gospel, moreover, implies a community and Epaphroditus has sacrificed himself for the life of this community. Such,
indeed, is the 'worship' ('*leitourgia*', cf. *ad* 2²⁵) which is acceptable to
God.

3¹ᵃ Sometimes taken as a conclusion to what precedes (Heinzelmann,
Lightfoot, Scott), or as an introduction to what follows (Lohmeyer,

E.P.P.—5

Matter, Vincent), **3¹** ought rather to be divided into two halves (Barth, Beare, Ewald, Gnilka, Haupt). Verse 1a still belongs to letter B and marks the transition with the appeal to Euodia, Syntyche and other of Paul's friends at Philippi (4²⁻⁷) in which the exhortation to 'rejoice in the Lord' reappears with urgency (3¹ᵃ; 4⁴); while v. 1b starts letter C (cf. Introduction §2). *'To loipon'* is actually used by the apostle both in the conclusion to a letter (2 Cor. 13¹¹; cf.4⁸) and to introduce an exhortation (Eph. 4¹; 1 Thess. 4¹; 2 Thess. 3¹). It is also associated with a reference to the 'brethren' (*'adelphoi'*) in 1 Thess. 4¹; 2 Thess 3¹; 4⁸; here they are mentioned in 1¹² (cf. 3¹³,¹⁷; 4¹,⁸). In the ancient world the term 'brethren' was already in use for members of the same religious community and is absent neither from the Old Testament (Jer. 22¹⁸) nor from the Qumran texts (1 QS 6, 10.22). Christian usage could go back to Jesus himself (Mk. 3³³; Mt. 25⁴⁰; 28¹⁰; etc.). Paul makes important use of the word in the plural to designate Christians;[1] even so it is no mere title but indicates profound affection (cf. 1 Cor. 5¹¹; 6⁵⁻⁸; 8¹¹⁻¹³; etc.).

The present imperative *'chairete'* reflects an enduring feature of the Christian life—its joy (Gnilka). Except for the special case of 4¹, it is used exclusively here in letter B (cf. *ad* 1⁴). The appeal again is to realise this 'in the Lord', that is, as springing from the acts at the same time humble and glorious of the One who is spoken about in **2⁶⁻¹¹**.[2]

LETTER C

To know Christ (3¹ᵇ–4¹)

With the second part of **3¹** we reach the third letter of the original correspondence between Paul and the Christians of Philippi, from which correspondence our epistle was compiled. There is no need to repeat the reasoning which led us to this conclusion (cf. *supra*, pp. 3ff), but merely to notice that the change in tone and of the matters at issue between **3** and the preceding chapters is quite obvious; the break is particularly evident in **3¹** itself, the two halves of which are hard to reconcile. Let it be remembered, however, that the apostle is here getting to grips with the same itinerant Jewish Christian preachers as those he was attacking in a more veiled and cautious way in the third part of the previous letter (1²⁷–3¹ᵃ; cf. *supra*, pp. 11ff) and whose kin will be found at Corinth when *2 Corinthians* is

---

[1] Sixty-eight times, 6 of which are in this epistle. But it does not appear in Ephesians or Colossians.
[2] Beare, and Lightfoot see an indication of 'farewell' in the *'chairete'*.

written. Boastful of their Jewish descent, they were demonstrating their Christianity by excellent 'signs'—ecstasies, speaking with tongues, and the like—which drained any theology of the Cross of its significance (v. 18) to the benefit of a theology of an already attained 'perfection' which has nothing further to expect (vv. 12ff). This also signifies confidence in oneself (v.3) and not in the grace of God alone and is lacking in communal *agapé*, so that the Christian life is simply being presented as some kind of competition.

It is therefore important for the apostle to define what 'knowing Christ' really means (v. 10). In general it involves sharing both in his resurrection *and* in his sufferings (v. 10), so that only thus can one have experience, through faith, of grace alone and turn away from all self-glorification (vv. 8–9). This latter is fully typified by the use which has been made of the Old Covenant (vv. 3–7). We also learn that experience of grace leads, surely but humbly, to a glory yet to come (vv. 12–21); and it is only in this humble and difficult companionship that the true community of 'brethren' is actualised (3^{15ff}; 4^1).

The tone is impassioned, the attacks violent, the argument often extremely concise (doubtless through reference to a 'catechism', vv. 7ff), making it difficult to discern any well constructed plan. Leaving aside the direct attacks in v. 2 and vv. 18–19 which are the framework of the chapter the following main sections may be detected:

1. Polemical introduction: vv. 1b–2.
2. A way of life left behind: vv. 3–6.
3. To know Christ: vv. 7–11.
4. The forward march: vv. 12–16.
5. Fresh polemical outburst: vv. 17–19.
6. The true hope: vv. 20–21.
7. Conclusion: $4^1 + 4^{8-9}$

1. *Polemical introduction* (3^{1b-2})

(1b) *To write the same things to you is not irksome to me and is of advantage to you. (2) Beware of the dogs! beware of the evil workers! beware of the mutilation!*

3^{1b} The things' ('*ta auta*') which Paul does not cease repeating are not appeals to joy (Dibelius, Lohmeyer) but warnings about 'dogs'. The warnings were doubtless made in writing ('*graphein*') rather than verbally (against Calvin, Michael, Gnilka) but there is no need to think of lost letters (Barth, Michael, Vincent); **2**, on our interpretation of it, is sufficient (cf. Lightfoot; W. Schmithals, *Paulus . . . 1965*, p. 53). The apostle also claims that his persistence ('*ouk oknēron*') can only be to his correspondents' advantage ('*asphales*'). The antithesis is so elegant that Michael suspects a literary quotation. V. Furnish (*NTS*

10, 1962–63, p. 83f) gives '*asphales*' the equally current meaning of 'specific', 'concrete': after the generalities of **1–2** Paul now wants to turn attention to practical points.

3² Abandoning the oratorical caution which the prologue to letter B displayed (**1¹⁻¹¹**), the apostle starts with a triple warning imperatively presented—'*blepete*'.[1] It is first directed against the 'dogs' ('*kunas*'). In Jewish eyes the dog is unclean and feeds on excreta (Gnilka) though it should not be concluded from this that Paul is attacking people of dissolute conduct (against W. Schmithals, *Paulus* . . ., 1965, pp. 60ff). Perhaps we should think of a baying pack harassing the apostle (Bonnard, Haupt)? But more probably the word would often rise to the lips of the apostle's opponents as an expression of their scorn for all who did not adhere to the laws of Moses; it was used in Judaism for the Gentile unbeliever (cf. Billerbeck, I, p. 724f; III, p. 621f). In which case Paul is merely returning the complement (cf. Barth, Dibelius).

The two qualifications which follow actually take up in mockery 'titles' with which these people trick themselves out. The noun '*ergatēs*' occurs again with Paul only in 2 Cor. 11¹³ where it is used of the 'super-apostles' at work in Corinth; and D. Georgi has shown (*Die Gegner* . . ., 1964, pp. 49–51; cf. also Gnilka) that in the latter case it was a current designation for itinerant preachers. But does not Paul himself elsewhere speak of his apostolic activity as a 'work' (cf. **1²²**)? The Jewish Christians who had arrived at Philippi could then set themselves up as 'workers' ('*ergatai*')—'Workers on behalf of Evil' ('*dolioi*'; 2 Cor. 11¹³) the apostle replies, 'in whom Satan disguises himself as an angel of light' (2 Cor. 11¹⁴).

Their Jewish connections are apparent in the third word Paul uses about them. 'Mutilation', 'cutting' ('*katatomē*') is a wordplay (cf. Rom. 12³; 2 Thess. 3¹¹) on the noun 'circumcision' ('*peritomē*'), the circumcision they extolled as the following verse leaves in no doubt. In reality, understood in a strictly literal sense, circumcision is nothing but a cutting.

2. *A way of life left behind* (**3³⁻⁶**)

(3) *It is we, indeed, who are the (true) circumcision, we whose service is (animated) by the Spirit of God, who boast in Christ Jesus and do not put confidence in ourselves;* (4) *although, for my part, I have good grounds for having confidence in myself. If anyone else thinks he can have confidence in himself, so can I—and more so:* (5) *circumcised on the eighth day, of the race of Israel, of the tribe of Benjamin, a Hebrew*

---

[1] Wanting to bridge the gap between v. 1a and v. 1b, G. D. KILPATRICK suggests taking it not as a warning but merely as an observation: 'You see the dogs . . .' ('"*Blepete*" Philippians 3.2' in *In Memoriam P. Kahle*, ed. M. Black and G. Fohrer, 1968, pp. 146–48). Although this is a possible reading it does not explain the threefold repetition of the word.

son of Hebrew parents; a Pharisee, in regard to the Law; (6) with regard to zeal, a persecutor of the church; with regard to legal righteousness, beyond reproach.

The reading '*theō*' instead of '*theou*' in v. 3 is a *lectio facilior* and is very poorly attested (ℵ𝑐, D*, P). P 46 resolves the difficulty by omitting the word. The *Koiné* in v. 6 reads a masculine ('*zēlon*') which was more usual than the neuter (cf. Acts 5[17]; 2 Cor. 9[2]) but identical in meaning. Some manuscripts (G, 464) add '*theou*' to '*ekklēsian*' by analogy with Gal. 1[13] and 1 Cor. 15[9].

In the face of those who take advantage of 'fleshly' prerogatives v. 3 enunciates the theme which will be developed in what follows, that true circumcision does not consist in an external mark but in a deep transformation of attitude. The illustration which follows is not merely a piece of autobiography, nor even primarily, as in *2 Corinthians*, a defence of his apostolic authority; he is quite simply using his own case as a particularly clear *example* (cf. v. 17) of what every Christian life should be. So the *apostle* does not appear here alongside or over the community but as the spear-head in the *common* struggle in which it should be engaged. This distinction is doubtless not without interest for current discussions about the nature of the 'ministries'.

3[3] The theological compactness of this verse is such that an echo of some catechetical instruction should be envisaged. Thus, the assertion that the church[1] is the true 'circumcision' is intelligible only on the basis of the more explicit passages Rom. 2[27ff]; 4[11f]; Col. 2[11]; Gal. 6[12f]; and we agree with E. Trocmé ('L'épître aux Romains et la méthode missionnaire de l'apôtre Paul', *NTS*, 7, 1960–61, pp. 148–53) that to a large extent the Epistle to the Romans is a reflection of Pauline catechesis. The apostle, therefore, stresses the link between the Old and New Covenants, yet in conformity with prophecies about the New Covenant (Jer. 4[4]; 31[31-34]; 32[37ff]; Ezek. 36[26f]; 44[1]; 1 QS 5.5, 26) he also insists on the need for a profound transformation of man's life. This is made possible by the Spirit which diverts a man from self and opens him to Christ Jesus. The present issue, however, is not that of the Spirit versus external ceremonial (Martin, Michael) but the Spirit as initiator of the New Covenant, at work in the depths of human nature, promoting a life for others, a life of love; such a life is the only worship ('*latreuō*') acceptable to God (cf. *ad* 2[25,30]).

Here 'flesh' ('*sarx*') primarily has the quite specific meaning of fleshly circumcision and membership of the Israelite race; but it also covers justification by the Law and even by man's own religiosity or spirituality.[2] Such 'flesh' is not in itself evil but is open to condemna-

---

[1] We have already said why the 'we' here should not be limited to Paul and his collaborators (against Tillmann).
[2] Cf. H. R. MOEHRING, 'Some remarks on "*sarx*" in Phil. 3.3ff', in *Studia*

tion in so far as it lays claim to being a way of salvation while this is only to be found in Jesus Christ. To 'boast in him' (Martin translates 'rejoice', 'exult' in him) is to acknowledge the objective principle of the eschatological and ultimate intervention by God in human history of which the Spirit is the subjective principle, and so to anchor oneself on something completely outside the self by having resort to faith.

3⁴ It is not from any weakness or cowardice or lack of personal assets that Paul recommends reliance upon Another. His message does not spring from frustration. The argument here clearly recalls 2 Cor. 11²¹ᶠ and 12¹ᶠ. First he will list the 'assets' he could presume upon by birth (v. 5) and then those he has acquired by his own efforts (vv. 5d, 6; Bonnard, Jones, Lohmeyer).

3⁵⁻⁶ With circumcision at the centre of the debate, Paul insists that he has been circumcised in accordance with strictest tradition (cf. Gen. 17¹²; 21⁴; Lev. 12³). The same is true concerning the 'race of Israel'—one is reminded of the '*Israēlitai eisin*; *kagō*' of 2 Cor. 11²². The word '*Israēl*' does not merely indicate ethnic origins but also and above all the glorious past of the Chosen People.[1] In addition, D. Georgi has demonstrated correctly that the word belonged to the apologetic vocabulary of Hellenistic Judaism (*Die Gegner* . . ., 1964, pp. 60–3).

The phrase 'of the tribe or Benjamin' which follows corresponds to '*sperma Abraam eisin; kagō*' in 2 Cor. 11²². There is no need to look for any particular quality possessed by the tribe of Benjamin; Paul is merely stressing his Jewish descent. It is also true that Benjamin enjoyed a measure of special prestige which nevertheless did not put it beyond reproach (Jg. 19²²⁻²⁶; 20³⁵; 21²⁰ᶠ; 2 Sam. 16⁵⁻¹⁴; etc.), a prestige no doubt originating from the fact that Benjamin, together with Joseph, were Rachel's only sons (Michael), and Benjamin was the one child of Jacob born in the Promised Land (Billerbeck). To this tribe the first king belonged (Beare), and this tribe, along with Judah, was the only one to retain its ancient territory after the division of the kingdom and then after the exile. But the reason for this respect could go back more or less consciously to an even earlier date: Benjaminites, nomads contemporary with Abraham, are referred to in the Mari texts, and while their identification with the ancestors of the biblical Benjamin is far from obvious it has been ably defended by A. Parrot (*Abraham et son temps*, 1962, pp. 42–51).

Paul is also a 'Hebrew', a term rare in the New Testament and

---

Evangelica, IV (ed. F. L. Cross), 1968, pp. 432–36; A. SAND, *Der Begriff 'Fleisch'*, 1967, pp. 131ff; E. SCHWEIZER, art. '*sarx*, etc.' *TWNT*, VII, 1964, p. 129f (ET *ibid.*).
[1] G. v. RAD, K. G. KUHN, GUTBROD, art. '*Israēl, Israēlitēs*, etc.' *TWNT*, III, 1938, pp. 356–94 (ET III, pp. 356–91).

which comes from the apostle's pen again only in 2 Cor. 11[22]. As opposed in Acts 6[1] to 'Hellenists' it bears a Palestinian stamp and is essentially linked with Semitic characteristics of language and culture (Dibelius). It was used more than '*Ioudaios*' by the Jewish 'mission' to bring out the antiquity of the religion of Moses, antiquity being to the world of that time a token of wisdom and authenticity (cf. D. Georgi, *Die Gegner . . .*, 1964, pp. 51–60).

But Saul of Tarsus is not content with being 'well born'; he attached himself to the Pharisaic party with its reputation for strictness not to say intransigence (cf. J. Jeremias, *Jerusalem in the Time of Jesus*, ET 1969, pp. 246–67). He pushed his zeal to the point of persecuting the church, and this activity did not appear as a secondary aspect of the life of Saul the Pharisee but as a real vocation, the high-water mark of the zeal which one could show on God's behalf ('*diōkō*' appears as a *terminus technicus* for Paul's attitude before his conversion—Acts 9[4]; 22[4,7,8] , , ,; 1 Cor. 15[9]; Gal. 1[12,23]). But writing to Christians Paul reveals the full tragedy of the heresy of his opponents: to push zeal, to push any religious fanaticism to its limit simply in fact leads to the persecution of the church (Lightfoot, Michael). The church is spoken of in the singular because behind its diversity it is one and to touch one member of the body is to assail the whole body (Martin). With respect to the Law ('*en nomō*') Paul was therefore 'righteous' ('*kata dikaiosunēn*') and 'beyond reproach' ('*amemptos*', cf. *ad* 2[15]). Once more the vocabulary is not easy to understand without the background of the Epistle to the Romans and reference to a 'catechism' about the 'righteousness of God' of which v. 9 will say more.

3. *To know Christ* (3[7–11])

(7) *But all my assets I regarded as loss for the sake of Christ.* (8) *And furthermore, I even reckon all things as loss for the superiority of the knowledge of Christ Jesus my Lord. For his sake I let myself be despoiled of all things and I reckon them as dung, that I may gain Christ* (9) *and be found in him, possessing not my own righteousness which the Law gives but the righteousness which God gives which is (obtained) by faith in Christ, the faith* (10) *which is a knowledge of Christ, of the power of his resurrection and fellowship with his sufferings; I am in the process of being conformed to his death* (11) *to attain, if possible, a resurrection (which is truly) from among the dead.*

BOUTTIER, M., *La condition chrétienne selon saint Paul*, 1964, p. 11f.
KERTELGE, K., '*Rechtfertigung' bei Paulus—Studien zur Struktur und zum Bedeutungsinhalt des paulinischen Rechtfertigungsbegriff*, 1967, pp. 160–78.
SIBER, P., *Mit Christus—Eine Studie zur paulinischen Auferstehungshoffnung*, 1971, pp. 99–122.

TANNEHILL, R. C., *Dying and Rising with Christ. A Study in Pauline Theology*, 1967, pp. 114–23.
VALLOTTON, P., *Le Christ et la foi*, 1960, pp. 85–91.

In v. 7 important manuscripts (P 46, ℵ*, A, G) omit the conjunction '*alla*' and this could be the original reading. The superabundance of particles in v. 8 is an embarrassment and P⁴⁶ and ℵ* omit the '*kai*'; P 46 and B give '*Christos (Iēsous)*' its original force of 'Messiah' by putting the definite article before it; A and the *Koiné* supplement the elliptical '*hēgoumai skubala*' by adding '*einai*'. A more weighty problem is posed by Westcott who puts a comma between '*dikaiosunēn*' and '*epi tē pistei*' in v. 9; to this we shall return later. In v. 10 it could be that a definite article should be read before '*koinōnian*' and '*pathēmatōn*' (*Koiné*, D, G), but in the following verse '*tēn ek nekrōn*' (most manuscripts), which raises particular problems, should not be changed to a banal '*tōn nekrōn*' (*Koiné*).

To base his life upon human, all too human, values is henceforth no longer possible 'because of Christ' ('*dia ton Christon*'). The passage revolves round this name and the knowledge one can have of it ('*gnōsis Christou Iēsou*', vv. 8–10), under which heading there is offered an extraordinary summary of Pauline Christianity, though the terse, allusive and polemical thought is not easy to unravel exactly. Whatever the previous history of the expression 'to know Christ' (cf. v. 8) it nevertheless seems clear here that its theological placement is not simply on a mystical plane nor yet on the level of jurisprudence, but, over and above both such levels which Paul uses simultaneously (Tannehill), is historical. The alternation of tenses is indeed striking—past, present and future. Knowing Christ involves first of all a particular attitude to the past and its values (vv. 7ff), and then also a reaching towards a future which although it is assured is nevertheless still to come (vv. 9ff). The present is lived in this dialectical tension and it creates a definite outlook which both embraces and goes beyond mysticism and legalism and which has no other name than 'faith' ('*pistis*'). And what is this faith if not the abandonment of all self-confidence in order to put one's entire trust in the grace of God, a painful yet patient expectation of glory? Faith is therefore a continuation in the life of the believer of the event of the Cross and Resurrection. The power of life which leads to Life (vv. 10–11) emerges, beyond all human expectation, out of misery and suffering.

3⁷ The apostle's movement away from the assets and values mentioned above is reminiscent of that of the hero of the Christological hymn in 2⁶ (Hendriksen). It is not impossible that Paul is alluding to the saying of Christ, 'What will it profit a man, if he gains the whole world and forfeits his soul' ('*psuchēn*', RSV 'life'; Mt. 16²⁶), for it has several points in common with this verse (Martin). In which case '*dia ton Christon*' should be taken as 'because of what Christ has said and done'. But the gain/loss antithesis was common in the

Judaism of the day (Billerbeck, I, p. 749), and in a looser sense '*dia ton Christon*' means 'because of what took place on the Cross, the effect of which is now continued within us' (cf. 1 Cor. 4^{10}; 2 Cor. 4^5). It is not certain that Paul is here referring directly to his conversion (with Bonnard, Dibelius, Ewald; against Gnilka, Michael, Michaelis) as the use of the perfect '*hēgēmai*' and not the aorist '*hēgēsamēn*' would suggest: the judgement passed upon 'fleshly' values has its basis in the past but is renewed daily. So the interest of the apostle does not lie primarily in autobiography but in parenesis; there is no narcissism in him, he is simply striving to instruct. And this is why, when speaking usually of conversion he lays the stress on divine grace but here accentuates human decision and judgement ('*hēgoumai*', cf. $2^{3,6}$; Lohmeyer). It is still true that divine grace far from annihilating the faculties of man stimulates them rather and recreates them in freedom.

3^8 This takes up and develops the previous verse and gives it concrete illustration. So the perfect '*hēgēmai*' becomes the present '*hēgoumai*' and the judgement it expresses extends to 'everything of value which is independent of Christ ('*hatina*'; Bonnard, Dibelius).[1] The '*dia ton Christon*' is expanded into the 'superiority of the knowledge of Christ Jesus my Lord'. This is a highly overloaded expression and one, moreover, unique in Paul. Are we to detect some influence from Hellenistic mysticism (Dibelius), from gnosticism (Bultmann, Schmithals)[2] or simply from Judaism (J. Dupont, *Gnosis* . . ., 1949, pp. 34–6)? The Pauline sentence doubtless combines these various currents of thought (Gnilka). But whatever its origin the 'knowledge' meant here is strongly determined by its object—'Jesus Christ my Lord'. Certainly, the genitive could be taken as subjective, i.e. the knowledge which Christ has of us (cf. Gal. 4^9; 1 Cor. 13^{12}; Gal. 1^{15}) which would be answered by the human 'knowledge' of v. 10 (P. Vallotton, *op. cit.*, p. 86f); but this is unlikely, and we would be inclined rather to find in this expression an allusion to some act of worship—baptism, confession of faith or proclamation of the Gospel. The stereotyped nature of the confession-acclamation 'Jesus Christ is Lord' (cf. 2^{6-11}, the hymn) and the fact that the term 'knowledge' is found very early on associated with the preaching of the Gospel and with baptism (cf. A. Benoit, *Le baptême chrétien au second siècle*, 1953, pp. 168ff) supports the suggestion. The apostle does not tire of referring, not to some vague speculation or some 'inner experience', but to his own and the whole community's actual experience Sunday by Sunday. This experience, which is that of one single Lordship, is in fact the only one which

---

[1] In '*alla menoun ge kai*' the '*alla*' takes up the opening of v. 7 and reinforces it with '*menoun ge*'. '*Kai*' stresses the verb which follows: 'and, furthermore, I even reckon that . . .'

[2] BULTMANN, art. '*gignōskō*, etc', *TWNT*, I, 1933, p. 710 (ET *ibid.*); W. SCHMITHALS, *Paulus* . . ., 1965, p. 67.

deserves to be distinguished from the rest ('*huperechon*'). This latter term no doubt carries a polemical point; of the four Pauline instances of the use of the verb three occur in this epistle (cf. **2³**).

Awareness and experience of this Lordship (the '*di' hon*' links quite directly with '*tou kuriou mou*') can lead only to a total abandonment of one's own 'glory' ('I let myself be despoiled') and scorn for any other way to salvation ('*skubala*' = 'refuse', even 'dung'—Calvin). Yet the Christian has not yet arrived; Christ, who has already given himself in many ways is still to be 'gained' ('*kerdēsō*'). Experience of his Lordship is therefore essentially a dynamic experience which sets one on the road. That road, from self to Christ, is a long one.

3⁹ To 'gain Christ' is also 'to be found in him'. The future tense of the verb undoubtedly points to the Last Judgement, and the passive which follows corresponds to an Hebraic way of referring to the action of God (cf. 1 Cor. 4²; 15¹⁵; 2 Cor. 5³; Gal. 2¹⁷; Mt. 24⁴⁶; Bonnard, Gnilka, Michael).[1] But what does 'in him' ('*en autō*') mean? An ecclesiological implication here seems to have little support (against P. Stuhlmacher, *Gottesgerechtigkeit bei Paulus*, 1965, p. 99f) and on the other hand what follows the expression enhances its legalistic flavour: 'to be found in him and to be justified is one and the same thing' (Bonnard). But the link with a Christian's present circumstances '*en Christō*' should also be observed (Gnilka); to be found 'in him' is to lack any glory of one's own and to be conformed to his death and sufferings in order to share in his life (vv. 10–11).

The cultic reference, to preaching and baptism, in the preceding verse is now followed by a reminder of the 'catechism' concerning the 'righteousness of God' (cf. *ad* **3⁶**). A thing is 'righteous' ('*tsad-dîq*'), according to Hebrew etymology, basically because it conforms to a norm or standard. The raising of man to the standard of his humanity as it was willed and created by God, cannot, in Paul's eyes, be achieved by man himself but only by God who thus shows himself righteous (in his Creation) by acting righteously ('justifying').[2] But here it is not really a question of '*dikaiosunē theou*' but of '*dikaiosunē ek theou*' over against a 'righteousness *derived from* the Law'. Then the Law comes to be regarded as a means of salvation and in that way takes the place of God. But faith is not in the same category; it is the anthropological point of contact where the righteousness of God impinges upon man ('*dia pisteōs*'). Faith has no value in itself; it merely turns one to Christ who is the object of faith ('*dia pisteōs Christou*'). It is again possible, of course, to regard

---

[1] Michaelis, P. SIBER (*op. cit.* pp. 111, n. 53) and Vincent prefer a present meaning for the verb.

[2] The meaning of the Pauline expression 'righteousness of God' has in recent years given rise to much discussion and the production of important studies. In addition to the work of Kertelge already mentioned a good survey of the problem will be found in P. BONNARD, 'La justice de Dieu et l'histoire', *ETR*, 43, 1968, pp. 61–8.

this as a subjective genitive with P. Vallotton (*op. cit.*, p. 88f); then it is Christ's faith (i.e. work) which justifies us, and this faith subsequently arouses man's faith ('*epi tē pistei*', at the end of the verse). This has the advantage of explaining the repetition of '*pistis*', but nevertheless it comes to grief from the parallels in Rom. 3[22,26,28,30]; 9[30]; 10[6]; Gal. 2[16]; 3[8]; etc. (cf. K. Kertelge, *op. cit.*, pp. 160ff). It must indeed be realised that in spite of defining its object and its eminently concrete and full Semitic connotation,[1] the concept of 'faith' has to be saved from any kind of whimsical interpretation, such as we have seen in 1[29] to be the case at Philippi. So Paul now feels constrained to give it definition—'faith is . . .' ('*epi tē pistei tou . . .*').

3[10] If, especially in Koiné Greek, the genitive of the articular infinitive can have either a final or a consecutive force (B–D §400; most commentaries) it is not easy to see exactly where to attach it here, and so it is better to view it as a complement of the noun '*pistei*' (Hendriksen, Westcott). The use of the personal pronoun '*auton*'—which grammatically should refer to God but in fact refers to Christ —only shows that the '*tēn ek theou dikaiosunēn*' of the previous verse is an explanatory addition and that the second mention of faith simply picks up the proper thread of the discourse.

Faith is thus also a form of knowledge, and we have seen to what extent this knowledge rests upon a tradition or 'catechism'. In its content, however, the word considerably exceeds the domain of mere knowing; it embraces all the wealth of the Hebrew '*yādhāh*' which is even used for marital relationship. To 'know' Christ is therefore to live with him in peculiar intimacy—though again the expression can be misunderstood, so Paul is quick to add the rider that this intimacy can only be translated into definite attitudes which carry the stamp of the Cross and Resurrection. That he sees these as one inseparable event is shown by the presence of a single definite article governing the whole expression (Michael; P. Siber, *op. cit.*, p. 111). Moreover, the inversion which mentions the resurrection before the death is not due to chance (Michael), nor to Paul's experience on the Damascus road (Bouttier, Huby), but as Siber has correctly seen, to polemic. To know Christ is to have experience of a life-giving power, but this power is shown only in the midst of difficulties, sufferings and death ('*pathēmata*').[2] Furthermore, the fellowship uniting Christians with Christ and with one another ('*koinōnia*') is forged *only* within such difficulties and sufferings. In this we meet again the grand theme of letter B (1[5,29f]; 2[19–30]), though the fulness of the thought expressed

---

[1] Cf. Vallotton, *op. cit.*, pp. 13–9.

[2] There is then no question here of resurrection at the Last Day but of a present experience (so Dibelius, Gnilka, Michael, Vincent, Siber; against Beare, Bonnard, Lohmeyer). J. A. Fitzmyer sees an adumbration of trinitarian theology in the tripartite '*dunamis—Christos—koinōnia*' ('To know him and the power of his resurrection; Ph. 3.10', in *Mélanges B. Rigaux*, ed. A. Descamps and A. de Halleux, 1970, pp. 411–25).

here is nowhere better expounded than in 2 Cor. 4⁷⁻¹⁰: 'We have this treasure in earthen vessels, to show that the transcendent power belongs to God and not to us . . .' This is why the Christian 'has been conformed to the death of Christ'. The words are so oddly reminiscent of Rom. 6¹ᶠᶠ, that one suspects an allusion to baptism. The Christian life therefore takes its origin from a death, the death of Christ, which translates itself for every believer into a death to sin and to self. Once more it can be seen why the 'glory way' of the apostle's opponents stands condemned.

3¹¹ Over against the starting-point of the Christian life (death with Christ) is now put its final goal (resurrection with him). The believer moves between these two poles. The polemical intention of what is being said is here especially obvious (cf. P. Siber, *op. cit.*, p. 118). On the one hand, the *future* of the verb is accompanied by a restriction: '*ei pōs*' = 'if possible'. Not that the apostle doubts the reality of the resurrection, but only one road leads to it—you don't have to take it. It is not God whom Paul is doubting but himself. A similar hesitation is found in 2 Cor. 5³. On the other hand, the unusual expression with the repeated '*ek-*' (and '*exanastasis*' is even a biblical *hapax*) can only mean a 'resurrection which is precisely a rising from among the dead'. To Live one must first Die.

4. *The forward march* (3¹²⁻¹⁶)

(12) *It is not that I have already arrived or already become perfect, but I pursue my course, striving to lay hold (of the prize), since I myself have been laid hold of by Christ Jesus.* (13) *Brothers, I for my part do not think that I have already laid hold (of it). But one thing is certain: forgetting what is behind me and straining eagerly forward,* (14) *I pursue my course towards the goal and the prize which God calls us to receive on high in Christ Jesus.* (15) *This is the way in which all we who are 'perfect' should behave! And if in any respect you behave differently God will enlighten you about this.* (16) *But from the point which we have reached let us go on in step.*

PFITZNER, V. C., *Paul and the Agon Motif. Traditional Imagery in the Pauline Literature*, 1967, pp. 139–53.

In v. 12, P 46, D*, (G), etc. add an interesting detail to make up for the lack of an object for the two verbs: 'or that I am already justified' (cf. 1 Cor. 4⁴). As usual the reading '*ei kai*' whose precise meaning is difficult to fix (cf. 2¹⁷) has given rise to variants, as has the form of the name 'Jesus Christ'. Variants in the following verses are unimportant, except for the reading of Tertullian and Origen in v. 14: '*anengklēsia*' ('irreproachability') instead of '*anō klēsis*'. Some manuscripts add '*kurios*' to the end of the same verse. In v. 15 ℵ and L have an indicative in place of the imperative '*phronōmen*'; as a *lectio difficilior* it could well be original. In v. 16 some readings repeat in various forms the verb '*phroneō*', adding to it '*kanōn*' as the 'norm' for '*stoichein*' under the influence of Gal. 6^{16}. The oldest manuscripts give the shorter text.

To readers who would claim to be 'perfect' ('*teleioi*', v. 15) and believe themselves to have reached the goal, Paul speaks again of what the Christian life is—a forsaking of what lies 'behind' (the past and dead values) and a reaching out to what lies ahead. From a literary angle the passage has some affinity with Rom. 9^{30ff} which deals with the Jewish quest ('*diōkō*') for righteousness.Christianity, too, is a quest though of a different order. But 1 Cor. 9^{24ff} is especially to be remembered where Paul compares the Christian life with a race in the stadium (cf. also 2^{16}; Gal. 2^2; 2 Tim. 4^7). The same figure occurs here in v. 12 (against Pfitzner who sees its appearance only in v. 13b). Finally, 1 Cor. 8 where the apostle confronts his readers' pretensions to gnosis should also be in mind; true 'knowledge' is what recognises its limitations, just as true 'perfection' is recognised as something to be unceasingly striven for.

3^{12} To express doubt about the possibility of attaining to the final resurrection (v. 11) does not mean, as some of the Philippians might believe ('*ouch hoti*') that Paul supposes he has already arrived at the goal at the *present* time. Quite the contrary! 'It' is not yet laid hold of ('*elabon*'). The object of this verb is not in fact expressed. Should it be assumed to be moral and spiritual perfection (Vincent), knowledge (Michaelis), resurrection of the dead (W. Lütgert, *Die Volkommenen . . .*, 1909), righteousness (P 46; D*; A. F. J. Klijn, 'Paul's opponents in Phil. 3', *NT*, 7, 1964–65, p. 281) or Christ himself (Dibelius; Pfitzner, p. 144)? Two other possibilities actually seem more likely: either the apostle already has in mind the metaphor of the race-track and the implicit object is the prize ('*brabeion*', v. 14) awarded there (Beare, Bonnard), or the object is deliberately unexpressed because the apostle simply wanted to suggest something incomplete (Ewald, Gnilka, Haupt; W. Schmithals, *Paulus . . .*, 1965, p. 70f). The verb '*teleō*', which is unique in Paul, was no doubt introduced here as a play on words with the quality of 'perfection' ('*teleioi*', v. 15) claimed by the Philippians; it means both to have attained a goal and to be perfect (cf. G. Delling, art. '*telos*, etc', *TWNT*, VIII, 1969, pp. 50–88 (ET VIII, pp. 49–87)).

As one who is on the way the apostle pursues ('*diōkō*') his course. The stress lies on the effort required because '*diōkō*' properly speaking does not mean 'to run' but 'to chase', 'to pursue after', 'to hunt down' (cf. *ad* 3^6). There is no doubt that the comparison of the race-track is already in mind since in 1 Cor. 9^{24} where it is clearly expressed the verbs '*lambanō*' and '*katalambanō*' reappear (cf. also v. 14). Even so it is not easy to determine the meaning of the second of these; it appears to be only a strengthening of the simple '*lambanō*' ('to take') and it can also have the philosophical meaning 'to understand' (cf. J. Dupont, *Gnosis* . . ., 1949, pp. 501–21). The apostle's striving has as its goal (*'ei kai'*) to 'lay hold of for good and all' (*'katalabō'*). But the force of the *'ei kai'* (which normally indicates concession, cf. *ad* 2[17]) is not merely to suggest the goal; it conveys a hint of doubt about its realisation: 'I do all I can so far as possible to attain the goal' (cf. B–D §§368; 375).

The motive (*'eph' hō'*) for this intense effort is not, however, a desire to forge ahead, to complete a task (a 'work'). In so far as everything has already been accomplished, it is a matter of making this achievement actual. In so far as the Christian has already been laid hold of by Christ he seeks in turn to lay hold of Christ.

3[13] The comparison of the race-course is developed further. One must push on ahead and not rest upon the laurels of a dead past (*'epilanthanomenos'*), whether as Jew or even as Christian, but unceasingly reach out (*'epekteinomenos'*) towards something other than oneself. The exhortation takes a note of urgency (*'adelphoi'*, cf. *ad* 3[1a]) yet it is expressed obliquely ('so far as I am concerned . . .').

3[14] The Christian 'race' has a goal (*'skopos'*, a Pauline *hapax*) which gives it its direction (*'kata'*); and it is crowned by a prize (*'brabeion'*, cf. 1 Cor. 9[24]) which here is 'the heavenly calling of God in Jesus Christ'. The use of the word *'klēsis'* ('call') applying neither to an individual vocation nor to baptism but to the End of time is unique for Paul and for the entire New Testament, so that attempts have been made to connect it with expressions in Philo or in apocalyptic (Lohmeyer); but we would rather suppose that it was introduced from the analogy with Greek games in which the foot-race was an event. Such games were organised and presided over by agonothetes or athlothetes whose office was highly respected. At Olympia they bore the name of *'Hellanodikai'* and 'after each event they had a herald announce the name of the victor, his father's name and his country, and the athlete or charioteer would come and receive a palm branch at their hands.'[1] This is the call to which Paul is alluding—but he makes it clear that what is at stake is not a sportsman's prize (it is from on high, *'anō'*) and the agonothete is none other than God himself and Jesus Christ his herald (*'en Christō Iēsou'*). Furthermore, this call sounds forth through the event of the Cross and Resurrection.

3[15] The contradiction between 'not that I am already perfect' of v. 12 and 'all of us who are perfect' of v. 15 is hardly explicable except by supposing that the Philippians boasted of being perfect (*'teleioi'*).[2]

---

[1] G. GLOTZ, art. 'Hellenodikai' in C. Daremberg and E. Saglio, *Dictionnaire des antiquités grecques et romaines*, III, I, 1900–1963, pp. 60–64, and E. SAGLIO, art. 'Agonothètes', ibid., I, 1, 1877–1962, pp. 148–50.

[2] Beare, Dibelius, Gnilka, Friedrich, Haupt; A. F. J. KLIJN, 'Paul's opponents in Phil. 3', *NT*, 7, 1964–65, p. 282; H. KÖSTER, 'The purpose of the polemic of a Pauline fragment (Philippians 3)', *NTS*, 8, 1961–62, p. 322f; W. SCHMITHALS, *Paulus* . . ., 1965, pp. 70ff.

However, this statement as it stands does not make it possible to determine what the heresy was at Philippi, whether a legalistic Judaism as Klijn thinks or an antinomian gnosticism as for Schmithals. Certainly, the term *'teleios'* is used elsewhere by the apostle himself for the 'maturity' which the Christian life should attain (1 Cor. 2[6]; 14[20]; Eph. 4[13]; Col. 1[28]; 4[12]), so he does not wholly reject the term which his readers are using. But as he has just explained, the true basis for perfection is Christological. From that starting-point, it is lived in a tension embodied in temporal existence. From this springs the Christian ethic—hence the verb *'phroneō'* which follows, which we have seen to play a great part in this epistle, denoting both actual behaviour and the motivation behind it (cf. *ad* 2[2]). 'In Christ' perfect behaviour can be none other than what the apostle has just described, so he has no doubt about convincing his readers. If, however, the reading in ℵ and L should be accepted which has the verb in the indicative (*'phronoumen'*) and not in the imperative the sentence would have to be read as an ironical question: 'Is this not how all we who are perfect think?' True perfection consists in thinking rightly and in recognising that the apostle is correct.

Even if this is not wholly the case, Paul does not doubt that his readers, who are probably boasting of all kinds of revelations (*'apokalupseis'*) which have been granted to them, should still profit from the genuine revelation, which comes from God and which will enlighten them about the truth. The verb *'apokaluptō'* has a rather special sense here, to be related to its use in 1 Cor. 14[30].

3[16] It remains true (*'plēn'*) that whatever the past differences between Paul and the church at Philippi have been they must walk boldly (*'stoichein'*; for the imperatival force of the infinitive cf. B–D §389) and in step (*'tō autō'*) along the way opening before them.

5. Fresh polemical outburst (3[17–19])

(17) *With one accord, brothers, imitate me and pay attention to those who proceed according to the pattern which you have in us.* (18) *For there are many, as I have often told you and now repeat with tears, who live as enemies of the Cross of Christ;* (19) *their end is perdition, their belly is their god and they esteem only what is shameful; their concern is in earthly things.*

BETZ, H. D., *Nachfolge und Nachahmung Jesus Christi im NT*, 1967, pp. 145–53.

In v. 18, P 46 adds *'blepete'* before *'tous echthrous'* no doubt by analogy with 3[2] (Gnilka); it only overloads the sentence.

These are not new opponents whom Paul is now attacking, as we have shown on pp. 12ff. There is actually no break between vv. 12–16

and vv. 17–21. In fact the metaphor of the race-track is continued in
the verb 'to walk, go' ('*peripateō*', vv. 17–18); the eschatological
perspective of vv. 11ff is given further precision in vv. 19ff, and the
'*skopos*' ('goal', v. 14) becomes '*skopeō*' ('to have as object', 'to have
in view', v. 17). Further, v. 17 is given as the inevitable consequence
of what precedes. Paul had had no intention of giving an 'objective'
account of his conversion; he merely wanted to show by a particularly striking and authoritative illustration what the Christian life
involved, and so now he draws the conclusion from what precedes—
'do as I do!' There were indeed others who set themselves up as
patterns of the Christian life and who flashed before the eyes of the
Philippians the enticing image of a 'glorious' ideal; hence the fresh
polemical outburst of vv. 18–19 whose very violence again shows
the danger which this ideal presented to immature faith.

3¹⁷ The 'I's' of the previous verses now take their full paradigmatic
force as Paul appeals to his readers to imitate him. Again the appeal
is pressing and affectionate, addressed to 'brothers' (cf. **3¹³**; **3¹ᵃ**),
and again also the stress is upon the communal nature of the imitation: 'Imitate me with one accord' ('*summimetai*', cf. especially
H. D. Betz, *op. cit.*).[1] Whatever otherwise may be the historical and
religious roots of Paul's notion of 'imitation',[2] the apostle often
presents himself to his readers as a pattern in order to emphasise the
importance of 'sufferings' (1 Thess. 1⁶; 2¹⁴; cf. 2 Thess. 3⁷⁻⁹) and of
self-giving (1 Cor. 11¹) in the life of one who 'imitates Christ' (1 Cor.
11¹; 1 Thess. 1⁶; cf. Eph. 5¹; 2⁶⁻¹¹). So it is not by chance that the
word arises again here in opposition to the 'glorious', perfectionist
ideal offered by the opposing preachers. The apostle does not however offer himself as the only pattern; in contrast to *2 Corinthians*
the apostolate itself is not immediately at issue; though Paul perhaps
wishes in this way to confirm the authority of those within the community at Philippi who remain loyal to him (cf. Timothy and Epaphroditus, **1¹** and **2¹⁹ᶠᶠ**). Never is this authority found to rest upon
membership of a hierarchy but upon a particular way of living.

3¹⁸ The emotion the apostle feels leads him to refer again more
directly to his opponents and it hinders the proper construction of
his sentence; the relative lacks a verb and '*tous echthrous*' must be
taken as predicate to the subject '*polloi*' (cf. Haupt). The first characteristic of his opponents is therefore their number. Doubtless their
field of activity is not limited to Philippi and they are to be found at
work in one guise or another in several churches founded by the

---

[1] Given the context of this epistle and the wealth of compounds in '*sun-*' it
contains (cf. *ad* **1⁷**) this interpretation is preferable to that of some more special
relationship with the apostle (Bonnard) or merely of a strengthening of '*mimētēs*'
(MICHAELIS, *TWNT*, IV, 1942, p. 669, n. 13 (ET IV, p. 667)). The word occurs
nowhere else in the whole of Greek literature.
[2] Beside Betz, cf. A. SCHULZ, *Nachfolgen und Nachahmen*, 1962.

apostle (Beare, Bonnard, Michaelis, Gnilka). If he has often had occasion to give warning about them ('*hous pollakis elegon humin*') that could only be in our letter B (1¹–3¹ᵃ) and during the exchanges which had taken place between Paul and Philippi up to that time (cf. 2¹⁹⁻³⁰). But now the situation has deteriorated and the apostle's supplication is 'with tears' ('*klaiōn*', cf. 2 Cor. 2⁴).

The heresy thus envisaged bears upon every aspect of the Christian life, especially the realm of ethics ('*peripatousin*') where its impact is 'contrary to the Cross of Christ'. The expression is unfortunately vague, though that is no reason for thinking Paul was not alluding here to some definite doctrine (Dibelius, Staab). Similarly Bonnard is over-cautious when he says, 'They are enemies of those who have put their trust in the Cross'. Although the term 'enemy' in a polemical sense is found only here in Paul, words of the '*stauros*' family appear in the Pauline corpus in three different contexts. The first is that of the Galatian dispute in which the apostle is trying to bring out the novelty of the 'religion' of the Cross in relation to that of the Law (Gal. 3¹; 5¹¹,²⁴; 6¹²,¹⁴). The second is the confrontation with the 'wisdom of the world' in *1 Corinthians*, where the Cross becomes the sign of God's foolishness (1 Cor. 1¹³,¹⁷,¹⁸,²³; 2²⁻⁸). And the third context is that of the Ephesian and Colossian Epistles where the Cross is understood primarily as a sign of reconciliation (Eph. 2¹⁶; Col. 1²⁰; 2¹⁴). Our passage lies precisely at the intersection of the three lines of approach just sketched. The 'enemies of the Cross' are those who refuse to recognise the decisive eschatological importance of the event of the Cross and Resurrection which inaugurates a radically new order of things (2 Cor. 5¹⁷); they are those, too, who do not accept the shameful character of suffering and 'folly' which must indelibly stamp this new way of life; and thus their activity can only issue in estrangement and a destruction of all the fellow-feeling brought about through the reconciliation of the Cross.

This, then, seems to be the meaning of the enmity to the Cross, and not any moral laxity,[1] or purely materialistic behaviour (Betz, Scott), or orthodox Judaism,[2] or apostasy at the time of persecution (Lohmeyer).

3¹⁹ The violent denunciation commencing in v. 18 now continues but in such general terms that they do not allow the personalities of those who are under attack to be discerned with any clarity. So it is only by the light of a general hypothesis about the identity of the adversaries who are in view in 3 that this verse can be illuminated.

---

[1] Beare, Haupt, Lightfoot, Michael, Michaelis; R. JEWETT, 'Conflicting movements in the early Church as reflected in Philippians', *NT*, 12, 1970, pp. 362–90; W. LÜTGERT, *Die Vollkommenen . . .*, 1909, pp. 10ff; W. SCHMITHALS, *Paulus . . .*, 1965, pp. 77ff.
[2] Müller, A. F. J. KLIJN, 'Paul's opponents in Phil. 3', *NT*, 7, 1964–65, pp. 278–84.

From a temporal and eschatological viewpoint Paul can only point to his opponents' 'end' ('*to telos*'): it will be perdition ('*apōleia*'), i.e. death without hope of return,[1] for their God is a perishable god, none other than their belly ('*koilia*'). Does this allude to excesses at table and to debauchery or the very opposite, to over-scrupulous attention to the purity of foods?[2] Or should the word be given a more neutral sense, equivalent to 'flesh' ('*sarx*'), as meaning that the conduct which is being denounced is not guided by the Spirit?[3] Neither the Pauline use of the term (Rom. 16[18]; 1 Cor. 6[13]; Gal. 1[15]) nor that of the entire New Testament in fact allows us to settle the matter one way rather than the other; in the New Testament 'belly' has a range of meaning, not necessarily pejorative and even including the mother's womb (cf. Gal. 1[15]). Having regard to the total context of this letter, the pride of these 'dogs' (3[2ff]) and the disorders that follow them on the community level (2[1-18]), one would be tempted to take it as: 'They have their eyes fixed on their own navel; their god is themselves!'

Their glory ('*doxa*') is the same; it is their shame ('*aischunē*'). There has been a desire to regard this as a fresh reference to excesses of all kinds, particularly sexual; unless it refers to circumcision (Barth, Benoit, Ewald-Wohlenberg, Müller). Yet only in a secondary sense does '*aischunē*' mean debauchery; in the Old Testament it even covers the experience of man in face of divine judgement (Gnilka). 'Glory', as we have seen, was one of the key words of the apostle's opponents. 'What glory is it,' he replies, 'which involves a betrayal of the Gospel, the putting of self first and the destruction of the Christian fellowship? Such glory is but shame!' These people again have their whole interest in 'earthly things' ('*ta epigeia*'); their outlook is sordid and bounded by themselves, and they follow only earthy impulses which lack power to raise them above ground-level. The importance of the verb '*phroneō*' in this epistle has already been considered (cf. *ad* 2[3]; 3[15]).

6. *The true hope* (3[20-21])

(20) *For we are citizens of heaven and it is from there that we eagerly await a Saviour, Jesus Christ the Lord.* (21) *He will transform our miserable body, conforming it to his glorious body, in virtue of the power and the dominion which he exercises over all things.*

[1] Cf. L. MATTERN, *Das Verständnis des Gerichtes bei Paulus*, 1966, p. 61f.
[2] For the former hypothesis: Beare, Dibelius, Friedrich, Michael, Michaelis; W. LÜTGERT, *Die Vollkommenen...*, 1909; W. SCHMITHALS, *Paulus...*, 1965. For the second: Barth, Bonnard, Ewald-Wohlenberg; BEHM, art. '*koilia*', *TWNT*, III, 1938, pp. 786–89 (ET *ibid.*).
[3] Gnilka; H. KÖSTER, 'The purpose of the polemic of a Pauline fragment (Philippians 3)', *NTS*, 8, 1961–62, p. 326f; A. F. J. KLIJN, 'Paul's opponents in Phil. 3', *NT*, 7, 1964–65, p. 283.

GUETTGEMANNS, E., *Der Leidende Apostel*, 1966, pp. 240–47.
STRECKER, G., 'Redaktion und Tradition im Christushymnus', *ZNW*, 55, 1964, pp. 75–8.
SIBER, P., *Mit Christus Leben*, 1971, pp. 122–34.

In v. 21 the *Koiné* smooths the somewhat abrupt construction, in which '*summorphon*' follows '*metaschēmatisei*' without a link, by inserting '*eis to genesthai auto*'; similarly it corrects the inexact '*autō*' into a reflexive '*heautō*'.

This particularly rhythmic sentence (Lohmeyer) is also marked by the unusualness of such words as '*sōtēr*' and '*politeuma*'. Some have thought to detect here some kind of previous hymn (Güttgemanns, Strecker). It could well be supposed that Paul ends the letter (3^{1b}–4^1) by an appeal to 'orthodoxy' and tradition. The thought is, however, eminently Pauline, particularly in v. 21, and is the logical conclusion of all that has already been said (Siber). The view we prefer is that, using traditional motifs, the polemical presentation of the nature of the Christian life is here brought to a close (Gnilka, Siber). The analogy between these verses and the hymn in 2^{6-11} (Stecker) only goes to confirm what we said of its authorship and the position of the passage in the epistle.

So if the Christian life is one of a yearning for the future ('*apek-dechometha*') it is a future so full of richness that the ecstasies and other 'glories' proffered by the apostle's adversaries are a mere nothing. And this wealth and this true Glory appertain in the first place to the Lord (v. 20) of the whole universe (v. 21). In the second place, it is a Glory which is not proportioned to our own efforts; it more than satisfies us because it has its origin outside ourselves. Yet it will not be for ever external to us; we shall be transformed into glory (v. 21a), and the assurance we can have of this transformation consists precisely in our present 'conformation' ('*summorphon*') to humility, even to the humiliation of the Cross. Sharers in the Death of Christ, we can do no other than share his Resurrection.

3^{20} The Christian is a citizen of heaven. 'It is unnecessary to stress the part played by the city in ancient life. It could almost be said that before being an independent person a man was a citizen.'[1] The Philippians, who lived in a Roman colony, would be particularly quick to grasp the metaphor (Bonnard, Dibelius, cf. also 1^{27}). The idea of a heavenly city is far from being original, however, and it is not too clear whether it should be traced back to Hellenistic conceptions[2] or Jewish speculations about the heavenly Jerusalem. The

---

[1] G. BARDY in the introduction to the *Cité de Dieu* by St Augustine (Bibliothèque augustinienne, 33, 1959), pp. 52–74 (p. 53); cf. also STRATHMANN, art. '*polis*, etc.', *TWNT*, VI, 1959, pp. 516–35 (ET *ibid.*).

[2] 'I understand,' he said 'you mean the city whose establishment we have described, the city whose home is in the ideal . . .' 'Well,' said I, 'perhaps there is a pattern of it laid up in heaven for him who wishes to contemplate it and so beholding to constitute himself its citizen [or: found a city in himself].' (PLATO, *The Republic*, 592b, Loeb Classical Library, vol. 2, ed. P. Shorey).

context gives a slight weighting to the second option, though here it is not actually a matter of the 'city' ('*polis*') but of 'sharing in the civic affairs or organisation of a city' ('*politeuma*'). In opposition to those whose impulses are basely terrestrial ('*hoi ta epigeia phronountes*', v. 19) Paul affirms that the Christian draws his hope and faith and motivation from *elsewhere*.

For this reason there is an expectation and a yearning ('*apekdechometha*'). The verb is primarily Pauline in the New Testament (6 out of 8 times) where it always refers to expectation of the parousia, notably in Rom. 8^{19-25}.[1] The subject of expectation is here said to be the 'Saviour', so it is a glad expectancy, not one of fear or resignation before apocalyptic cataclysms which are to come (Hendriksen). The modern reader is at first surprised to learn what little use the New Testament makes of the title 'Saviour', accustomed as he is to seeing it given an important place in the devotion and the theology of the churches. Paul only has it here (cf. however Eph. 5^{23}) and only the *Pastorals* and *2 Peter* give it a special place. The reasons for such silence are not easy to discern.[2] Let us simply note that for the apostle the terms 'to save' and 'salvation' refer essentially to the final stage of the work begun by God through Jesus Christ, namely decisive laying aside of the coming wrath (Rom. 5^9; 1 Cor. 3^{15}; 5^5; 1 Thess. 5^{19}) or, as here, the ultimate acquisition of Glory.[3] The present status of the Christian he prefers to express in terms of 'justification' or 'life in Christ'. Salvation, therefore, cannot be reduced to some sort of event in the individual's life as was then the case with Hellenism in which, from healers to initiates in some mystery religion or other, via the philosophers (after Epicurus), everyone claimed to be a 'saviour'. It was perhaps to avoid any confusion of meaning with these that the apostle seems reluctant to give Christ the title of Saviour. The polemical bearing of this chapter, however, afforded a unique opportunity to use it. The link between 'today' and 'tomorrow' does not reside within ourselves but with him alone who is today confessed as *Lord* (cf. 2^{11}) and who will also be the Saviour.

3²¹ Our assurance of glory to come does not rest with us but in the Lord himself, whose 'power over all things' should inspire us with complete confidence (v. 21b; cf. 1 Cor. 15^{27ff}, inspired no doubt by Ps. 8^7). Yet further, this Lord is 'the first-born of many brethren' (Rom. 8^{29}), therefore inasmuch as we truly participate in this Christ-Lord so shall we also participate in his glory. Now to 'par-

---

[1] The construction '*ex hou*' would normally mean that it is from the 'city' that the saviour is awaited (Lohmeyer), but one could also take it as a *constructio ad sensum* and link the relative with '*ouranois*' (Gnilka; Michaelis; cf. 1 Cor. 15^{47}; 2 Cor. 5^2; Gal 1^8; 1 Thess. 1^{10}).

[2] Cf. O. CULLMANN, *The Christology of the New Testament*, ET² 1963, pp. 238–45.

[3] Cf. FOERSTER-FOHRER, art. '*sōzō*, etc.', *TWNT*, VII, 1964, pp. 966–1024 (especially pp. 1013ff), (ET VII, pp. 965–1024, especially pp. 1012ff).

ticipate' here on earth means primarily to share his 'humiliation' ('*tapeinōsis*'). The kinship in expressions between 2[6-11], 3[10f] and this present verse is very striking: the '*schēma*' of 2[7] recurs in the '*metaschēmatisei*' of 3[21],[1] the '*etapeinōsen*' of 2[8] in the '*tapeinōsis*' of 3[21], the '*morphē*' (2[6]) and '*summorphizomenos*' (3[10]) in '*summorphon*', '*dunamis*' (3[10]) in '*energeia*', and the '*pan-pasa*' of 2[10f] in the '*panta*' of 3[21].

7. *Conclusion* ([4[1]]; 4[8-9])

(1) *Since this is so, my dear and beloved brothers, my joy and crown, stand firm in the Lord, my beloved!*

D* and 209 suppress the second '*agepētoi*' which in B and 33 is followed also by the possessive '*mou*'.

The '*hōste*' ('this being so') links this verse with what precedes.[2] It therefore closes letter C with an exhortation to stand firm ('*stēkete*') which originally was followed by the recommendations of vv. 8 and 9 (cf. *infra* pp. 146ff). To 'stand firm' is to not give way to heresy but continue in the straight course marked out by the Gospel; it also means 'holding together' in face of the dangers which threaten the unity of the fellowship (cf. 1[27] '*stēkete en heni pneumati*'); and, finally, it means facing up to all the difficulties and even sufferings involved in the Christian life and not taking refuge in any kind of disembodied spirituality. This is why such steadfastness must be 'in the Lord', that is in submission to the one Master of the community, the meaning of whose Lordship has been so forcefully depicted in 2[6-11].

From this perspective the apostle's readers can be no less than his 'brethren', his 'joy' and 'crown'.[3] The theme of joy, which is characteristic of letter B (cf. *ad* 1[5]) is found only here in letter C. It is brought in particularly through the metaphor of the 'crown' ('*stephanos*'), as in 1 Thess. 2[19]: You are our hope, our joy, our crown in whom we shall boast ourselves in the presence of our Lord Jesus at his return.[4] So our verse stands in the eschatological perspective opened up by vv. 20–21. The 'prize' of the race (3[14]) for which the apostle strives, the 'crown' (cf. 1 Cor. 9[25]; Prov. 16[31]) is thus none other than the fellowship of those he has led to Christ (cf. 1[6]; 2[15ff]; 2 Cor. 3[2]).

[1] The verb here marks the depth and reality of the transformation.
[2] Barth, Bonnard, Friedrich, Haupt, Martin, Matter, etc.; against Lohmeyer.
[3] For '*epipotheō*', cf. *ad* 1[8]. '*Epipothētoi*' is a N.T. *hapax*.
[4] Cf. W. GRUNDMANN, art. '*stephanos*, etc.', *TWNT*, VII, 1964, pp. 615–35 (ET VII, pp. 615–36).

Letter B, fourth part (*continued*)

Final recommendations (4²⁻⁷)

(2) *I beg Euodia and I beg Syntyche to reach agreement in the Lord;*
(3) *and I ask you, true companion, to help them; they have striven
along with me for the Gospel, as have Clement and my other fellow-
workers whose names are written in the book of life.* (4) *Rejoice in the
Lord; I shall not cease to say, Rejoice!* (5) *Let your moderation be
known to all; the Lord is near.* (6) *Let nothing make you anxious but
in every circumstance make your needs known to God with prayer and
petition, with thanksgiving.* (7) *And the peace of God, which far surpasses all trivial arguments, shall guard your hearts and your thoughts
in Christ Jesus.*

The question posed by v. 3 is to know whether '*suzuge*' should be read
as a common noun or a personal name. Some good manuscripts (P 16
vid, ℵ*) have a slightly longer text than the majority of witnesses: 'Clement
and my fellow-workers, and the others whose names . . .' In v. 4 it would
be better (with Ewald and against most commentaries and Nestle) to
attach the adverb 'always' to the second verb ('I will always say it again')
rather than to the first ('Rejoice always') because the second verb is future
('*erō*'). The variants in v. 7 are not sufficiently well supported to create
any problem: A reads 'the peace of Christ' instead of 'the peace of God';
G has 'body' for 'thoughts' and P 16 lumps together 'thoughts and body'.
Lohmeyer thinks these readings are favourable to his thesis about martyrdom. P 46 ends with 'the Lord Jesus' instead of 'Christ Jesus'.

Originally following 3¹ᵃ these verses also formed part of the ending
of letter B. After having spoken about Timothy and Epaphroditus,
Paul turns now to other particular cases (vv. 2–3); he ends with
exhortations of a general kind but in which the note of joy has once
again a central place. And so beyond the difficulties which beset the
community at Philippi (v. 2; cf. 1²⁷–2¹⁸) the future lies open, wherein
the dynamic of the Gospel can operate (v. 3) and a Saviour who
brings reconciliation and peace is close at hand (vv. 5ff).

4² Women always played an important part in the Pauline communities (cf. Rom. 16), notably at Philippi (Acts 16¹ ³ᶠᶠ), so it is not
surprising to find two of them named here who doubtless had been
mixed up in the dissensions of the Philippian community (cf. '*to auto
phronein*' and the '*to auto phronēte*' of 2²). We have no other knowledge of these two, except that their names are well attested in Greek
(cf. Arndt-Gingrich *Lexicon*, *ad loc.*). The thesis of the Tübingen

school of last century which saw the two women as allegories of the Jewish-Christian and Gentile-Christian communities deserves no mention except as a curiosity. In conformity with the attitude he has adopted throughout letter B the apostle continues to go out of his way to use persuasion; the verb *'parakalō'* in the sense of 'counsel', 'suggest', 'beg' (cf. Phm. 8f) occurs twice. The thing which matters is to bring these two women back 'before the Lord' (cf. *ad* 2[19]).

4[3] In any case their past pleads in their favour and should induce them to return to a better frame of mind. They are well aware of what the true Gospel is, on behalf of which they have contended alongside the apostle (*'sunēthlēsan'*; cf. 1[27]!). So they should be given help (*'sullam-banomai'*, cf. Lk. 5[7]). The mediator for this reconciliation is a mysterious person who now appears and it is not easy to know whether we are given his name as 'Syzyge' or his description as 'placed under the same yoke, yoke-fellow', 'companion'. Supporters of the alternatives are fairly equal in numbers. It is said on the one side that if it were not a proper name the Philippians would not know who was being addressed and that frequently in Greek a common noun is transferred into a name.[1] On the other, the name 'Syzyge' is said not to occur.[2] Furthermore, the adjective *'gnēsios'* qualifying the noun hardly seems applicable to a personal name and Benoit, Ewald and Müller's interpretation ('Syzyge the well named') seems forced (Michaelis). In fact *'gnēsios'* means 'legitimate', 'authentic' (2 Cor. 8[8]; 1 Tim. 1[2]; Tit. 1[4]) and is found in 2[20] qualifying and certifying Timothy's mission. Our view then is that it is Timothy, who has arrived in Philippi to re-establish harmony, whom Paul is addressing in this way (Friedrich), rather than Epaphroditus (Lightfoot), Silas (G. Delling, art. *'suzugos'*, *TWNT*, VII, p. 749f (ET p. 748f)), Luke (T. W. Manson, 'St Paul in Ephesus. The date of the Epistle to the Philippians', *BJRL*, 23, 1939, p. 199) or, according to the far-fetched notion already denounced by Calvin, the apostle's own wife.[3] As he insists yet again upon the communal spirit, in a context in which five composites in *'sun-'* occur in two verses, it is understandable that the apostle wanted to stress one quality of his representative which would follow from that spirit and which at the same time accredited him fully for the task Paul had suggested to him.

But Euodia and Syntyche were not the only ones to strive alongside the apostle! There are all his 'fellow-workers' (*'sunergoi'*; the word is frequent in Paul) whose 'prizes' have not perhaps been out-

[1] Barth, Benoit, Ewald, Gnilka, Haupt, Müller, Staab.

[2] Bonnard, Dibelius, Friedrich, Lightfoot, Michael, Michaelis; G. DELLING, art. *'suzugos'*, *TWNT*, VII, 1964, pp. 749–50 (ET VII, pp. 748–50).

[3] She could even have been Lydia! Even if the adjective can really have a marital connotation, it is masculine here. W. SCHMITHALS suggests in this connection that originally a personal name (e.g. Timothy) occurred here in the place of *'suzugos'* and that the redactor of the epistle thought it necessary to remove it and replace it with a less definite form of address (*Paulus* . . ., 1965, p. 55).

standing here below but whose names are written in that 'book' where God inscribes the names of the chosen to whom he promises life (Dan. 12^1; Ex. 32^{32ff}; Ps. 69^{29}; etc.): 'God *knows* them, and he knows they belong to him' (Barth). Among these elect is one Clement, whom it is useless to try to identify further since the name was extremely common at that time (cf. Lightfoot, pp. 168–71).

4^4 For one last time the Philippians are given an appeal for joy, a joy which comes from the sense of involvement of the apostle and his correspondents in the great work initiated by the Lord of all ('*en kuriō*'), with a view to the full manifestation of his salvation (cf. v. 5). Once more, it is not then a question of the joy of martyrdom (Lohmeyer), nor that of men who might never meet again (Gnilka), but rather the joy of believers who know, because the signs of it are obvious, that the future stands open (observe the future tense 'I will always repeat') and its realisation is on the way.

4^5 'The Lord is at hand'. Unique in the New Testament, and no doubt inspired by the Aramaic '*Maranatha*' ('the Lord comes'; 1 Cor. 16^{22}), the expression indicates in the first place the temporal proximity of the Lord's return (Bonnard, Dibelius, Gnilka, Haupt). Yet this 'diachronistic' interpretation does not exclude but actually supports a 'synchronistic' interpretation: the Lord who *came* so close to humanity (2^{6ff}) as actually to share the human lot is still near at hand (Calvin; cf. Ps. 145^{18}). For this reason the Christian outlook is resolutely centripetal, not centrifugal; and so the solution to the problems of the Philippian church is not to be found in some kind of introspection but in a desire to turn outwards toward others ('*pasin anthrōpois*'). The community will then find the 'moderation' ('*to epieikes*') in which it is so tragically defective—for this is how '*epieikes*' is to be understood and not with the majority of translations as 'meekness' or 'gentleness' (cf. Preisker, art. '*epieikeia*', *TWNT*, II, 1935, pp. 585–87 (ET II, pp. 588–90)). Far from inducing exaggeration, disorder and bombast the nearness of the Lord induces balance, equilibrium and peace.

4^6 To say equilibrium is also to say prayer; prayer and more prayer, as Paul puts it here by using the pleonasm '*tē proseuchē kai tē deēsei*'. And the prayer of petition ('*aitēmata*') can only be at the same time a prayer of thanksgiving ('*meta eucharistias*'), for has not everything already been given? So the Philippians are not to be anxious about anything ('*mēden merimnate*'), whether it be concerning the fate of the apostle, the development of their own community or the future of the Gospel. 'Therefore I tell you, do not be anxious . . .' (Mt. 6$^{25-34}$).

4^7 As often at the end of his letters Paul now comes to speak about peace, '*eirēnē*'.[1] So the desire with which the letter opened (1²) occurs again; we have come full circle, and the apostle's whole purpose, however passionate or violent sometimes, was only to lead finally to the one thing that matters—the peace of God. Above all this means that peace should reign between the Philippians themselves on the one hand, and between them and Paul on the other.[2] But such a good relationship is possible only—and this is the force of the genitive '*theou*'—because Peace has been established between men and God through Jesus Christ (Rom. 5¹; cf. Eph. 2¹⁴ᶠᶠ). So peace is more than a simple inward certitude of feeling; it is a bond uniting various participants and characterised by righteousness and a balanced progress (cf. the Hebrew '*shālôm*').

And so this peace 'passes all understanding'. The qualification has not so much a general or philosophical bearing as a limited and practical one: the 'understanding' ('*nous*') which the Philippians put into their dissensions ought in the end to be subjected to the peace which God gives (cf. Bonnard). It is not by chance that the verb '*huperechō*' ('to go beyond', 'surpass') is found three times in this letter out of four Pauline instances because the essential question at Philippi was to know who or what was 'superior', out-topping the rest (cf. 2³; 3⁸). And it is no surprise then to learn that the 'hearts' and 'thoughts' of the readers need to be 'guarded' ('*phroureō*', a military term), the hearts because they are the seat of the will and hence of all conduct both individual and social, and the 'thoughts' ('*noēmata*') because, whatever Paul's very high regard for intelligence elsewhere,[3] left to itself intelligence risks going astray. Hence of the six Pauline instances of '*noēma*' five occur in *2 Corinthians* in connection with the heretical 'sophistries' of the apostle's opponents (cf. J. F. Collange, *Enigmes . . .*, 1972, p. 93). The limits put upon the 'heart' and true 'understanding' are 'in Christ', i.e. they arise from the Great Work of God springing from the historic fact of the Cross and Resurrection, still continuing today.

[1] Rom. 15³³; 16²⁰; 2 Cor. 13¹¹; 1 Thess. 5²³; 2 Thess. 3¹⁶. For the word itself, cf. FOERSTER, V. RAD, art. '*eirēnē*, etc.' *TWNT*, II, 1935, pp. 398–418 (ET II, pp. 400–20).
[2] Cf. Rom. 14¹⁷,¹⁹; 1 Cor. 7¹⁵; 14³³; Eph. 4³; Col. 3¹⁵.
[3] Cf. P. BONNARD, 'L'intelligence chez saint Paul', in *L'Evangile hier et aujourd'hui* (*Mélanges F. J. Leenhardt*), 1968, pp. 13–24.

Letter C

Conclusion (continued) ((4^1); 4$^{8-9}$)

(8) *Finally, brothers, apply your mind to whatever is true, noble and righteous; to whatever is pure, pleasant and honourable; to whatever is virtuous and worthy of praise.* (9) *Put into practice what you have learnt and received of me, what you have heard and seen from me; and the God of peace will be with you.*

At the end of v. 8, D* and G, puzzled by the rather unusual use of *'epainos'* have given it definition by adding *'epistēmēs'* ('praise in knowledge').

Originally these verses followed directly upon 4^1 and ended letter C. In relation to 4$^{4-7}$ they make a sort of doublet for which it is hard to see any justification if the letter is taken as a unity. The *'to loipon'* ('finally') opening v. 8 corresponds to the same expression in 3^{1a} and both announce conclusions, one of letter B and the other of letter C. In addition, the theme of 'imitation' of the apostle (cf. *ad* 3^{17}) underlying the second letter and absent from 4$^{2-7}$ reappears forcefully in 4^9.

The form of the discourse at this point is particularly polished and rhythmical, though there is no need to look for a precise metre. Two sentences end with imperatives preceded by a *'tauta'* ('all these things') which summarises the points previously mentioned, and the two sentences outline the task confronting the Philippians as having two aspects: they must 'reflect' (*'logizesthe'*) and 'act' (*'prassete'*). The whole strength of Christianity lies in the union of these two imperatives. The norms which should guide the action are a union of discipline (v. 8), tradition (v. 9a) and instruction gained from life (v. 9b).

4^8 First, the discipline. It is often thought surprising that the list of 'virtues' submitted by the apostle to his readers has nothing distinctively Christian about it but springs out of a kind of 'natural morality'.[1] But the actual situation of the church at Philippi must not be forgotten. In face of the quibbling and the more or less specious arguments of his opponents Paul insists on the need for rigorous moral reflection and a return to commonsense, and sometimes it would be better to pay heed to quite simple but solid truths even if they are pagan rather than to so-called Christian 'revelations'.

[1] The terms used are those of popular Stoic morality (Beare, Dibelius Gnilka), certainly influenced also by their LXX usage (Lohmeyer, Michaelis).

This does not mean, however, that such 'simple truths' had no connection to maintain with the Christ event (the Revelation); v. 9 shows that on the contrary they are both founded upon this event and stand under its scrutiny.

So in the first place reasoning must be 'true' (*'alēthē'*), not in any metaphysical sense of the word 'truth' but in the sense of 'truthful', as the one other Pauline instance in 2 Cor. 6[8] shows; other people are not to be deceived. Likewise *'semnos'* ('noble', 'honourable') in 1 Tim. 3[8-11] describes the bearing of men who are no scandal-mongers. Thinking should be 'righteous' (*'dikaia'*), i.e. conforming to the norm, 'right' (cf. *ad* 1[7]), and 'pure' (*'hagna'*), i.e. with pure intentions, as in 1[17] and 2 Cor. 6[6].

'Prosphilē' ('pleasant') connects still more directly with the actual circumstances of the community at Philippi. It applies primarily to social or community relations; it occurs only here in the New Testament and has no place in the lists of virtues current in antiquity.[1] Likewise, *'euphēma'* (lit. 'well-spoken of') of which only the cognate *'euphēmia'* ('good reputation') is found in Paul (2 Cor. 6[8]). It is harder, on the other hand, to determine the precise force of *'aretē'* (Pauline *hapax*). It is a typically Greek word with no Hebrew equivalent.[2] In this particular context it should not be given its general meaning of 'virtue' but the closely related one of 'esteem', or 'excellency'. Indeed, with it is linked *'epainos'*, 'worthy of praise', also a term from the public life of antiquity (H. Preisker, art. *'epainos'*, *TWNT*, II, 1935, p. 584 (ET II, p. 587f)). Paul therefore requests his readers to fix their attention (*'logizesthe'*) on the specific conditions for a communal life.

4[9] Yet it is not sufficient to think 'rightly'; something must also be done (*'prassete'*), and again it is necessary that people should see (*'eidete'*) what it is to be a Christian. For this 'doing' the apostle, bearer of the living evangelical tradition (*'parelabete'*),[3] offers himself as a pattern—the pattern of one who has experienced Strength out of Weakness, not of one with a debased sense of superiority (cf. 1[29f]).

---

[1] Cf. S. WIBBING, *Die Tugend- und Lasterkataloge im NT und ihre Traditionsgeschichte unter besonderer Berücksichtigung der Qumran-Texten*, 1959.

[2] Cf. J. N. SEVENSTER, *Paul and Seneca*, 1961, pp. 150–54.

[3] The verb does not necessarily have a fixed and formally defined sense (as in 1 Cor. 11[23]; 15[13]; Gal. 1[9-12]; Gnilka, Lohmeyer), it can also be more neutral (cf. K. WEGENAST, *Das Verständnis der Tradition bei Paulus und in den Deuteropaulinen*, 1962, p. 113f).

Letter A

Thanks for gifts sent (4¹⁰⁻²⁰ (+4²¹⁻²³))

(10) *I have had great joy in the Lord in seeing your concern for me now at last revive; this concern did not lapse but lacked opportunity.* (11) *I do not say this under the pressure of need; for I have learnt to be independent in every situation.* (12) *I know how to face deprivation as well as abundance; I am trained for every situation, for satiety as for hunger, for abundance as for want.* (13) *I can endure all things in Him who strengthens me.* (14) *Nevertheless, you have done well to associate yourselves with my affliction.* (15) *For you well know, you Philippians, that when the Gospel was in its beginning, when I left Macedonia, no other church than you was associated with me by a profit-and-loss account.* (16) *Even to Thessalonica you sent several times to supply my needs.* (17) *Not that I seek the gifts; what I do seek is the profit which accrues to your account.* (18) *I have all that I need, abundance and superabundance, now that Epaphroditus has brought me your gifts, a sweet odour, a sacrifice God receives with pleasure.* (19) *So my God will abundantly supply every need of yours, according to his riches in Christ Jesus.* (20) *To God who is also our Father be glory for ever and ever. Amen.*

GLOMBITZA, O., 'Der Dank des Apostels. Zum Verständnis von Ph. 4.10–20', *NT*, 7, 1964, pp. 135–41.

This pericope offers few striking variants. In v. 13 the *Koiné* makes it explicit that it is Christ who strengthens the apostle. The end of v. 16 has some variations in detail, probably due to the un-literary forms of expression. Thus the best manuscripts (ℵ, B, G^{gr}, etc.) read 'You sent to me ("*moi*") for ("*eis*") my need'; P 46, A, have 'You sent the necessities' i.e. 'what I needed' (no '*eis*'); and D^c, P, 'You sent for my ("*mou*") need'. In v. 19 Ψ, D*, G, etc., have the aorist infinitive '*plērōsai*' instead of the more normal and better attested future '*plērōsei*'.

We find ourselves confronted here with the first of the three letters, a brief note of thanks addressed to the Philippians by the apostle when he received the aid they had sent him through Ephaphroditus (v. 18). The independent nature of the pericope, its curious position as a 'thank you' passage at the end of a letter which used to be thought a unity, and the necessarily long period of time which passed between the receipt of the gift and the writing of the first chapters of the epistle, all point to the independent composition of these verses, even prior to the rest of the epistle.

In this connection some (as Dibelius, Gnilka, Lohmeyer) have spoken of 'thankless thanks' and it is true that the apostle's thanks are expressed in a curious manner as though something held him back from a full expression of his pleasure. So C. O. Buchanan thinks the Philippians transgressed some firm instruction of the apostle's by sending him assistance ('Epaphroditus' sickness and the letter to the Philippians', *EvQ*, 36, 1964, pp. 161ff). We know that Paul was exceedingly jealous of his financial independence which elsewhere caused misunderstandings, especially at Corinth.[1] The situation actually seems quite different here. Verse 17 is most striking: 'not that I seek (*"epizētō"*) a gift'. This can only mean that the Philippians were able to imagine he did seek gifts; and how was that possible if their own gift was entirely spontaneous? So we may suppose that contrary to his usual custom the apostle solicited help from a church, perhaps because he was on somewhat cool terms with the local fellowship (cf. 1^{15-18}) and did not want to appeal to them (cf. Glombitza) and yet had need of money either to advance the enquiries for proving his Roman citizenship or for fresh evangelistic projects he had in mind. The fact remains that from this angle it is easier to understand the 'now at last' (*'ēdē pote'*) in v. 10, Paul's concern to show that he would have been able to do without such gifts (vv. 11–13) and that the Philippians are the only people he did approach in this way (vv. 15–17). Hence also the deeper implication of the request as an involvement of the community at Philippi in the Gospel (v. 14; cf. Glombitza). Preaching is a work of the community, and often the only way of showing fellowship is what today is called an 'offering' (v. 18).

4^{10} Like letter B which will follow it, this brief note is stamped with the mark of joy (*'echarēn'*).[2] This joy is 'in the Lord', for it is caused by the renewed brotherly concern recently shown by the Philippians towards the apostle, which testifies to Christ's Lordship over his church. This brotherliness has 'sprouted afresh' (*'anethalete'*)—a New Testament *hapax* and in any event a rare verb, the prefix expressing either the thrust of the new foliage or its renewal, but the latter suits the sense of what is said in vv. 15ff better. So it can be taken either as: 'you have revived so far as concern is involved' (intransitive: Gnilka, Haupt; N. Baumert;[3] cf. Ps. LXX 27^7; Wis. 4^4), or as: 'you have revived your concern for me' (Beare, Bonnard, Dibelius, Scott; cf. Ecclus. 1^{18}; 11^{22}). But he avers that this 'reviving' is belated (*'ēde pote'*: 'now at last'; cf. Rom. 1^{10}). Most commentators are in two minds about seeing a veiled reproach, believing that Paul is merely expressing his relief at seeing at last the arrival of what he was waiting for. This interpretation is possible but what follows in

[1] Cf. D. GEORGI, *Die Gegner . . .*, 1964, pp. 234–41.
[2] As in 2^{25}, it is an epistolary aorist (against Michael). The adverb *'megalōs'*, which has the same meaning as the more frequent *'mala'*, is only found here in the New Testament.
[3] 'Ist Ph. 4.10 richtig übersetzt?', *BZ*, 13, 1969, pp. 256–62.

the text does not commend it. The concern of which the Philippians have given proof is marked by the same verb '*phronein*' the importance of which we have stressed in 2^{3ff}. In 1^7, using the same expression ('*phronein huper*'), the apostle reverses the relationship and voices his concern for his readers (on the expression again cf. Haupt and N. Baumert, *art. cit.*, p. 260f).

The '*eph' hō*' at the end of the verse can either be taken as a causal preposition dependent on '*echarēn*' and expressing a fresh reason for joy,[1] or as a simple relative referring to one of the ingredients of the preceding statement.[2] Whichever the case, these words can hardly be taken as anything but an attenuation of the veiled reproach expressed at the beginning of the verse: it is not the Philippians but the circumstances which were responsible for the slow arrival of help. '*Akaireisthai*' is, indeed, a rare word denoting lack of a 'suitable opportunity' ('*kairos*').

4^{11} One objection, at all events, must be got rid of at once ('*ouch hoti*'; cf. B–D §480.5); Paul does not speak under the pressure of need ('*husterēsis*', cf. Mk. 12^{44}). But this objection does not bear so much upon the expression of joy (most commentaries) as upon the reservation which follows it in v. 10b: the reason for appealing to the Philippians' charity has not been need. For in the hard school of the apostolate (2 Cor. 11^{23ff}; Bonnard) Paul has learnt to be independent ('*autarchēs*') in all circumstances, or, with anybody (O. Glombitza, *art. cit.*, p. 136f; '*en hois cimal*'). 'Autarchy' or 'self-sufficiency' had an important place among the virtues which the Stoic philosopher is under obligation to acquire. But Paul gives the concept a very un-Stoical meaning: a man does not find true freedom within himself but in God who gives it to him (v. 13).[3] Only because he has learnt to depend on God alone has the apostle acquired true liberty (Bonnard, Glombitza).

4^{12-13} Paul now explains why poverty could not be the motive force of his conduct and wherein his independence consists. It has been said that these verses were composed of two three-lined strophes (Friedrich, Gnilka, Lohmeyer). Although it is true that the passage is rhythmical in form a verse structure is not obvious. We prefer Nestle's punctuation: the first two infinitives each preceded by 'I know' ('*oida*') introduce the list which follows, itself reminiscent of the catalogues in 1 Cor. 4^{11}; 2 Cor. 6^{3-10}; 11^{23f}. So Paul's apostolate is characterised by a paradox which is none other than a reflec-

---

[1] So most commentaries; B–D §235.2; cf. Rom. 5^{12}; 2 Cor. 5^4; 3^{12}.

[2] N. BAUMERT (who gives a very good résumé of the various attempts at translation, *art. cit.*, pp. 256ff). He gives the second '*phronein*' the sense of 'to be proud': '. . . your concern for me, of which ("*eph' hō*") you are proud (cf. v. 15f), but lacked opportunity to express it.'

[3] Cf. A. BONHOEFFER, *Epiktet und das NT*, 1911, pp. 109f, 291, 355f; J. N. SEVENSTER, *Paul and Seneca*, 1961, p. 113f; LIGHTFOOT.

tion of the Cross and Resurrection—satiety and hunger, abundance and deprivation. The humiliation ('*tapeinousthai*') recalls Christ's action referred to in **2⁸**; it applies not only to material conditions but also to an inward attitude (Lohmeyer, who, however, as always, is thinking of martyrdom). The 'abundance' ('*perisseuein*') which occurs twice here is a typically Pauline term for describing the new era which Christ's coming will inaugurate (cf. **1⁹,²⁶**). To this is added 'satiety' ('*chortazesthai*', a Pauline *hapax*) in opposition to 'hunger' ('*peinan*'; cf. 1 Cor. 4¹¹) and 'want' ('*hustereisthai*'; cf. 1 Cor. 8⁸; Lk. 15¹⁴). These various verbs are used some in the active, some in the passive, thereby expressing that the varied circumstances through which the apostle passes are the result both of his own will and of a will imposed upon him.

Paul thus finds himself 'trained', 'initiated' ('*memuēmai*'). The verb is a New Testament *hapax* and is characteristic of the mystery religions, though an allusion to them here is unlikely, unless it is to be understood that the 'mysteries' into which the Christian is initiated do not lie outside everyday reality but actually within it to the extent to which it is illuminated and transformed by the power of the Gospel. Hence the surprising conclusion which breaks completely with the Stoic ideal and is in purest Pauline strain: 'I can (endure (Bonnard, Gnilka)) all things through him who gives me power' ('*endunamounti*'). In **3¹⁰** 'power' ('*dunamis*') was clearly indicated as being that of the resurrection.

4¹⁴ But it is also necessary to come to grips with the genuine and deep sense of 'sharing' which the apostle has asked of the Philippians (Glombitza) and which is the mark of fellowship, not of a fellowship whose end is itself but one which finds expression in action on behalf of the Gospel (cf. **1¹²ᶠᶠ**). The result of their financial aid is precisely to make the Philippians sharers in this struggle ('*thlipsis*'), which is *the* ultimate struggle and which is characterised by testing (cf. biblical meaning of the word). The apostle stands in the front line of this battle, though the entire church strives along with him.

4¹⁵ Why does the apostle now feel the need to enumerate the various gifts the Philippians have already had occasion to send him? Certainly not in order to prick the self-satisfaction of donors who may have boasted of their actions (Michael). It could more easily be taken as intended to reassure 'brethren' who may have thought they had not done enough for him (Bonnard, Gnilka); or, if we punctuate differently, it could give the reason for what precedes: 'you have shared in my tribulation, as you well know. For . . .' (cf. Ewald-Wohlenberg). But Calvin seems nearer the mark when he states that Paul says this 'in excuse for what he has often received from them.' The emphasis is essentially on the fact that the Philippians ('*Philippēsioi*' is a sign of affection, as in 2 Cor. 6¹¹ and Gal. 3¹) have been the only ones ('*oudemia ekklēsia ei mē humeis monoi*') to have acted in this way. The apostle cannot then be accused of living at the expense of the communities founded by him and the Philippian community ought to be conscious of the distinction which it is given. Distinction is the right word because—and this is the second emphasis of vv. 15–16 (cf. vv. 14 and 17f)—the Philippians from the beginning have been involved in an especial way (*'ekoinōnēsen'*) in the great advance of the Gospel.[1]

This was from the beginning (*'en archē'*). It is surprising to find the beginning placed in Macedonia (*'apo Makedonias'*). It should not be imagined that the apostle actually started his missionary activity in Macedonia around the 40's A.D.[2] nor that any mission in this area prior to his own be dismissed as of no consequence (O. Glombitza, *art. cit.*, p. 140). Paul is no doubt putting himself at the Philippian standpoint (Dibelius, Ewald, Scott) and at the same time that of the missionary activity for which he was entirely responsible (Friedrich, Gnilka, Lohmeyer). In his earlier missionary activities he is actually shown in second place to Barnabas (Acts 13–14) and the stay in Galatia does not really seem to have been planned, so it is possible that he may have regarded Europe as the mission field which fell particularly to his lot and the true starting point of his 'Gospel'.

4^16 Even (*'hoti'*)[3] as early as his visit to Thessalonica (*'kai Thessalonikē'*; Benoit, Bonnard), the first stage after Philippi (Acts 17^2), the Philippians' especial concern for the apostle had had opportunity to show itself. But that was only the beginning. The expression *'kai hapax kai dis'* can actually be taken either in the restricted sense of 'once, or even twice' (Bonnard, Friedrich, Lohmeyer, Vincent) or more generally as 'more than once' (Gnilka, Lightfoot, Michaelis). L. Morris[4] has shown that the latter is indeed the meaning to be given to these words, and his analysis at several points intersects B. Rigaux's in connection with the one other New Testament instance of the usage (1 Thess. 2^18; B. Rigaux, *Les épîtres aux Thessaloniciens*, 1956, *ad loc.*). Moreover, in 1 Thess. 2^9 Paul claims not to have lived at the expense of his readers, adding that he has had to work hard for this reason, so the aid from the Philippians was far from meeting all his needs.

4^17 The concern the apostle shows to justify himself, the picking up of the *'ouch hoti'* ('not that') of v. 11 and the repetition of the verb

---

[1] *'Eis logon doseōs kai lēmpseōs'*, 'in the matter of a balance-sheet of profit and loss'. The expression belongs to the commercial vocabulary (cf. papyri texts cited by Lohmeyer), but was already used metaphorically in Jewish writings (Billerbeck).

[2] M. J. Suggs, 'Concerning the date of Paul's Macedonian Ministry', *NT*, 4, 1960, pp. 60–8.

[3] With Haupt, Müller, Vincent. But the conjunction could be parallel to the *hoti* at the beginning of v. 15, so continuing the account of the 'knowledge' (*'oidate hoti'*) the Philippians had (so most commentaries).

[4] L. Morris *'kai hapax kai dis'*, *NT*, 1, 1956, pp. 205–208.

'*epizētō*' ('to seek') show that he was trying to guard against some reproach (Calvin). So he returns to the fact that his sole concern has been to associate the Philippians with the Gospel (v. 14) and thereby to increase, not his own (monetary) capital but his correspondents' at the Day of Judgement. The vocabulary is borrowed from commerce ('*eis logon*'; '*pleonazō*') with an eschatological undertone ('*karpos*'; cf. 1[11,22]; Bonnard, Gnilka, Lohmeyer, Michaelis). The thought is therefore basically the same as that expressed in 2[16].

4[18] Even if there might have been doubt about the apostle's intentions in the past it should be completely removed because he now asks nothing further of the Philippians, he has all that he needs and more than enough. Thus the verb '*apechō*' can mean 'to give a receipt' (Bonnard, Gnilka, Lohmeyer). Furthermore the significance of Paul's request and his correspondents' response is clear: the true recipient of the gift has been God himself to whom it provided an acceptable ('*dektēn*')[1] sacrifice. The wording is from the Old Testament: '*osmē euōdias*', 'sweet odour', in connection with an incense offering (Gen. 8[21]; Ex. 29,[8,25,41]; etc.); and '*thusia*', 'sacrifice', 'offering'. We meet here again with both the terminology and the thought of 2[17]. The apostle's activity and the financial help of the Philippians which support it form a unity the 'judge' of which is God. '*Euarestos*' ('acceptable') in Paul essentially refers to man's relationship with God (Rom. 12,[1f]; Col. 3[20]; Tit. 2[9]). There is something here about the meaning of money and of church 'offerings' which deserves consideration.

4[19] But God is not merely the One who judges, he is primarily the One who gives (cf. Rom. 2[4]; 9[23]; 11[12]; Eph. 1[7-18]). Inasmuch as he has satisfied ('*peplērōmai*', v. 18) the needs of Paul himself ('*eis tēn chreian*', v. 16) so he will satisfy ('*plērōsei*', v. 19) the Philippians in theirs ('*pasan chreian*'), whether material or spiritual. In order to show this mutual relationship in which God is the agent Paul uses the expression '*my* God', which with 1[3] is unique for him. The Philippians will receive full satisfaction '*en doxē*', i.e. in the glorious Age to come (Lohmeyer, Michaelis)—or 'abundantly', 'gloriously', since the construction with '*en*' may reflect an Hebraic adverbial form. It would then be better to attach the phrase to the verb '*plērōsei*' than to the noun '*ploutos*'. And the verb has the further qualification 'in Christ Jesus'. There is no reason for adhering to Michael's suggestion that 'in glory' has been added by a copyist and that the original reading was 'riches in Jesus Christ'. The enriching of the Philippians will thus be marked both by the historical sign of the Cross and of the Resurrection, promised glory arising from present misery.

[1] All the accusatives cannot, with Lohmeyer, be made to depend upon the verb '*peplērōmai*'—'I am filled with the odour . . . etc', an allusion to the apostle's martyrdom. For Epaphroditus, cf. *ad* 2[25].

4²⁰ The passage **4¹⁰⁻²⁰** ends with a doxology which expresses very well its deep purport: the apostle's gratitude is addressed above all to God; it is he who, through the mediation of his church at Philippi, has succoured his servant. The doxology is also strongly marked by the liturgical tradition, as in Rom. 16²⁷; Gal. 1⁵; Eph. 3²¹; 2 Tim. 4¹⁸. Hence the Hebraic expressions 'unto the ages of the ages' and 'Amen'; hence also the repetition, after v. 19, of the word 'God'; and probably also the title 'Father' extended into 'our Father'. The designation is very frequent in Paul (cf. *ad* **1²**) but is particularly in place here since it is a matter of God showing mercy to his servants.

Greetings (4²¹⁻²³)

(21) *Greet each one of the saints in Christ Jesus. The brothers who are with me greet you.* (22) *All the saints greet you, especially those of Caesar's household.* (23) *The grace of the Lord Jesus Christ be with your spirit.*

ROLLER, O., *Das Formular der paulinischen Briefe*, 1933, pp. 68–78.

In v. 23 the *Koiné* replaces 'spirit' by 'all' and adds the *subscriptio* 'written from Rome by Epaphroditus'. Most manuscripts end with an 'Amen', which both B and G lack.

Whichever the letter—A, B, or C—which these verses originally ended, they are very Pauline in style. All the epistles actually end similarly; but it would be wrong to regard it as a mere stereotype. By considerably developing the brief *'errōso'* ('farewell') which usually ended letters at that period the apostle again brings out the real quality of the relations between Christians and of those realities which might be said to 'obsess' them—'Jesus Christ' (twice), 'Lord', 'saints', 'brethren', 'grace'. The last verse quite obviously repeats a liturgical formula, a sign that the apostle's letters were read during public worship and also of the importance of worship as the context of the Christian life.

4²¹ In writing to a disunited community Paul does not want even on this last occasion to take sides for particular individuals (cf. prologue **1¹ᶠᶠ**); this is why he uses the singular *'panta hagion'*, 'each one of the saints' and also why, contrary to his usual custom, he will mention no one by name in these final greetings. His correspondents are 'saints' ('holy ones') because they belong to the people of the Holy God (cf. *ad* **1¹**) and as in the opening address this belonging is stamped with the seal 'in Christ'. Hence it is better to attach the expression to 'saints' rather than to the verb 'greet'. Bonnard, who holds the opposite view, appeals to Rom. 16²² and 1 Cor. 16¹⁹ where, however, only 'in the Lord' appears, the meaning of which is not the same (Müller). The apostle himself is not in isolation; he too belongs to a group of 'brethren' (cf. *ad* 3¹ᵃ) who associate themselves with his greetings.

4²² Are the 'saints' who now join in the apostle's greetings the same as the 'brethren' in the previous verse or do they form a larger group of whom the brethren are the nucleus? It is hard to say. At all events, Paul feels the need to affirm that the community with which he is surrounded is a real one and to name one of its constituent groups. 'Those of Caesar's household' are not the Emperor's kinsmen but slaves or freedmen belonging to him and to be found virtually throughout the Empire in the administrative service. So in 1877 at Ephesus the following inscription was discovered: '*curum agunt collegia lib(ertorum) et servorum domini n(ostri) Aug(usti) i(nfra) s(cripta)*' (G. S. Duncan, *St Paul's Ephesian Ministry*, 1929, p. 110). So the reference here to 'those of Caesar's household' in no way supports the thesis of a Roman imprisonment. Why does Paul make special reference to these people? Perhaps to reassure his readers about the conditions of his captivity (his 'guards' join in his greetings; Gnilka) or because there were special connections between Christians of the Roman colony which was Philippi and the Imperial services (Michaelis).

4²³ That the apostle has recourse here to a liturgical formula arises from the highly stereotyped form taken by the benedictions with which he ends his letters. So grace ('*charis*') is mentioned in all the epistles. It is the beneficent and saving action of the Lord towards men as revealed in Jesus Christ; so the source of this action is always expressed in the same way (except for *Colossians* and *Ephesians*), the grace having as origin and agent the Lord whom the church confesses (cf *ad* 2¹¹).[1] In confessions of faith the Lord is always said to be Jesus Christ, i.e. the man Jesus of Nazareth, crucified under Pontius Pilate and raised on the third day. By the spirit ('*pneuma*') which the grace should reach (cf. Gal. 6¹⁸; Phm. 25) is meant the whole personality most especially in its mental and 'spiritual'[2] aspects. Thus we meet again in this final desire the preoccupations expressed by the apostle throughout his letter, notably already in 1⁹⁻¹¹. If the 'Amen' attested by most manuscripts was original it could have been in the

---

[1] In Rom. 16²⁰⁻²⁴; Gal. 6¹⁸; 1 Thess. 5²⁸; 2 Thess. 3¹⁸ it is 'our Lord'. 'Jesus Christ' always appears except in *Ephesians* and *Colossians*, abridged to 'Jesus' in Rom. 16²⁰ᵇ and 1 Cor. 16²³.

[2] Cf. E. SCHWEIZER, art. '*pneuma*', *TWNT*, VI, 1964, p. 433 (ET VI, p. 435). Compare with 1 Thess. 5²⁸; 2 Thess. 3¹⁸; 1 Cor. 16²³; Rom. 16²⁰⁻²⁴.

apostle's own hand, authenticating what has just been said ('it is true'; cf. Rom. 16^{22}; 1 Cor. 16^{21}; Gal. 6^{11}; Col. 4^{18}; 2 Thess. 3^{17}) or, in harmony with the reading of the epistle in the liturgy, the response of the assembly to it.

ANALYTICAL INDEX